dancer

Who Saved

Her

Soul

Book Three
in the
Zodiac Series

An Atlantis Entertainment Novel

J. S. Lee

Axellia Publishing

First Edition, June 2019
Published by Axellia Publishing

Print ISBN: 978-1-912644-23-0
eBook ASIN: B07S9BZ8MM

Cover design by Natasha Snow Designs;
www.natashasnowdesigns.com

Edited by C. Lesley
Proofread by S. Harvell

This book is a work of fiction. Any references to historical events,
real people, or real locations are used fictitiously. Other
characters, names, places and incidents are the product of the
author's imagination. Any resemblances to actual events,
locations, or persons—living or dead—is entirely coincidental.

CONTENTS

DEDICATION

To those still chasing their dreams

It might not be the same path as everyone else, but we'll get there eventually!

And for Kai (EXO), and Rosé (BLACKPINK) for being my visual inspirations

THE ATLANTIS ENTERTAINMENT UNIVERSE

Young Adult Contemporary Romance
(As Ji Soo Lee)

Zodiac

The Idol Who Became Her World
The Girl Who Gave Him The Moon
The Dancer Who Saved Her Soul
The Leader Who Fell From The Sky

Coming Soon

The Boy Who Showed Her The Stars

K-101

For those of you unfamiliar with K-pop / K-Dramas / Korean culture, here's a short handy guide:

Names

Names in Korean are written family name then given name. It's not uncommon to use the full name when addressing a person—even one you're close to.

차예린 is the Korean way of writing Cha Yerin

이승진 is the Korean way of writing Lee Seungjin

조미연 is the Korean way of writing Cho Miyeon (The 'Mi' is pronounced like the 'mi' in minute)

후다솜 is the Korean way of writing Hoo Dasom

If you are interested in how to write and pronounce the characters names, please go to https://www.jisooleeauthor.com/characternames.html

Surnames (Family names)

As the western worlds combined, we ended up with a lot of variation in surnames. In Korea, although there is variation, you will find a lot Kims, Lees, and Parks.

BTS, for example have Kim Namjoon (RM), Kim Seokjin (Jin), and Kim Taehyung (V). They all share the same family name, but are not related.

To try to keep things as easy to follow as possible, I have tried to make sure that all characters don't have the same surname *unless* they're in the same family. The one exception to this is Minhyuk and Seungjin. (To cut a very long story short, in the first version of this book, Minhyuk's name had to be Lee. Then I scrapped the whole story and re-wrote it. As I'd already published Zodiac 1, it was too late to change it. One day I may share that version with you).

Oppa (오빠), hyung (형), noona (누나), and oennie (언니)

This one gets a little confusing at first. The first thing you need to know, in Korea, age is a very important thing. It's not uncommon for you to be asked your age before your name because you need to be spoken to with the correct level of respect (known as honorifics). To show this, there's actually several ways to speak to address a person and it usually depends on your age (an exception to this might be in a place of work where someone younger than you is more senior to you). But I'll keep this simple and limit myself to terms used in the book.

Traditionally, oppa, hyung, noona, and unnie are terms used to describe your older sibling—depending on what sex you are and what sex they are. If you are male, your older brother is hyung and your older sister is noona. If you are female, your older brother is your oppa, and your older sister is unnie (technically, 언니 when Romanized is oenni, and 형 is hyeong, but unnie and hyung have become the more standard way of writing this). However, this can often be transferred to people you are close to. A girl will call her older boyfriend oppa. An idol will call his older groupmates hyung.

Sunbae (선배) and Hoobae (후배)

Along the same vein, sunbae (senior) and hoobae (junior) may be used as an alternative when using experience as a basis, rather than age.

Teacher (선생, 선생님, or 쌤)

A teacher in Korean is a seonsaeng. Because teachers are a respected profession, you will often find 'nim' (님) tagged on the end—선생님 / seonsaengnim. In America (or other western countries), teachers are often called Mr. (or Mrs. Etc) Family name. In Korean, they will be called Family name Teacher. If was a teacher, I would be Ms. Lee, or in Seoul, Lee Seonsaengnim. Even teachers will address other teachers this way.

This might differ with a student addressing the teacher if they have a good relationship with a teacher, to become ssaem (it's like an abbreviation of seonsaengnim), and then I would be Ji Soo ssaem.

The reason I'm including this is because one of the teachers will be referred to as Woosung ssaem.

Other

Comeback: this is an odd one for most people. Your next single isn't just your next single. It's a comeback—and it doesn't matter if you've waited two months or two years.

Kakao: Kakao is a messaging app similar to Whatsapp or Wechat.

SNS: What we would call Social Media, Koreans use the term Social Networking Service. Included in this would be **V Live**, an app which allows Korean idols to communicate with their fans (a bit like Instagram Live)

화이팅: Fighting, or 'hwaiting' is a word commonly used as encouragement, like 'good luck' or 'let's do this'.

Maknae: a term used for the youngest member of a group.

'Ya!': The Korean equivalent to 'Hey!'

Yeobo: Honey, a term endearment

Abeoji: Father

Eomeoni: Mother

Ahjussi and Ajumma: The literal translation is middle-aged man or woman, respectively. The US equivalent would be sir or ma'am—a respectful way of addressing someone.

제 X 장: Chapter (pronounced jae X jang)

Mixtape: Unlike in the western world, a mixtape is not a collection of songs burned on a CD. In the K-pop world, it's more of an unofficial album. It is usually created by one member in the group, but it's not a solo album. Songs are released on platforms like Soundcloud where fans can download for free. However, as this is K-pop and there are usually exceptions to the rule, some artists (Jooheon and I.M of Monsta X and J-Hope of BTS, for example), have released 'mixtapes' which have physical album sales.

Nenek: This is Malay (one of the languages of Singapore) for grandmother

Character Bios are also available at the back of this book

More terms and information is available on Ji Soo's website:
www.jislooleeauthor.com/k101

AUTHOR'S NOTE

Although South Korea is a developed country with a GDP in the top 15 of the world, when it comes to values and beliefs, many Koreans value tradition. While some of this is certainly admirable and respectful, when it comes to things such as appearance / public perception, *some* can take this to the extreme.

One of the characters in this book is dealing with her parents separating and getting a divorce. Until recently, this was not a common thing in South Korea, and even now, the country still has a relatively low divorce rate compared to many of its western counterparts.

Unfortunately, despite this, divorce is still seen as a taboo subject and many families will go out of their way to hide their marriage status because of it. Many will still keep up the appearance of being married.

Your name and your reputation are one of the most valuable things you have, and people can (and will) do what they can to protect it.

제1 장

Z

Yerin

"Wh**hat do you mean the card has been rejected? That's not possible. Swipe it again."** I glowered at the sales assistant.

"I'm sorry," the woman said, apologetically. "The transaction has been declined again."

"Ugh." I reached over and snatched my card back. "If this is how you treat loyal customers, I don't want to shop here anymore, anyway." I abandoned the eight hundred thousand won worth of clothes, flipped my hair over my shoulder and turned on my heel, marching out of the shop with my head held high.

I, Cha Yerin, was not going to allow anyone to think that this was anything other than a mistake on the department store's part. Even if it was my bank's fault!

I stormed down the mall to the food court. This required bubble tea. All I had wanted was a few new outfits for this week at school, a welcome break from studying … and the arguing at home. I ordered a strawberry bubble tea, paying with cash.

Taking a seat at the edge of the seating area so I could survey the mall, I sipped at my drink. Then I pulled out my phone and called my father.

He didn't answer.

Too irritated to stay at the mall, I left. I hailed a taxi, barely acknowledging the driver for longer than it took to give my address. When his eyes widened, I flipped my hair and pulled out my phone, flicking through my phone, checking the various SNS until I arrived home.

As it was the weekend, I was required to go home instead of staying in the dorms. For everyone else, going home was optional and most people chose not to, instead, staying at the SLA.

I, however, had to suffer with my mother being the principal of the Seoul Leadership Academy. It had its advantages: SLA was the most exclusive school in Seoul, and if my mother was the most important powerful person there, I was second.

Our house was enormous. Sitting in the Pyeongchang-dong district, on a clear day, I could see as far as SLA in Gangnam. The taxi dropped me at the gates, and I could see him trying to peer behind the tall wall that surrounded the property. Good luck.

Inside I dumped the shopping I had managed to purchase in the hallway, scowling at the fact our housekeeper wasn't there to take them from me. Rude.

I could hear voices from the kitchen, so I walked along the airy hallway, wondering what it was that looked different today. Something was off, and I couldn't put my finger on it.

The voices belonged to my parents. They were

arguing again. I'd been ready to tell my father about the declined credit card, but now I had no desire to get in the middle of it.

"I don't understand it, Chiyoung," my mother was saying. "How can a bank freeze a school bank account? I was supposed to pay the gardeners today, and all of the payments bounced."

"I don't know, yeobo," my father replied. "Let me look into it."

"You have been looking into it for weeks. You deal with financial trading every day, so how are you struggling to perform this task?"

I peered into the kitchen, keeping out of sight. My mother was behind the island counter, a half-consumed glass of red wine on the counter in front of her. My mother was one of those women who exuded grace and dignity. She never left her bedroom without her hair and makeup in place. In fact, I couldn't remember the last time I had seen my mother bare faced.

Father was in a suit, despite it being a Sunday. That was odd. Sunday was reserved for golf, not work. The suit looked a little crumbled though; like he had worn it for more than a day . That wasn't right, either.

"Financial work is not easy," Father protested. "I can't just access the information like that."

"Everything is on the internet. The only thing stopping me from accessing it is that you have all the passwords," Mother glowered at him.

"And rightly so," Father snapped, finally losing his patience. "I am the master of this house and its financials are my responsibility."

"The school is my responsibility!"

I almost squealed as Father lashed out, sending

the wine glass soaring across the kitchen. "You are only the principal of SLA!" he yelled as the glass exploded, sending shards of glass and wine raining down everywhere. "I own SLA, like I own SLU, like I own this house. The financial responsibility is mine, and if people are complaining that they are not getting paid, you need to direct them to me!"

I slowly backed out of the room, tears lining my eyes. My father was not someone who shouted easily, and I hated seeing him like that. My mother was quick to argue with everyone. Goodness knows how long they had been arguing for him to react like that.

I walked back through the house and went to my bedroom. Safely inside where I couldn't hear the raised voices, I sat down at my desk, staring out across the city through my window. I wiped at my eyes until the view was no longer blurry.

The ornate clock which hung on my wall above the desk told me it was nearly three in the afternoon. I had a couple of hours before I had to return to the SLA, and I had homework to finish.

At SLA, Sunday nights were my one evening of freedom—provided I had managed to complete my homework … at least for the next couple of weeks. Mother would be in soon to check and seeing as how she was already in a foul mood, I didn't want to provoke her further.

I focused on the textbook in front of me, working through the assignment questions. I lost track of time until Mother came in. "Have you not finished yet?" she asked, sounding both disappointed and irritated.

"I have one last question," I told her.

"If this was an exam, it would be over now."

If this was an exam, I'd know how long I'd have to do it. Instead of saying so, I pushed the workbook towards her. Mother poured over the workings out, her expression getting darker. Internally, I sighed, forcing my gaze on the desk in front of me. "There are three incorrect answers on this assignment," she said, slowly. "Three out of twenty. You will correct them before you hand them in. I will not have the daughter of the principal submitting anything as disappointing as this."

"Yes, mother."

She dropped the workbook on the desk in front of me, then walked out of my room. I pulled it to me with a sigh. As per usual, she hadn't indicated which of the problems were incorrect. I would have to go through them all again.

I rubbed at the back of my neck, then reached for my pencil. One of the incorrect answers was my incomplete one. Two left …

It took me longer to check the answers than it did to work them out the first time around. Once I was sure which they were, I made the amendments. Satisfied, I packed my school bag and walked downstairs, ready to go back to school.

I hated studying by myself. I did better when there were others with me. Mother was adamant that studying in a solitary manner was much more effective. Seeing as that was a battle I was never going to win, that was why she made me return home every weekend.

I left my bag by the door, next to the unclaimed shopping bags. Seriously, where was our housekeeper? Mother was in the living room, reading a book. From this angle, she looked like a poised dignitary. When she noticed me lingering in the doorway, she sighed, sliding a bookmark into the book and setting it down on the table beside her. "You took your time. I assume they are correct now?"

"Yes, Mother."

She stood and I followed her out to her Range Rover. Most of the journey was spent in silence, until we grew close to the school, and then the inevitable lecture started. "You dream is to go to an American Ivy League University. I don't understand how you think you will be able to accomplish that if you do not study. Those kinds of grades will only get you into Seoul Leadership University, and that's only because your father owns it. You are not naturally smart, Yerin. I keep telling you, you must study to accomplish these goals."

"Yes, mother."

Mother's dream had been a SKY university—one of South Korea's elite institutions—but my grades weren't perfect, and SKY required perfection. After years of tutors and coaches telling her to lower her standards, she had accepted Harvard or Yale as an alternative.

I didn't care. I wanted to study in America, but only because it would put distance between us.

I didn't like studying and both places required that. My goal was to use them to find a suitable husband. One rich and powerful, who could look after me. Who could get me out of this place.

We arrived back at the school. Mother parked in her spot, close to her office. Mother didn't live at the school like I did. She had come in, in part to drop me off and ensure I went straight back to school, but mainly so she could do her inspections. She liked to check things at the end of the weekend so she could compile a task list for the janitorial staff.

Thanks to having to redo my homework, it was later than I had planned. The sun had set, and my evening was escaping from me. Sunday night was the night Kareun, Eunbyeol, and I would watch our dramas. The one we were watching at the moment had my favorite idol staring in it: Sukwong from the group Deity. He was the most beautiful person on the planet.

Deity—and K-pop—was my secret pleasure. Mother would kill me if she ever found out I liked K-pop. It was no secret that she disproved of the idols in our school at the moment. "They say that those who are too dumb for school become idols," she'd announced one weekend over breakfast. It was the weekend after several members of Bright Boys had returned to SLA. "They can't even do that properly."

I walked back to my room, wondering for the hundredth time why my mother had allowed their enrollment. A few of them had been students here before they had signed with Atlantis Entertainment, but the rest hadn't. More importantly, the reason they had returned to the school was because they had been caught up in a huge scandal.

I remember it being all over the news when it had happened, just before school started back up. At the time Mother had said it wasn't a surprise and just reinforced the idea that those with no future either became idols or criminals—or in this case; both.

I pushed open the door to my room, finding my roommate, Kareun, and our other friend, Eunbyeol, already on the bed, the television on. "You said you would wait!" I cried, annoyed.

"You said you would be on time," Kareun

shrugged. "If you're not going to keep your promises, why should I?"

I narrowed my eyes and glared at her.

Kareun was a bitch.

Set to join her mother's fashion line when she graduated, Kareun knew exactly what she was going to be when she left school: the top designer of the fashion world. Although she was stunning enough to be a model with her slim figure and a face shape to die for, she was going to be a designer.

According to Kareun, designers needed to be ruthless.

And so she was.

She had also been my best friend since kindergarten. Of course, that didn't stop her from being a bossy bitch.

"Start it again. I'm here now," I demanded, catching a glance of Sukwong. Damn, that man was gorgeous.

"No!" she responded. "You should have returned when you said you would."

She might be my best friend, but there were times when I really wanted to slap her. I glanced at Eunbyeol, who just shifted uncomfortably. Eunbyeol had joined our group when we started at SLA.

I deposited my bag on my bed. "Kareun, it wasn't my fault. Just start it over."

"No," she repeated. "You come back on time."

Great, she was in a pissy mood.

The hell with that. I dug my phone and earphones out of my bag and then walked out of my room, flipping my hair over my shoulder as I did so. I had no intention of only watching half of the show, and I didn't want to stay in there while it was on.

I stuck my earphones in my ears and set the music playing. Hyuna's singing filled my ears. Her voice raised my spirits slightly and I started wandering the dorm. Although there was a common room, I didn't want to be in it. I didn't like people and it would be full of them. Instead, I found myself outside.

It had rained during the day, but the clouds had disappeared a few hours ago. The night was cool and the humidity down. It was pleasant to be out in. I was back in the parking lot. Mother's car was still there.

That ruled out going into the school.

Instead, I walked back inside, heading to the roof, taking the stairs, despite the four-inch heels I was wearing. I was too irritated to go back and change now. Up top, it was cool with a pleasant breeze. I walked to the edge, staring down at the ground below. Situated between the SLA and SLU was the shared running track. I stared down at it, appreciating the peace, before moving over to an area where chairs and tables had been left. I sat on one of them, resting my head in my hand as I propped it up with my elbow on the table.

How was it Sunday night already?

제2 장

Seungjin

I collapsed onto the sprung wood floor, breathing heavily. Sweat was running down my forehead from my wet fringe, dripping off onto my knee as I bent over to restart the music video.

Life sucked.

All I had ever wanted to be was an idol.

The last thing my brother ever wanted me to be was an idol.

My dad? There wasn't much he could say on the matter considering he owned an entertainment company.

For years, I had spent every available moment dancing, pushing myself to learn moves and routines from YouTube when none of my family would allow me to take lessons. It wasn't even that money was an issue: Dad had created and owned Atlantis Entertainment, and thanks to B.W.B.B., and lately, Onyx, we had money.

They just didn't want their family to be one of the cogs that kept the machine running.

I wasn't stupid. I knew that being an idol was not an easy option in life. With eyes on you 24/7, you had to look and act the part all the time. Schedules were crazy, and during promotions, you'd be lucky if you ever got more than a few hours' sleep. People thought it was easy, but it really wasn't.

But it was still all I wanted.

Dancing was what I loved most, but I didn't want to just be a backup dancer.

I pressed play and watched the latest NCT Dream music video again. Given the choice, SM Entertainment would have been my first company on the list. They had some amazing groups, but some even better dancers. NCT were a prime example of that. Dream, U, 127—all the units were slick. It was something I aspired to be like.

Unfortunately, being the son of Lee Woojin meant no other company was going to accept me. Which left me with Atlantis.

So I had continued to practice and practice until my blisters had blisters and my socks were constantly stained from blood. When I wasn't dancing, I was working on my vocals—you couldn't be in an idol group without being able to sing or rap. I couldn't rap. I'd tried … my singing wasn't the best, but it was better.

The opportunity had come, and I had auditioned for my own company. My dad and brother had been part of the judging panel. I wasn't sure if they had simply accepted me because they didn't want the negative press that surrounded rejecting your own family, or if they, if *Dad*, had finally realized how much I wanted this.

I'd thought it was the former, but as time passed, I was beginning to feel like it was the second option.

I wanted to punch someone, but considering a fight was what had put me in this situation, I stood, started the music video for the thirtieth time, and started dancing along. I was determined to learn every member's part and so far, I only had Jisung and Renjun's parts down.

Dancing was my escape. I allowed the concentration to take over and the angry thoughts ebbed away with the beat.

Or, at least, they did until the song ended.

Then I had to start it again, keeping up the momentum, until, finally, I dropped to the floor, gasping for breath as I stared at the ceiling. The door behind me opened, sending a cool draft in. I turned my head, finding my brother scowling down at me.

"What are you doing here?"

"Practicing."

Sejin's mouth twisted, like he was sucking on a sour lemon. "What good is that going to do you?"

"I want to be ready for when Bright Boys have our comeback," I told him, rolling up into a sitting position.

"Until you can tell me what happened with Hyunseo, Jaehoon, and King, there won't be a comeback."

"Why are we all being punished for this?" I asked him. Sweat ran down the side of my forehead and into my eyes. I had to blink rapidly to try to clear it.

"Because one of you punched an innocent member of the public and the rest of you are covering for him." Sejin folded his arms. "Because you were in a nightclub, drinking, underage."

"Hyung," I started, but Sejin cut me off.

"How many times do you have to be told, when I am at work, I am not your brother."

"There is nobody around," I pointed out. I loved my brother, but things had slowly been changing between us. He had never liked the idea of me being an idol, but the bigger issue seemed to be the appearance of our half-sister.

Apparently, while my father was married to my mom, he'd had an affair. The other woman had run off to America, pregnant. Dad didn't even know until a few years ago. That was when my mom divorced him. From all the arguments I'd heard, this woman wasn't his first, or his last, and she had finally had enough. Now she was in another city.

I missed her.

As for this half-sister, it wasn't exactly her fault that my parents had divorced, but I wasn't interested in meeting her. Which Sejin would know if he ever spoke to me about it.

Dad had brought her in to manage another group at Atlantis: my sunbae group, H3RO. Actually, that wasn't true. He'd brought her to Seoul to eventually run Atlantis, I guess. Which was why Sejin was pissed off with the world. He'd told her to not only manage H3RO, but to also revive their careers and get a number one single—after years of being inactive.

Would you believe it: she accomplished it!

Maybe she could help me with this 'break' Bright Boys were on …

"We are still on Atlantis property," Sejin snapped.

With the sweat still dripping into my eyes, I reached up and wiped my forehead, brushing my hair to the side at the same time, then wiped my hand on my damp T-shirt. "Did you need me for something?"

"I was told you were here, and I wanted to see that for myself, considering Bright Boys had all been explicitly told that all activities were suspended. That includes practice times."

"Hyu— Sejin, *buhoejangnim*," I said, stressing the 'Vice Chairman' before he could tell me off again. "The practice room was vacant. I checked."

"You are stopping someone from using it, but that's an irrelevant point," he told me. "You were told not to use it. You were also told to get back to SLA and reflect on your actions, not your reflection," he added, pointing at the floor to ceiling mirror behind me.

If he wanted to act like that, so be it. I stood and walked out of the room, brushing past him as he half blocked the doorway, but refusing to give him an apology: regardless of what he said, he was my brother before he was my boss.

When he was out of sight, I stuffed my hands in my pockets and scowled at my shoes. I was tired and hungry, but I wasn't ready to go back to the SLA dorms yet; even if curfew was looming. Yes, I needed to shower, and yes, I needed to eat, but I shared a dorm room with Jaehoon and Minhyuk—King—and I didn't want to see them.

It wasn't that I didn't like them, because I did, but I was still annoyed with them about the whole Hyunseo situation. Whatever had happened, had happened after I had left that night. Those two, along with Sungil, a guy who had been a trainee with us before he'd abandoned Atlantis, had witnessed it all, and none of them were sharing the details.

"Lee Seungjin!"

I turned at my name being called and found Kim Youngbin, the leader of another Atlantis group, Onyx, waving me over. Curious, I walked over. "Youngbin-hyung," I said, giving him a smile.

Although he was nearly ten years older than me, he and I had a good friendship. If I was honest, he was more of a brother than Sejin was, hence why I didn't call him sunbae, even though it would have been more proper to do so.

"You look …" he tilted his head. "Have you been dancing all afternoon?"

I nodded.

"Want some chicken? There's a place close to SLA that does good food." When I hesitated, he grinned. "My treat."

It wasn't really a secret that we were back at SLA. It had been all over the news that Bright Boys activities had been suspended, as Sejin had said, so we could reflect on our actions. But it didn't mean we had to hide out in the school dorm … "Sounds good to me."

We walked to the restaurant chatting mainly about H3RO's comeback. I knew Youngbin had taken an active part in producing the album with H3RO's leader, Tae, even though he wasn't credited on the album: long story short, my brother was a jerk.

We walked into Roosters and took a seat. I'd never been in it before, although it had always smelled good on the rare occasion I had walked past. There was a section at the back that was almost private due to the tall room divider, and as far as I could tell, the only thing back there was the kitchen, which meant, for Youngbin who was in a popular group, and me, who was trying to keep a low profile, a private place for us to eat. "I've been trying to get in touch with you," Youngbin told me, once we'd ordered. "I would have sent you a Kakao message, but I couldn't find you."

I frowned. "Why would you? I'm a rookie: we're not allowed phones yet."

"You're a suspended rookie no longer at the dorms and in easy reach. Surely that's a good enough reason to have yours," he pointed out. "But that's not what I wanted to say. I spoke to Holly."

I set my can down and stared at him. "What does she want?"

"She asked me to give you her number," he explained. He leaned back in his chair, kicking his legs out in front of him so he could pull something out of his back pocket: his phone.

"What does she expect me to do with that?" I asked dumbly, referring to the number and not his phone.

"I don't think she *expects* anything from you." Youngbin unlocked his phone and scrolled through it. "She said there was no pressure to meet her, but if you felt like you wanted to meet up at some point, she would love to hear from you. It sounds like she didn't know anything about you either because she said she'd understand if you didn't."

"That's not going to happen," I informed him. I didn't care whether she knew or not: she was the reason Sejin was in such a bad mood. If he found out that I'd met with her …

"You know, for what it's worth, I like her. Tae was telling me she had all this thrown at her and she has been working as hard as they have to get that number one." Youngbin tucked his legs back under the table.

"Have you got a pen?"

I shook my head. I didn't even have any money on me. I'd only agreed to come because Youngbin was paying.

"All I am going to say is think about it. She seems decent enough ... unlike your brother."

I let out a long sigh, shaking my fringe out of my face. It was a universal fact at Atlantis that Sejin was not a popular person. At least not with the idols. With the board and the managers ... the non-group managers ... he was popular: their annual bonuses ensured that. He knew how to run a profitable company ... "Whatever," I muttered.

"Your order." A tray of chicken was placed between us. I barely paid any attention to the server until Youngbin asked him a question.

"Do you have a pen?"

"Sure," the guy responded.

I looked up, watching as he pulled a pen from behind his ear, then realized who our server was. I stood up abruptly, sending my chair flying. "What are you doing here?!"

Min Taekyung, TK, stepped back, eyes wide when he realized I was the one he was serving. "I work here," he returned, boldly. "If you don't like it, you can leave."

"You know him?" Youngbin asked me.

"He's the jerk whose brother is telling lies to everyone who will listen!"

"My brother was assaulted by Hyunseo!" TK snapped, his eyes darkening. "Gukyung spent a night in hospital thanks to your leader. Just because he's an idol doesn't mean he should get away with attacking

17

someone!"

"Your brother is a liar!" I yelled at him, my hands balling into fists. "Your brother isn't just ruining Hyunseo's life; he's destroying everyone's in Bright Boys!"

"What is going on back here?" a voice demanded. I half glanced at the restaurant's owner.

"Did you know you're employing the family member of a liar" I asked.

"I'm employing a man who turns up to work on time, does his job, and does it well," the owner countered.

"I think we should leave now," Youngbin interjected, but not before I had turned and swiped the chicken off the table.

It hit the wall sending sicky, greasy smears down the wall as it fell to the floor. "You need to watch yourself," I said, jabbing my finger at TK. First; he turned up in my class at SLA, then he turned up where I was eating? That wasn't an empty threat. I stormed to the door, ignoring Youngbin who was both apologizing to the owner, and shouting after me.

Youngbin didn't catch up with me. It wasn't until I got back to the school that I realized that I never took Holly's number.

Oh well … it wasn't like I was going to do anything with it …

I was still hungry and the idea of returning to my room was just as unappealing as it had been an hour ago. It was, however, almost curfew time.

I jammed my hands in my pockets. With any luck, cleaning up that chicken would make TK late and he'd get a detention for it.

Instead of returning to my dorm, I detoured from the lift to the stairs to the roof. I liked it up there. There was a spot which was protected from the wind but meant I could practice in peace. I was tired from dancing and had no desire to do that, but I had left the book we'd been reading in Korean class when I had been up there last.

I'd been using it to stop my chair wobbling.

I pushed open the roof door, turned a corner, and found someone in my seat.

Cha Yerin.

She was in my class and best friends with Geom Kareun. Kareun was the unofficial president of my fan club and one of my fan sites. Yerin ... I wasn't sure about Yerin. I had a feeling she liked Bright Boys though. Who wouldn't?

She looked up at me, two dark eyes sparking in the moonlight. There wasn't much light, but her face was puffy. Either she needed to lay off the fried food, or she had been crying. Looking at her thin figure, it was probably the second option.

Girls and tears. I'd rather be in the room with Jaehoon and King. "You're sitting on my book," I told her.

She frowned, then slowly stood, looking at where she had been sitting. "I'm fairly certain I'm not."

I pointed at the chair's leg. "I'm fairly certain you are."

She looked again, plucking the book out. "That's exactly how I felt about it," she muttered, handing it over.

"Why are you up here?" I asked, taking it. "Your throne looks a little different here."

Everyone knew Yerin was the Queen Bee in this school. There wasn't a day that went by without her pointing out to someone who her mother was. I had no idea why she did that: I did everything I could to deny the fact I was Lee Woojin's son at Atlantis. After my first week as a trainee, it was obvious that everyone thought I was there because of who I was.

I bet the same people didn't think that now.

"It's none of your business," she responded, curtly.

No, it probably wasn't. I didn't know her. She didn't know me.

I doubted we ever would.

제3 장

Seungjin

October

Life was getting progressively worse. It had been
almost three months since we had been sent
back to SLA and nothing had changed apart
from the season. Hyunseo was getting closer to a court
date; something the news was constantly reminding the
public of. The rest of us—or most of us—were still at
SLA, waiting in limbo.

I hated the fact that my career was depending on
the outcome of that court case!

I had tried to speak to Dad about it, but his
response was simply that Sejin now took care of that
side of things, not him.

Whoever had thought, or still thought, that I was
there through favoritism needed to dig out the evidence
and show it to me, because I was just another name in
a database to them.

Which was why I was surprised when Dad sent
me a Kakao message asking that I come home at the

weekend for brunch. We'd never done brunch. Hell, I'd had to look up the word to find out it was some weird mashup of breakfast and lunch.

I was sitting at the dining table we had not used since my mom had left, wondering what was going on. It seemed far too formal for him to discuss my future, and then Sejin walked in, talking to my grandmother.

I stood as she walked over to the table. "Good morning, halmeoni," I greeted her.

She moved over, enveloping me in a hug. "How are your grades? I hope you will be able to get into a SKY university."

I gave her a pained smile, not responding as I sat back down.

My grades sucked.

I was there to pass time while I waited for Atlantis to release us from the dungeon our careers had been thrown into. My grades were probably not going to get me into a university at all, never mind one of the three most prestigious universities in South Korea.

I had no desire to go to university. Dancing was in my blood, not academics.

"Why must you waste your time on fruitless things like you do?" she demanded when I didn't say anything. "An idol is not an honorable job. Why can't you be more like your brother?"

I tuned out. I'd been hearing this comparison for years. Not once had my father or brother spoken up for me. Why would today be any different?

And then the door opened. I looked up as our butler entered, declaring 'Holly Lee ssi'.

My half-sister.

I'd seen her a couple of times in passing at

Atlantis, but I'd made sure she'd never seen me. She was shorter than me, so she didn't get her height from dad like Sejin and I had.

"You're late," my grandmother snapped at her.

She knew who she was. And she was expecting her?

At what point had my family suddenly decided to allow the illegitimate child into the house? I wasn't against this. I was curious more than anything; as more time had passed, I had wanted to go say hello. It was just, the voice in the back of my mind kept telling me that if I angered Sejin, Bright Boys were done. So I did nothing.

Holly moved around the table, taking the only free seat: next to me. I watched her warily, still unsure what was happening as everyone watched her in an awkward silence.

"This is your grandmother." Finally, someone, Dad, said something.

Before he could turn to me, my grandmother set her hand on the table, just forcibly enough to make the chopsticks next to her bowls rattle in their holder. "You will call me Park Sonha."

"I'd like to call you something else," Holly muttered under her breath. It took me a second to translate it from English and I had to bite back my smile.

Grandmother's eyes narrowed. "I beg your pardon?"

Without missing a beat, Holly reached for the cloth napkin (we used them less than we used the dining table) and set it in her lap. "It's a pleasure to meet you after all these years," she told her politely. "My mother speaks so fondly of you."

Grandmother snorted. "Your mother was a gold digger."

I stared at my plate, unsurprised. When I'd found out Holly existed, Grandmother had wasted no time in telling me that Holly's mother had been after Dad's money, and after failing to seduce him and break up the marriage, had intentionally gotten herself pregnant.

"*Eomeoni*!" Dad cried. The mortification on his face was the most emotion I'd seen from him in a long time.

"It runs in the family," Sejin muttered from beside Grandmother. I had a strong suspicion he wasn't trying to be quiet.

I turned and watched Holly, curious as to how she would handle our family. Judging from how, under the table, her hands had fisted around her napkin, I was going to bet this wasn't going to end well.

Moments later, the napkin was dropped on the table as she stood. "Well, this was worth getting out of bed for," she announced. Without another word, she marched back around the table and out of the room.

I watched her leave. It wasn't exactly as explosive as I had expected, but that was the first time I had seen anyone stand up to my Grandmother. I wasn't sure it was deserved, after all, her mom had tried to split up my family, but it had taken a certain level of guts not to sit there and take it like I had seen so many of Sejin's ex-girlfriends do in the past.

While my dad was busy telling Grandmother that she shouldn't have spoken to Holly like that, I made my own exit from the room. I wasn't sure why I was following after her, but I guess I was curious.

I somehow beat her outside, finding a Range Rover I didn't recognize in the drive. I was willing to put money on the fact Dad had bought it for her. She didn't strike me as someone who drove a Range Rover.

Actually, she didn't strike me as a gold digger.

Thanks to Sejin's extensive research, I had seen that that type of woman all had something in common: they took far too much care with their appearance.

Not that it was wrong. I liked a girl who looked after themselves, but Holly wasn't one of them. She wasn't untidy. She had worn a nice dress for the brunch, but it wasn't designer.

I walked over to the SUV and leaned against the driver's door, waiting. Either she had gone snooping, or she had ended up in the library. Moments later, she left the house, walking over. She stopped when she saw me. "Hi," I said, realizing I'd not worked out what I was going to say to her.

She stared back at me. "Hello."

I pushed away from the door and said the first thing that came to my mind. "Do you want to go somewhere a little less uncomfortable for some breakfast? There's a place near the Atlantis dorms which serves really good porridge?"

She seemed curious, and a little hesitant, but she nodded anyway, unlocking the door. I moved around to the other side and got in before Dad or Sejin came out and stopped me.

Aside from her telling me she was going to park at the dorms, the ride was spent in an awkward silence.

I kept sending sly glances over at her. She didn't have Dad's height, but I could see the resemblance. She looked more like him than I did, anyway. She just didn't have his mannerisms: he would never have tapped at the steering wheel. She also seemed to have a habit of chewing her lip.

Ever since things had gone wrong for Bright Boys, I had taken to carrying a mask and cap with me at all time, even when I was at school. Of course, I couldn't wear them while at school, but they were there if I ever left campus. Today was no different. Even though I had dressed smartly for the brunch as Grandmother was there, they were hiding in my back pocket.

Holly parked the SUV in the parking lot under the dorms I had once lived in, then I led her down the street to the restaurant I had told her about. This was why I was never in Roosters: much as I loved chicken, it wasn't good for you. I was an idol and I worked hard to have the abs I did. Porridge was better than fried chicken.

It was also run by the friendly Han Yeonsoo who would always give me larger portions than other customers got. She reminded me a little of my mom.

Yeonsoo gave me a bright smile, leading me to a table in the back. It was just before the lunchtime rush, but the table was out of the way, just in case. I asked for my usual, but I waited while Holly picked something from the menu.

Other than speaking our orders, we sat in silence until the porridge was in front of us. This had seemed like a good idea back home, but now it was just us, I wasn't sure where to start. I knew nothing about her, and I wasn't good at asking for help.

Holly let out a long sigh. "I'm sorry I've not spoken to you before now. I don't have the greatest relationship with Sejin and I wasn't sure if you would want to meet with me either."

"I got your message from Youngbin. I contemplated calling you a few times," I told her. Although I'd left him without taking it, as soon as I'd gotten my manager's approval to get a phone, I'd gotten him to send it over. I played with my porridge, not really looking at what I was doing. "I thought you'd be like them."

"Them?" she questioned.

My family. I couldn't say that though. My eyes dropped to the bowl in front of me. "They don't like the fact I'm an idol. I think they're happy that things are going wrong with Bright Boys because they want to disband us too."

"I'm sure that's not the case."

"Which bit?"

Holly, who had eaten as much of her porridge as I had, set her spoon down. "Seungjin, I am not here to get in the middle of things with you and your family."

"We're your family too," I pointed out. "And I don't want you to get in the middle of things, but you've saved H3RO. Can't you save us too?"

"I'm H3RO's manager, not Bright Boys."

This was not how this conversation was supposed to go! "But Dad is trying to get you to take a senior position at Atlantis, so you'll be able to do something then, right?" I asked, desperately.

"If I didn't know any better, I'd think you were making moves on my girl," a familiar voice announced.

I looked up at Jun, pulling a face. "Gross. She's old." She was also my sister, but that wasn't public knowledge, so I had to settle for the next gross fact on the list.

It earned me an expected smack around the back of my head. Jun was a member of the group who Holly was saving: H3RO. He was the maknae of the group, and only a few years older than me. I liked Jun. He was fun. But he was still my sunbae.

"Ya!" he cried in mock irritation. I wasn't sure why—she was older than he was. He took the empty seat next to her, making me frown as he pulled Holly's barely touched bowl of porridge towards him.

Holly snatched up her spoon before he could and used it to smack the back of his hand. "I don't think so, mister." She pulled the bowl back. "And come on, you know he's my brother."

What?

I stared in confusion.

"But noona!" he whined.

How did he know? *Why* did he know? Why was he acting so informal with her? She was his manager! Noona? That was inappropriate!

"Oh, have it, I'm full anyway," she muttered, pushing the bowl back. She rolled her eyes before looking at me. "Look, I don't know what's happening with Bright Boys, but for now, just keep your head down."

"She's right," Jun agreed, mouth full of food. "Keep out of the spotlight for a bit."

Holly turned to Jun with a frown. "Why are you here?"

He pointed at the bowl. "I was hungry."

Another question I wanted to know was how he knew she was here. Much as I liked him, he'd made it so we couldn't talk about Bright Boys. Much as I wanted her help, I kind of wanted to get to know her too.

Maybe …

Either way, I couldn't do that with Jun here either.

I was playing with my porridge again, wondering how I was going to be able to escape when my phone bleeped at me. I pulled it out of my pocket: it was an alert that BTS were going live on V Live.

Meh.

It was good enough …

I stood. Holly's attention switched back to me. "I have to go. Do you like bowling?" I wasn't sure why I asked that, but I'd committed. "Want to do that; next time?"

I waited for her response then headed for the door, pulling on my mask and cap.

What was I doing? She had no power to save Bright Boys.

The only one who was going to save my career was me.

The question was, how?

제4 장

Z

Yerin

nother week, another weekend. I was back at home, in my bedroom, studying. There had been an exam in my Moral Education class and I had come in fourth. Last weekend, when I had tried to study for the class first thing on Monday morning, I had been distracted by my parents arguing again.

Something was going down at SLA. When the voices had finally gotten too loud to concentrate, I'd opened the door and sat at the top of the stairs, resting my head against the wall.

"... you're always asking!"

"Because you're never answering!"

"The reason that school is falling into disrepair is because there are more students," my father had snapped. "More students mean more wear and tear, and the fact you keep accepting more and more scholarship students every year means the school gets less money. You want more money, get some richer kids in whose parents are prepared to repaint the entire building."

"I don't want a building painted; you fool!" my

mother had yelled at him. "I want the leak in the third-floor boys bathroom fixed!"

"I've told you, I don't have access to that information."

There was the sound of something breaking. It sounded like glass. At this rate, there was going to be no glassware left in the house. "Then if you can't answer that, you can explain why the credit card was declined again. Do you know how embarrassing it is to be out for coffee with the ladies and not being able to pay?"

"There must be a mistake," my father had hurriedly told her. "I will go to the bank first thing tomorrow. In the meantime, take this."

"I don't need the money now, you fool!" my mother had screamed. "I needed it yesterday!"

I had pulled my headphones out then, sticking them over my ears and turning시끄러 (Shut Up!) by U-Kiss on, loud enough to drown out the arguing.

The shouting match had continued for about another hour before my father had left the house. At which point, any concentration I'd had earlier, had gone.

So far, today was turning out to be more productive. I'd finished up two assignments, and then turned to the notes of the Moral Education class from last week, ready for tomorrow's exam.

Then the déjà vu set in.

The shouting was closer this time: upstairs, instead of downstairs. Judging from the volume, my parent's bedroom door was open.

I set my pen down, walked over to my bed, and lay down on my stomach, pulling a pillow over my head. I'd left my headphones at school like an idiot.

The pillow did nothing.

"What do you mean it's all gone?" Mother shrieked. "How can it all be gone?"

My father's response was quiet. He wasn't shouting anymore.

"That wasn't your money!"

I yanked the pillow off my head and tossed it to one side, rolling over and sitting up. I still couldn't hear my father, but now ... now I was curious. What money? I walked over to the door and pulled it open a crack.

"I asked you about those bills!" my mother continued to yell. "I asked you and you said it was a mistake, and now you're telling me it's gone?"

"The business failed," my father told her. "I had people to pay. I couldn't have them going without their salary. How are they going to feed their families?"

"Their families?" Something flew across the room and hit the wall with a bang. "What about your own family? What are we going to eat?"

"Yeobo—"

"Don't you dare call me that!" Something else went bang. I winced. Mother was livid if she wasn't allowing Father to call her his favorite term of endearment.

But if money was missing ... I wouldn't let him call me that either.

"We are not going to go hungry," he said, trying to assure her. "I will get the money."

"How?" Mother demanded. "I spoke to the bank. There is no money! The fact you've not allowed me near the Academy accounts tells me there's no money there either." There was a long pause, and then the sound of skin hitting skin. "You stole from the Academy?"

"Borrowed!" Father said, hurriedly. "I borrowed it. I'm going to return it."

"HOW?" Mother bellowed. "You've already said your business failed. How can you make money when you're going to declare it bankrupt?"

"Nerin, let's not get hysterical. I borrowed the money so that I don't have to declare bankruptcy. As soon as things start to pick up—"

She slapped him again. "No, Chiyoung. I am not listening to this anymore. You will get out of this house and I will work out how to fix this mess you've caused."

"Ne— Nerin …"

"GET OUT!"

There was the sound of movement, and then my father appeared in the hallway, walking towards the stairs—and my bedroom. He looked up and caught me staring. "Yerin," he said, softly. "I'm sorry."

I slammed the door shut, staring at the white painted wood.

I felt …

I didn't know how I felt.

Numb.

Sick

Confused.

Disappointed.

Angry.

All of them, all at once.

How could he do that?

Outside of the room, I heard the front door close. Moments later, the door to my parent's bedroom slammed shut.

For some reason, a single thought filled my mind: this was going to be the last time I saw my father.

Irrational, with absolutely no reason for thinking it, the idea consumed me.

I pulled the bedroom door open and ran down the stairs, out of the door. My father's car was already pulling out of the gates. "Abeoji!" I screamed. When the car didn't stop, I ran after it, down the drive, and out onto the street. I could just see the car turning the corner at the bottom.

With that thought still taunting me, I charged down the road, building up speed as I tore down the steep hillside. At the bottom, I didn't stop, running out into the road. I couldn't see the car.

He was gone.

The next thing I knew, a horn was blaring. and I was lying on my back.

No, that wasn't quite right. I was lying on my back on something both firm and soft: a person, and not the sidewalk. Arms were wrapped around me like a security blanket.

Beneath me, the person struggled into a sitting position, bringing me up with them. "Are you insane?" I turned, finding a person wearing a cap and a mask, but I would recognize those eyes anywhere. He tugged the mask off his face. "It's me," he said. "Lee Seungjin."

"What are you doing here?" I asked him.

"Saving you from getting run over. What are you doing in the road?" he demanded. "Where are your shoes?"

I glanced down at my feet. One was covered in a sock, the other, a sock and a slipper. My gaze went to the road, but it was empty. A fleeting image of losing it as I ran down the hill returned to my memory.

It was quickly burned away by the memory of my

father's car disappearing around the corner.

I burst into tears.

It wasn't like one of those moments in the dramas where the guy wraps his arms around the girl and she cries and everything looks misty and romantic.

I mean, my view looked misty, but that was because of the tears.

Seungjin, pushed me away from him and jumped to his feet. "Why are you crying? What is wrong with you?"

I'd been in the arms of a gorgeous idol—it didn't even matter that he wasn't my Bright Boys bias (Kareum had made it clear Seungjin was hers. Mine was Ryan)—and then he had pushed me away. For some reason, that was what I chose to focus on. Maybe because it was easier than telling him I was never going to see my father again?

I cried louder, wailing, as I sat at the edge of the road. My body and my feelings in the gutter.

"Stop crying," Seungjin hissed at me.

I couldn't, even if I wanted to.

"Cha Yerin, stop it!" He took a few steps away from me, looking at me like I had gone mad.

Maybe I had.

For some reason, despite the obvious discomfort, he didn't leave me. He kept his distance, but he stayed.

I appreciated that.

When the tears finally ran dry, and my head felt thick and woolen, I brought my knees up and rested my cheek on them. Seungjin moved in front of me. "Are you done?" he asked. He was still looking at me like I was insane.

I nodded, although it was sideways.

"You want to tell me what that was about?"

"Not really."

He scratched at the back of his head, looking up and down the street. "You can't stay there."

"I'd rather stay here than go home."

A hand appeared in front of my face. I stared at it. "At least move out of the road."

Considering no passing car had stopped, nor had any tried to park where I sat, I wasn't sure it was necessary, but in the back of my mind, it started to dawn on me that I, Cha Yerin, was sitting in a gutter without any shoes on. I sat up, staring at Seungjin. "Give me your cap," I ordered.

He looked like he was going to deny my request, but suddenly, the hat was pulled off of his head and shoved onto mine. "Now get up."

I did, taking the few steps onto the sidewalk. And then I was crying out in pain. Before I could fall, Seungjin swooped in, his hands wrapping around my waist to keep me upright.

I ignored the warmth of his hands as I lifted my foot. There was blood on the sock.

With an irritated sigh, Seungjin let go of me, almost causing me to fall, but then he was in front of me, crouching down. "Get on."

"What are you doing?"

"How far do you think you can walk like that?"

I looked down at my foot, testing my weight on it. "I'll be OK," I muttered.

Seungjin looked over his shoulder at me, arching an eyebrow. "Sure."

I was about to prove to him I could, then it dawned on me that I could get a piggyback ride from

Lee Seungjin. I would be insane not to. I wrapped my arms around him as he scooped me up, my thighs resting on his forearms.

Without a word, he started walking up the road I'd come running down.

Lee Seungjin …

I was getting a piggyback from *Lee Seungjin* of Bright Boys. Kareun was going to be so jealous.

I sighed.

Kareun was never going to find out.

If I told her that Seungjin had carried me home, I'd have to explain why I'd needed carrying in the first place and she—or anyone else at SLA—could never find out about my father.

How much trouble was he in?

The fact he was stealing money was mortifying. No doubt that would make the news soon. I cringed, resting my head against Seungjin's shoulder blade. Oh hell; everyone was going to find out.

"What are you sighing about back there?" Seungjin asked.

"Nothing," I responded, curtly. "Just keep walking."

"I didn't realize you lived in this neighborhood. I assumed you'd live close to the Academy."

The further up the road we went, the more spaced out the houses were, hidden behind tall stone walls. The advantage to the neighborhood was that privacy. "We moved here a few years ago. We used to live a few streets over."

Would father go to prison? What would happen to us? Were we going to lose the house? Mother had said many times she didn't need to work thanks to father's money, but now he had none, would that still be the case?

Would I need to move into the SLA dorms full time?

Oh no … was I going to become one of those scholarship kids?

What about my college plans? Harvard? America?

"Put me down."

"Don't be silly."

"Put me down!" I cried, trying to wriggle free.

Seungjin lowered himself to the ground to let me free and I stumbled away from him towards one of the tall walls lining the street. I collapsed into it, my hands bracing myself as I tried to catch my breath.

This wasn't how the last eighteen months of school were supposed to go.

"Fake it until you make it," Seungjin told me.

I turned, staring at him. "Huh?"

He gestured to me with a frown. "Whatever you've got going on: hide it. Fake it. Pretend everything's OK. Eventually it will be."

"What would you know?" I asked.

Seungjin shrugged. "About your life? Nothing. About mine? More than you."

"Obviously," I said, flipping my hair over my shoulder. "But your life isn't such a secret. Your father is the President of Atlantis Entertainment, and you're a rookie idol on an enforced hiatus because your group has been caught up in a scandal."

"And do I look bothered by it?" he asked. "Do you think that's all that's going on in my life?"

I turned around fully so I could face him. "Have you ever caught your reflection at school? It's like there's a thundercloud following you around. And if TK is ever within five feet of you, which, as we're in the same class, is all the time, you look like you want to punch anyone who speaks to you." I laughed, but it sounded hollow. "Fake it until you make it? Seungjin, you're not faking anything. Your faking is that bad, I'd advise not going down the K-drama route unless you take some serious acting lessons."

Maybe the words were harsh, but they were true.

He stared at me with his hands jammed in his pocket. Just like in class, he looked like I was someone he wanted on the receiving end of a punch. I raised my chin, refusing to feel intimidated by him.

"You don't know half of what I'm hiding," he growled at me. Then, he marched back down the hill, leaving me where I was.

I watched him go, scowling at his back. Hiding? His life was too public to hide anything, and if he thought he had bigger problems than me, he needed to think again.

제5장

Seungjin

November

The door to Holly's office slammed behind me, the noise echoing around the waiting area outside it. Her secretary, Sejin's old secretary, stared at me in disbelief. Screw her. Screw Holly.

"Seungjin?"

I turned and looked at Hyunseo, the leader—former leader—of Bright Boys.

Rage was thrumming through me.

I marched up to him and punched him. "Don't you ever speak to me again!" I spat at him. "You're the reason Bright Boys doesn't exist anymore."

He was five years older than me and stronger than me, but he didn't say anything. That angered me even more. Not even an apology? I hated him.

I hated Hyunseo.

I hated Holly.

I hated my dad.

I hated them all.

Why had I ever thought that she would be able to save us?

I'd mistakenly believed that blood would get us through this. That my father, my brother, and my sister—half-sister—would make everything right. They owned and ran Atlantis. It wasn't like they didn't have the power.

They just didn't have the loyalty to do so.

Well, screw them.

I didn't need any of them.

Holly had said they would terminate our contracts if that's what we wanted. Well, that's exactly what I wanted. I would go to SM Entertainment. I'd heard rumors of plans for another NCT unit. I'd audition and transition.

My family might not think I was good enough, but I would show them all when I got accepted into SM.

I walked out of the building, taking the main entrance, unnoticed. Six months ago, I wouldn't have been able to do that. There had been fans who would wait outside and now there were none.

I didn't need to go back to school to keep a low profile and have the public forget me: they already had.

I sat down on a bench, staring up at the digital display which was currently advertising H3RO's latest comeback.

The one place I really wanted to go right now, was SM, but I had enough sense to realize this anger wasn't the right thing to take with me. I needed to calm down first. Only, I couldn't. I was angry at everyone and this time, I didn't have a coffee table to flip.

I marched back into the building, taking the lift back up to the top floor, only, instead of heading to

Holly's office, I went straight for my dad's. I ignored the warnings from his secretary and barreled in. Dad was in the middle of a conversation with some guy I vaguely recognized as working in the legal department, but I didn't care. "Did you know?"

It was rhetorical. Holly had already said he knew, but I wanted to hear it from him.

"Son, I am in the middle of a meeting."

The fact he was sitting there, calmly, like I was nothing, had my blood boiling. "She has disbanded Bright Boys!" I yelled. "And you don't even care."

My dad let out an exasperated breath. "Seungjin, I am your father. I have always cared about you, and I always will. But Holly will be overseeing things from here on out."

"Dad!"

"No, Seungjin. Discuss this further with Holly."

"Why are you all trying to ruin my life?" I cried, marching out of the room. I wasn't going to get anything further from him.

There was no point discussing anything with Holly. Sejin had already told me she'd spent her life in America studying English Literature, so she knew absolutely nothing about this industry. I ignored the voice in the back of my mind which was trying to point out the fact she *had* managed to revive H3RO's career, and instead, I went to my last hope in the building.

Sejin.

I wasn't surprised to find the area outside his office empty. Since Inhye had quit her job as his secretary to work with Holly, he hadn't found anyone he liked (a few weeks ago, I'd overheard him telling Dad he needed to send her back). I was surprised when I walked into his office and found it empty.

Confused, I pulled out my phone and called his number. It rang and rang before going to his voicemail. "Hyung, where are you?" I asked, leaving a message. "Holly disbanded Bright Boys. How can you let someone who knows as much about this industry as a duck, dictate a group's contract?"

"Well, that's the first time I've been compared to a duck."

I turned around and glowered at my half-sister. "What do you want now?"

"I was hoping we could talk without you running off. I would like to explain my plan to you, Seungjin, because I really do want to help you."

"You disbanded Bright Boys!" I growled. "I don't want to speak to you. I want to speak to someone who can undo that and actually help me! Why isn't Sejin here? He should be here, fixing this mess."

Holly looked sad at that. "Seungjin, I know we're not close, but I promise you that I'm here to help you."

"Yeah, it seems like it."

She took a deep breath. "Besides, Woojin gave me full reign to deal with Bright Boys, so even if he was here, he wouldn't have the power to do anything."

"WHAT?!"

All the anger that had been flowing around me really did disappear as it was replaced with despair … hopelessness …

There had to be something my brother could do. "When was that decided?" I'd seen him only a week ago and no one had mentioned it.

"It was a very sudden decision," Holly told me.

There was something about the way she said it

that had me narrowing my eyes. "There's more to it than you're telling me."

"There is," she admitted, surprising me. I had expected her to lie. "Only, I can't tell you what that is."

"Of course you can't."

"Seungjin, can we *please* sit and talk. Preferably without destroying furniture?"

"You mean, can you talk at me?"

"No," she said, firmly, shaking her head. "I want to have a discussion with you. I want to explain things so you can see what I'm trying to do, and I want to know what you think."

"I can tell you that: this is career suicide, no *murder*. You're destroying our lives."

"OK," Holly said, her lips settled into a thin line as she folded her arms. "I'm done with this. You are eighteen. Your life has not been destroyed, so let's turn the melodrama down a notch, shall we?"

"That's easy for you to say!"

"Yes," she agreed. "It is easy for me to say, because I have the gift of distance which you don't. My primary focus here has been trying to get H3RO back in the charts, not looking at this mess that you're all caught up in, but because so many people have asked me to look at this—including you—I have done. I am getting as much sleep as H3RO, and I'm not the one who is an idol. I'm new to this—"

"Exactly!"

"SEUNGJIN, JUST SHUT UP!" Holly bellowed at me.

I blinked, taking a step back. But I shut up, mainly because I was surprised to hear her yelling at me like that.

"Thank you," she grunted with an irritated sigh. "I have looked at this again and again. Bright Boys will not recover from this. Not under Bright Boys. You were a new group who hadn't built up the loyal fans you needed, and frankly, considering Hyunseo got physical, I'm wouldn't expect loyal fans to stay loyal to that. You might not have been there, but two other members were. That's a third of your group. I could pull all three out, but that's what your name is associated with."

Holly waved vaguely towards the long empty table at the back of the room. Silently, I walked over and took a seat. I fully expected Holly to go to the other side of the table, but she didn't, pulling out the chair right next to me and sitting down in it. That confused me: Sejin wouldn't have done that.

"You guys need some good publicity right now, but with everything still in the air from Hyunseo's court case, we can't do that. All we can do is distance you from him and show everyone you are good kids."

"I'm not a kid," I objected.

Holly rolled her eyes. "You're still in school. Stay in school. Woojin has done some deal with the academy you're at and we will be partnering with them. Your lessons will be as much performance based as they will be academic. I've gotten some of the artists, coaches, and choreographers at Atlantis to agree to teach at SLA so you can all still learn and improve. Two months, Seungjin. That's all I'm asking for."

"And then what?"

She stared at me, chewing at her lip.

"You don't have a clue, do you?"

"I have a plan," she said, holding a hand up. "Look, I have commitments to H3RO, and my focus has to be on them, but I have something in mind for you guys. I want to re-debut as many of you as I can. But part of that outcome depends on you being at SLA. Woojin is discussing some of the legalities with Park Yongdae, and I need him to confirm things before I say anything. But if you go back to SLA, you will know yourself."

That was the name of the man Dad was talking to. "You expect me to find out tomorrow with everyone else?"

Holly sat back in her chair, clasping her hands together in her lap as she set me with a leveled look. "I'm going to lay it out for you, Seungjin."

"You mean you haven't already?"

"I have been holding back because I don't want to hurt your feelings, but I think the only way you will ever trust me is if I tell you this." She sighed. "Or you'll hate me forever ... The problem both you and I have is our name. Our name combined with working in our father's company. It comes with expectations. Much as I don't like how he went about it, what he's doing for me is helping me. No one knows who I am. Right now, no one has many expectations for me other than failure. The second everyone finds out who I am, they're going to think I got the job because of who my father is. I've got the opportunity to show people what I'm capable of with everyone here working against me. At least I can thank that ... At least I can thank Sejin for something."

"And you're saying I don't?"

"Seungjin, most people think you debuted because your family own Atlantis."

"Go to hell," I growled at her, standing and marching towards the door. I was done with this conversation. I was done with her.

"I never said I believed that!" she cried. "I think you have talent. I just want the world to see that too!"

I didn't respond, instead slamming the second door of the day in her face.

I left Atlantis and returned to school, but once again, I didn't want to go back to the dorm room. No doubt everyone would want to discuss what was happening next and I didn't want to do that.

Because I thought Holly was right.

She was just the first person to actually come out and say that to my face.

No, that wasn't strictly true: Sungil, King and Jaehoon's friend, had told me that a few times before when we'd both been trainees together. He was probably the only person who hadn't been afraid to. The others probably thought it too, but they didn't want to risk their contracts with Atlantis by upsetting the son of the Chairman.

That thought hurt.

I headed up to the roof and my small pocket of sanctuary needing some time to sit by myself and think. Or not think.

Needless to say, I was irritated to discover Yerin was there. "Of course," I muttered.

As soon as she saw me, she stood, smoothing her skirt, and then her long hair. "Lee Seungjin," she said, almost formally.

"What do you want?" After trying to help last weekend, she had spent the week at school ignoring me.

"I never thanked you for last weekend."

I arched an eyebrow, watching her in suspicion. "No, you didn't."

"Well, thank you."

I shrugged, expecting her to leave. She didn't. "You're welcome?"

"Why didn't you tell anyone?"

What? "Why would I?" I asked. "It's your business to share your parents are divorcing, not mine."

Yerin was tiny. Not only was she short, but she was slim. However, she had the pent up rage of a tiny dog. She charged over at me, shoving my chest and pinning me against the wall.

"My parents are not getting divorced and if you start spreading rumors like that, I will kill you."

I stared down at her, trying not to laugh. I could have this situation reversed in a second if I wanted to. However, I'd been exactly where she was about two years ago when my parents were going through a divorce. "I won't say anything," I told her, instead.

"I just told you, they're not getting a divorce." Her words sounded more desperate than final.

From out of nowhere, I had the urge to wrap my arms around her and hold her.

I shook my head, wondering where that idea had come from, then instead stepped out of her hold. "Fine, they're not getting divorced. But whatever is going on in your home is not my business. *That's* why I didn't say anything."

"You'd better not say anything. Or I'll—"

"Kill me?"

"Yes," she said, firmly.

I walked over to the chairs and sat down in one of them, thrusting my hands into my pockets. Leaning back, I stared up at the dark sky. It was somewhere between inky blue and purple, with clouds blocking out the stars.

"What are you doing up here?" Yerin asked.

I glanced over at her. She hadn't moved, but was staring at me, curious.

I was going to tell her it was none of her business, but instead, I decided to tell her truth. "Bright Boys was disbanded."

Yerin's mouth fell open. "No!"

"Yes," I shrugged.

"I can't believe it!" she cried, moving over and sitting in one of the spare seats. "Are you OK?"

I shrugged. No, I wasn't OK. I was far from OK. But I wasn't going to admit to that. "They have a plan. It will be OK."

"This is all TK's brother's fault!" she fumed.

I gave her a sharp look. "What do you know?" It was no secret that the person Hyunseo had punched was TK's brother: it had been all over the news for weeks. Only, the media was painting it as Hyunseo's fault. I still had no idea what had happened, but the other members were adamant it wasn't Hyunseo's fault—even if they still refused to share the details.

Angry as I was, I'd trained with Hyunseo for more than a year before debuting. In the year since, he had *never* come across as violent. He worked out a little, and he was probably the strongest member of the group, but he wouldn't even flick our foreheads as penalties on the variety shows we'd been on. I'd punched him and he'd never punched me back.

"I spoke to Sungil."

"Sungil told you what happened?"

Sungil, Jaehoon, and King had been there and none of them would say anything to the other members of Bright Boys, but Sungil had told Yerin?

"No," Yerin said, pulling a face. "But he did say it wasn't Hyunseo's fault and Min Gyukyung, TK's brother, was making it up."

I calmed down a little at that. Although I still didn't like Sungil all that much.

I leaned forward, resting my elbows on my knees as I stared down at the ground. I'd been forgetting someone important in this blame—Min Gyukyung.

I was still angry that Bright Boys had been disbanded. I didn't expect that anger to go away anytime soon, either. However, I needed to look at the future now. One that didn't involve Bright Boys. Or, at least, Bright Boys as it was now, if Holly was to be believed.

SM Entertainment was still an option, but maybe it was worth giving this plan of Holly's a shot. If nothing else, the scandal was too fresh for SM to consider me. I would need to separate myself from this current image before I auditioned there.

But how could I do that when Hyunseo's court case was scheduled for December?

Unless I got the court case to go away.

I sat up and looked at Yerin. "How much power do you have at this school?"

"What do you need?"

"To make Min Taekyung's life miserable."

"Why?"

"To get Hyunseo's assault charges dropped. You said yourself, he was being blamed for something that wasn't his fault."

Yerin wrapped a lock of hair around her finger as she considered it. "You don't want to go for just TK. His father works here—that's how he's a student here.

You need to go after his dad too."

I considered it, almost saying no. But desperate times called for desperate measures. And I was getting desperate.

"What did you have in mind?"

제6 장

Yerin

"Are you sure we should be doing this?" Eunbyeol asked, nervously.

I looked over at the girl who had her hair braided into pigtails and scowled. "Why not?"

"I don't know, it's just … it feels …"

"If you feel so strongly against it, you can help them clean it up," Kareun told her. She folded her arms and glowered at Eunbyeol until Eunbyeol shook her head.

"It's fine," Eunbyeol said, hurriedly.

I hadn't gone home over the weekend. Mother had said she'd had things to finalize for the Academy and I could study there instead of at the house. It had left me on edge all weekend. Even Kareun and Eunbyeol had seemed perplexed at me not going home.

I still hadn't told them. They were supposed to be my best friends, but I couldn't do it. Of the two, Eunbyeol was the one to be less judgmental about it, but if I told her and not Kareun about it, I would never be forgiven. At the same time, for some reason, Kareun was one of the last people I'd trust with that secret.

"Look, we're doing this for Bright Boys," I told them. Only a few hours after Seungjin had told me, the news had broken across SNS. It was official: Bright Boys was no more. "This is to help clear their names."

I'd told them the plan, but carefully kept Seungjin's name from it. My family was going through problems, and the last thing my mother would want to do is expel her daughter for causing trouble at school … if she found out I was behind it. Seungjin, who had told me he had to be kept out of it, had things to lose.

The added bonus was that, if the news that my father had been stealing to save his company broke, and if my parents did decide to divorce, this act would secure my position, and no one would mess with me.

I glanced around the room. It was nearly the end of breakfast. Seungjin and the rest of Bright Boys weren't present. He'd made sure they'd all arrived early and left just as we had arrived. TK wasn't here either. Which meant it was time.

I got up and walked over to the kitchen staff. "Unless you want my mother to have an unscheduled inspection, I suggest you all leave and do not come back until later."

My mother was an intimidating woman. She ran a tight ship and had exceptionally high standards. An inspection was not something anyone wanted. The last one had resulted in the chef being fired.

The four women scattered.

I returned to my table, climbing up on top of it. The action already had most students paying attention to me. I flipped my hair over my shoulder and took a deep breath. "Whatever is left in your trays, I want you to do this." I took the tray Kareun handed me, held it over the table, and dumped the contents on the floor. "Now."

Not a single person objected.

I kept my breath held so I could let it out in private.

Instead, around me, trays became empty as their contents slopped to the floor and tables. Some students even looked entertained at the process.

As food and chaos rained down around me, I stepped down off the table and then walked out of the cafeteria to get to class. The other students filed in behind me, taking their seats. Finally, Sungil, King, Jaehoon, and then Seungjin walked in, taking their seats. Seungjin paused in front of my table, just long enough to share a smile with me.

I finally let out that breath I had been holding onto, feeling relieved. More than anything, I hoped it would help Seungjin. The bell rang and I looked around the classroom. TK hadn't appeared. Neither had the annoying American transfer student who sat next to Seungjin, Lucinda.

Why wasn't I surprised?

Nam Woosung, our teacher, walked into the room. "A last-minute change to our schedule: Principal Cha would like us all to report to the auditorium for an important announcement."

For some reason, that sent my heart pounding. I stood, keeping my head held high as we all filed down to the auditorium and took our seats. Eunbyeol and Kareun were either side of me, discussing how happy they were that we were missing our Moral Education class, and hopefully we wouldn't have time for our quiz.

I was sitting in silence, trying not to fidget. My mother hadn't mentioned anything about a surprise assembly. She walked up onto the stage, and to the podium tapping on the mic. There was a brief blast of feedback that had everyone wincing but falling silent.

"Thank you for joining me in this unscheduled assembly," she said, as though it had been optional. "I am here today to share with you some exciting news which will see big changes to the Seoul Leadership Academy. Starting today, SLA will be working in partnership with Atlantis Entertainment."

The room burst into life and I found myself staring at my mother in disbelief. Something wasn't right here. My mother cared more about the school and its reputation than anything other than her own reputation—and that was so heavily tied up with the Academy that they might as well be the same thing.

Mother hated idols, K-pop and the music industry in general. As far as she was concerned, if the music wasn't classical, it was disgrace to music in general. Idols were simply cash-cows for corporations. There was no way she would have joined forces with an entertainment company unless the school was in trouble, and by default, her own finances.

How much damage had my father done?

I sat with my head facing the front, ignoring the looks Kareun and Eunbyeol were giving me. They'd known me for forever: they knew this too. I kept my back straight, my manicured fingers gripping my knees so tightly I could feel them digging in.

"… going forward. Most classes will remain the same, however, there will be changes made to the afternoon timetable to accommodate this. Your parents have been notified and we have assured them, as we assure you, those of you wishing to focus on your studies, will continue to receive the top-class education that you have received until now. All of you will now have the opportunity to train with choreographers and vocal teachers from Atlantis Entertainment. At the end of each academic year, you will also be given the chance to audition with Atlantis Entertainment."

I sighed, fully expecting to hear Lucinda complain at some point about how it made no sense for an academic year to run from January to December. As far as I was concerned, it made more sense than an academic year based on farming cycles when she was from, as she was always pointing out, New York. Maybe her family were farmers? That would explain why she didn't want to tell me. I would keep that a secret too.

The room burst into noise again, tearing me from my thoughts of the American. Half of it was excitement, the other was concern. SLA had a reputation of sending students to world renowned universities, creating politicians, world leaders, lawyers and doctors. This wasn't a school which had ever sent a student into the K-pop industry. *Ever.*

"Silence, please!" my mother cried. I closed my eyes as she got the school to fall into silence. "I would like to introduce to you Lee Woojin of Atlantis Entertainment."

My eyes snapped open. A tall man with a long thin face stepped out of the shadows. He was old, easily in his late fifties. I recognized him at once. As well as being the Chairman of Atlantis Entertainment, he was also Seungjin's father. "Hello, students," he said. "To show the commitment of both the Seoul Leadership

Academy and Atlantis Entertainment, we will be enrolling some of our trainees and former rookies here."

Why was Seungjin's father on the stage?

I turned, finding Seungjin at the back of the auditorium with the rest of the members of Bright Boys enrolled at SLA: King and Jaehoon from our class, and Dongyeol and Apollo from the year above. And Ryan Tseng … that surprised me. He hadn't been here at all this semester. Where had he come from? I had to fight to keep the giddy smile from my face—Ryan Tseng was back at SLA! Yes!

All of them were sitting silently, watching the stage, despite the fact I wasn't the only one to recognize Seungjin's father.

"As Principal Cha has stated, this school will continue the route of academia as it always had, but now it walks hand in hand with entertainment. We hope that both sides will provide options for everyone to excel in. I look forward to seeing some of you joining the roster of Atlantis Entertainment in the near future."

The assembly ended soon after that. When it did, Kareun and Eunbyeol immediately turn to me. "You knew about this?" Kareun demanded.

I flipped my hair over my shoulder and shot her an irritated look. "Of course," I lied. "Mother told me not to say anything."

"Since when do you listen to your mother?" Kareun exclaimed. "We're supposed to be your friends. You're supposed to tell us everything."

I shrugged it off, getting to my feet so we could return to our classroom. There was no point in arguing on this one: she was right. But it didn't mean I was going to tell her. Somehow, no one had questioned, *yet*, why Atlantis was partnering with SLA.

Maybe they wouldn't.

Maybe I would be lucky.

It was midmorning when TK turned up, accompanied by Lucinda. I had to pick up my textbook and hide my face behind it so no one could see me laughing. Judging from the state of them, they had spent all morning cleaning the cafeteria.

Admittedly, it probably meant TK's father was spared from being fired: as the janitor, he would have been responsible for ensuring the cafeteria was clean. Normally, the kitchen staff monitored it, and some of the students would keep on top of a general clean-down, but the amount of food we'd left would certainly have been a responsibility that would have fallen to him, even if he wasn't working at that time.

SLA had a uniform: a white shirt, gray blazer, and either a gray skirt for the girls, or a pair of gray pants for the boys. At this moment in time, neither of their shirts were white. TK had a giant wet patch on his back, and a stain from the breakfast soup ruining his sleeve. I was also certain I could see a beansprout in his hair. Lucinda didn't look much better. There were pieces of kimchi on her skirt and something smeared down her leg.

Gross.

I was also still surprised. I hadn't thought she would help, which further confirmed my suspicions that she was here on a scholarship too. She clearly knew her way around a janitor's cupboard.

"What time do you call this?" Nam Woosung, our teacher, was asking them. "School hours are not the time to be having romantic interludes."

Omo! Were those two ... something?

"If I was going to have a romantic interlude," Lucinda said to Nam Woosung, "It would be somewhere more romantic than the cafeteria, cleaning up other people's mess."

"You didn't think to clean yourselves up first?"

"If I have to suffer cleaning up other people's mess, then the other people can suffer through this." She stared pointedly at Seungjin—how on earth did she know that? Why wasn't she looking at me?

With a sigh, Nam Woosung waved them away. Lucinda and TK walked over to their seats. Lucinda sat next to Seungjin, and TK was in front of them both. As they passed me, I caught a whiff of them and nearly retched. Body odor and fish.

It took ten minutes for it to become unbearable. I stood, interrupting the class. "Woosung ssaem, this is revolting!"

Woosung turned from the board to face me, arching an eyebrow. "Cha Yerin, what is revolting is the behavior of students who think it is acceptable to throw perfectly good food all over a room and leave it to other individuals to clean up. However, if the individuals who orchestrated and participated in that revolting act were to confess, I would allow your two classmates to go clean up without gaining any demerits. Assuming they want to, because it doesn't look like they are bothered."

The fact he wasn't calling me out directly told me he didn't have direct proof, but he knew it was me behind it. I sat down and flipped my hair over my shoulder. "I don't know what you're talking about." I have him a nonchalant shrug and then reached into my bag, pulling out the bottle of expensive perfume I carried with me. I squirted it in the air, then aimed it at Lucinda and TK. They were too far to be covered in it, but it made me feel better.

Why on earth had they not gone back to their rooms to shower? That was disgusting!

The bell finally rang for lunch and I shot out of the classroom, desperate for fresh air.

"Can you believe her?" Kareun grumbled as we walked to the cafeteria.

"Who?" Eunbyeol asked.

"Lucinda: she helped him clean up and then came to class looking and smelling like a beggar."

"They must be friends," Eunbyeol muttered.

I rounded on her. "And that gives her the right to come into the classroom without showering? She sits next to Seungjin."

"I was just saying she was probably only doing it to help a friend out," Eunbyeol muttered, shrinking away. "I didn't say she should have come to class like that."

"Seungjin-oppa deserves better than how he is being treated at the moment," Kareun snarled.

We got out food and sat down at a table by the window. I looked around, amazed at how clean the cafeteria was. I couldn't see a spot of kimchi anywhere. For some reason that irritated me. This had been an attempt to help Seungjin out, and it had failed.

Now what could I do?

I yawned and glanced at the clock on the wall. We still had some time before class, and I was still thirsty. "I'm getting Oksusu-cha," I told the other two. The end hatch had a self-service hot drinks area, and I hurried over to it to make myself a cup of hot corn tea. As the tea bag was stewing in my cup, I walked back to the table and found Kareun chewing a piece of gum as she wrote on a piece of paper with a thick marker.

쓰레기—sseuregi. "Trash," I read aloud. "What's that for?"

"We're going to show Lucinda what happens when she messes with our idols."

"I'm not sure—"

Kareun whirled around to glower at Eunbyeol. "You're not sure about what?"

Eunbyeol swallowed. "A ... About how you're going to stick it."

"I've got that covered," she snapped. She got up and started walking out of the cafeteria, the paused and looked over her shoulder. "Well?"

"Is she PMSing?" I grumbled to myself as I followed after her.

We got halfway back to the classroom when we almost walked into Lucinda. She took one look at us and rolled her eyes. "Oh, my favorite people."

I stepped in front of her, using a hand to support my elbow. "Lucinda." I took a sip of my drink.

"Yerin."

My fingers tapped at the edge of the paper cup. "I always had my suspicions of you."

Lucinda glowered at me. "Yerin, I have less than an hour of lunch to go back to my dorm and get showered and changed, so unless you move to the side and let me pass, Gandalf, I'm going to spend the afternoon stinking out the classroom too. And that will also be your fault."

"I think you shouldn't make any accusations unless you have the evidence," I pointed out. Sure, I may have orchestrated it, but she had no proof.

"You're not going to move, are you?" she asked with a sigh. "So be it. What earthshaking news have you got to share with me?"

"News?" I scoffed, shaking my head. "No, I'm here to tell you to stay away from Korea's idols."

"I honestly have no idea what you're talking about."

Was she honestly blind? "Lee Seungjin."

"Seungjin? Again? Really?"

"Stay away from him," Kareun echoed.

"Let me say this slowly, just in case my Korean pronunciation is off, but I do not like Seungjin—"

"Why?" Kareun demanded. "What's wrong with him?"

She had the audacity to look at us like we were crazy. "While I do not deny that Seungjin is very attractive, I am not attracted to him. I have no intention of trying to date him. You will find no threat from me."

"And yet you insisted on sitting your dirty self down next to him," I pointed out.

"Yes, well some people decided to trash the cafeteria, so there is that?" she retorted.

Out of nowhere, Kareun stepped forward, pulling her gum out of her mouth and sticking it to the back of the piece of paper she was holding as she did so. "He is too good for you!" she cried, lunging forward and slamming it on Lucinda's shoulder.

Lucinda let out a cry of pain, then, pulling the paper, let out another small shriek as it pulled out a chunk of hair it had been caught up in. She screwed up the paper and launched it at Kareun.

Before I could stop her, Kareun snatched my

drink from me, pulling the lid off. Some of the hot water slopped onto my hand as she flung it at Lucinda.

I was too busy nursing my hand to pay much attention to the fact King had appeared from nowhere and whisked Lucinda away. I turned to Kareun, ready to kill her. "Are you insane? You got that on me!"

"Ugh," she muttered. "Come on."

Sometimes, my best friend was a complete bitch.

제7장

Seungjin

"We need to talk," I told Yerin as we walked to our next class. She had been reading a text message and looked upset. "Are you OK?"

She stepped back to the side, letting the rest of the students file past before looking at me. "What's up?"

"You look upset," I told her, putting my original topic aside. Upset was an understatement. She looked miserable.

"You wouldn't understand."

"OK, enough of this," I snapped at her. "I don't know why people think idols don't have a clue about real life problems, but we are human too and we all suffer. I'm not a robot. I can empathize."

Yerin's upper lip turned upwards. Bizarrely, that slight sneer was kind of attractive on her. "You wouldn't understand because my mother wants me to attend these performance classes," she snapped at me, before jabbing me in the chest with a finger. "You wouldn't understand because *you*," there was another jab," Want to be an idol and want to do these classes."

"Oh," I mumbled, feeling dumb. "You don't?" I asked, suddenly surprised.

"Harvard," she barked. "I am going to Harvard. I am going to America. This does not make that happen."

She was right. I didn't understand.

I scratched at the back of my head. "Look, I need to talk to you."

She narrowed her eyes as she looked up at me. "What are we doing now?"

"We need to stop this."

"The conversation? OK," she shrugged and turned on her heel.

I reached out, grabbed her wrist and tugged her back. She spun, crashing into me. The next thing I knew, she was in my arms, clinging on to me. I stared down at her. She had beautiful eyes. I'd noticed that before. They really stood out when she lined them with the smoky pink eyeliner she was wearing now. It brought out a warmth in them.

Scandal!

The word shot through my mind like a bullet and I quickly stepped back. "TK. And by default, Lucinda. It needs to stop, Yerin."

"This wasn't what you were saying yesterday," she scoffed.

I leaned against a locker and shook my head. "Yesterday Ryan hadn't pointed out that what we were doing could be considered bullying."

Ryan, an older member of Bright Boys ... a former member ... damnit, that was doing to take some getting used to ... Ryan had somehow guessed that I'd played a part in the cafeteria being trashed and told me to stop it: I was a decent person and decent people didn't act this way.

I wasn't sure I would go so far as to call myself a decent person. I was growing more bitter and angry as the days passed. I wasn't sure Yerin was a decent person either. But we were both better than how we were acting.

"It's not bullying," she said, pulling a face at the word. "It's making sure someone gets what they deserve."

"Maybe, but I'd rather let the universe fix things."

That earned me another eyeroll. "Karma? You want to sit around and wait for karma?" I shrugged. "Karma isn't a thing. Going out and making sure people aren't taking advantage of you, standing up for what's right—that's how you fix things. TK is the reason you're attending these stupid classes."

"TK's brother is the reason I'm taking these classes."

"Well, TK is the reason I'm taking them," she snapped.

"What does that mean?" I demanded.

Yerin ignored me. This time, when she walked off, I let her. How was it TK's fault? Hadn't she said her mother was making her take them?

I followed her to the newly repurposed classroom. Desks had been taken out and one of the walls had a floor to ceiling mirror covering it. I saw Jaehoon and walked over to him. "How does anyone else not see how ridiculous this is?" I asked him.

"I know," he agreed. "But what else can we do?"

"Maybe tell Sejin what happened that night?" I

suggested.

"Even if I did, it's too late. Bright Boys is no more."

I shot him a withering stare. "They would re-debut us now, and we wouldn't have to go through this." I pointed at the mirror where I could see the rest of the class lingering around. "No one has a clue."

"Then maybe we should show them," Jaehoon suggested. At that, he dropped into a deep lunge, stretching out.

I gave my reflection a look. Suck it up, I told myself. This was the only way and I knew it. I joined Jaehoon by doing my own stretches.

It didn't take long for the door at the back of the classroom to open and a familiar face to enter, causing me to smile for the first time in a long time: Ro Chanheon.

Ro Chanheon was a choreographer at Atlantis. He was a good one too. And best of all, he was one of the few people in Atlantis who liked me despite who my family were. He knew I could dance.

Unfortunately for almost everyone else, his presence wasn't a good thing—even if they didn't know it yet. He was a person who believed in the strict use of honorifics; something not uncommon in South Korea. He demanded respect: for himself, and for the dances that he taught.

As Lucinda was currently discovering. Even I had to wince when she started to talk to him informally. All things considered, her Korean wasn't that bad. She'd been getting better. I'd noticed that from sitting next to her. Well, her speaking was getting better. Her writing was abysmal. However, when it came to conversation, she always seemed to default to informal.

Most of the teachers cut her some slack with that. They could tell she was trying. She was a few months younger than me, but I wasn't going to get offended if she spoke informally to me.

Ro Chanheon was not the type of person to cut anyone any slack. Right now, he was giving her a hard time about being in this class. He was convinced she was here because of Onyx and BTS.

The next thing I knew, I was following a crowd to a classroom further down the hallway. This one had a microphone and speakers set up at the far end. It looked more like a noraebang setup than the recording studios I was used to.

Ro Chanheon moved over to it, picked out a song and held the microphone out to Lucinda. I looked at the song choice and winced.

The first time I'd ever met Lucinda was back in the summer. She had gone to a private performance of King's as Sungil's date (I did not buy that one for one moment), and afterwards, we had gone out to a noraebang for some karaoke. Lucinda had surprised me. She was a good rapper—in English, at least. Her singing, however … she had a very narrow range and struggled whenever anything left it.

I joined Jaehoon, Sungil, and King and discovered they were discussing the same thing. "I'm not sure you could class that as singing," Sungil was saying. "Lucinda was awful."

I didn't disagree, but I couldn't help but think that was uncalled for, for a boyfriend … I had nothing but a gut feeling, but if anyone had been dating Lucinda, it was King. "That's not a nice thing to say about your girlfriend," I pointed out although my attention was fixed on King to watch his reaction.

There it was: the glimmer of surprise.

Sungil looked between the two of us, frowning. "She's not my girlfriend anymore."

"Chanheon is going to destroy her. He seems to think she's over here to be an idol," Jaehoon added.

"Is she?" I asked, once again directing the question at King.

"I don't know."

Before I could press further, Lucinda started singing. It wasn't as bad as I remembered: it was worse.

To be fair to her, the song choice, Valenti by BoA, was not a good one for her. But it didn't make for a pleasurable listening experience.

"How do we make it stop?" Jaehoon asked.

I wanted to know the same thing. Much as I hadn't liked how she'd helped TK out, making her do this was not something I wanted to witness. She did not look comfortable and I wasn't that much of a monster.

Ro Chanheon made her sing two verses and a chorus. I knew how seriously he took his job, and how seriously he insisted every one of us had taken it, but this was unnecessary. As far as I was aware, Lucinda had never expressed any interest in being an idol.

According to King (not Sungil …), Lucinda was a dancer he had met on several occasions when they had attended the same dance academy in New York. She'd moved out here to explore more of that.

Actually, I was looking forward to seeing her dance. King was an excellent dancer too, so if she was as good as he was saying she was, I wanted to see it.

When the Ro Chanheon did kill the music,

Lucinda was greeted by a lackluster applause. I don't think any of us really knew how to react to it.

Except Yerin.

"Thank god!" Yerin exclaimed. "My vacuum cleaner sucks less than that. It also makes less noise."

I let out a long sigh as I turned and caught her flipping her long hair over her shoulder. As pretty as she was, she was pretty annoying.

... Had I just called her pretty?

I mean, she was ... but why had that been my first thought?

There was no way I could have a crush on her.

None.

At all.

It was Yerin.

... Aw, hell ...

"What's wrong with you?" Jaehoon asked me, suspiciously.

"Second-hand embarrassment," I muttered.

I managed to get through the rest of the class by pushing that thought to the deepest recess of mind.

By the end of the day, I felt tired, but good. Being back at school meant that I was in a classroom sat behind a desk instead of in a practice room. I'd missed it. I was prepared to stay and dance some more, but other members of the class had taken it over.

The hell with that. I would head to my spot on the roof and dance up there.

I'd walked three paces out of the door when Ro Chanheon barked my name. I turned back to him. "Have you been practicing?" he asked.

"As much as I can with Sejin banning me from the Atlantis practice studios," I told him.

That earned me a scowl. "You don't need a practice studio to dance. You need space and the drive to do it."

"I just mean that it was difficult to dance when I have exams and assignments to concentrate on."

Chanheon pursed his lips. "And what about your singing?"

"I sing," I muttered, not meeting his eyes.

Rarely. I sang rarely. I wasn't the strongest vocalist.

The admission earned me a clip around the ear. "You need to sing as much as you need to dance, if not more so."

"Yes, sir," I grumbled, rubbing at the back of my head.

"I'm serious, Seungjin. That new Vice Chairwoman, your sister, has been working on a plan for a new male idol group, and my sources on the board tell me she's not committed to re-debuting all the former members of Bright Boys. We both know your vocals are your weaker point, and I'm not a vocal coach. If you don't want to be stuck in high school with exams and assignments, you need to practice singing too."

I stared at him, trying to hide my anger. I wasn't angry at him; I was once again, angry at my supposed sister. Half-sister. She had promised me she was going to make things right and it had barely been a day before she had gone back on that.

"I will," I said with a bob of my head, hoping the growl in my voice wasn't as apparent as I thought it was.

Without giving him any opportunity to say anything else, I turned and left him there. I went straight back to my dorm room, slamming the door behind me.

Inside, I found Jaehoon stretched out on his bed, staring at the slats of King's above him. He turned to look at me as I marched in and dropped into the chair at my desk.

"What's the matter with you?"

"My family sucks."

Jaehoon arched an eyebrow. "I never wanted to say it before, but your brother is a jerk."

"He abandoned me to go start a new group in China," I grunted. "Who does that? Why didn't he stick around and save Bright Boys? Why did he have to let that woman destroy us?"

"Oh."

I looked up and found Jaehoon looking awkwardly at me. "What?"

"When you were saying your family suck, I thought you were finally acknowledging the stuff Sejin did."

"What did Sejin do?" I demanded.

Jaehoon sat up and scratched at the top of his shoulder. "I don't think your sister is that bad," he told me. "I mean, yes, it sucks that we were disbanded, but she didn't throw us out or throw us back in the dungeon like so many other companies would have done."

"What are you talking about?" I scoffed. Atlantis didn't really have a dungeon. Depending on who you spoke to it was either a dungeon or a basement, but neither of them were meant literally. It was simply a term for being taken out of the public eye to wait for that opportunity to come back and be released. For some idols, that never happened until their contracts ended. "All she did was change dungeon to a school, and frankly, I'm not sure that's any better."

"Seungjin, she brought in Ro Chanheon. He's one of the best dance teachers and choreographers at Atlantis. And I've heard Ruzt is being brought on board too."

"You're happy about that?" I asked in surprise.

Jaehoon had been set to feature on a mixtape Onyx's Jiwon was releasing. Even though a mixtape was more of an unofficial release than an official album— fans would be able to download the songs for free—it was a huge thing for a rookie rapper to do. Then everything had gone down with Hyunseo and Atlantis had pulled him out of there faster than he could blink, only to replace him with Ruzt.

"It wasn't Ruzt's fault." He shrugged, leaning back against the wall and crossing his legs in front of him. "But I'm going to get the opportunity to be coached by him. Of course I'm happy about it."

"At least somebody is happy about it."

"I've heard she also convinced Sa Hyesun to come in as a vocal coach."

I swear my heart stopped beating. Sa Hyesun was a vocal teacher at Atlantis. She was good at her job, but she hated me, and I had no idea why. I gave Jaehoon an uncomfortable smile. I'd told Sejin about it once and he'd told me to grow a pair; that she was tough on everyone, which was how she delivered the results she did.

"Seorin has told me so many times that all the vocalists in Cupcake are dying to work with her."

My eyes narrowed at that, but for a different reason. "I thought you had stopped speaking to Seorin."

"I have barely spoken to Seorin since Cupcake debuted." He turned his head to stare at a paper crane that always sat on the small shelf above his bed. The pink paper was fading now. They had been dating when they were both trainees, but they had broken up just before Cupcake debuted.

"If you think all of this is so good, why are you here instead of practicing?"

"Why are you?"

Because I was angry.

Because no matter what I wanted to do, there was always someone in my family that was set against me doing it.

Because I was getting to a point where I wasn't sure if I even cared anymore.

제8장

Yerin

I hated running. There were better ways to keep thin than running around a track. Even more than I hated running, I hated running in the rain. I had spent an hour doing my hair and makeup before class this morning. I didn't need forty minutes in the pouring rain to ruin it.

And yet, here I was, running around the track between SLA and SLU, for *Lucinda*. Just because she had never bothered to learn the language before moving out here, why was I being punished for it?

The only thing that I had felt a sliver of satisfaction at was the fact Hong Baekhee was running around that track too. The girl needed to lose several kilograms. She wasn't unattractive. In fact, she had once been quite pretty, but she had piled on the weight at SLA. Which was why I was so confused as to why she was in the performance classes.

My mother was making me be here so I, her good, obedient daughter, could prove to the naysayers that a student could keep her academic ranking *and* participate in the performance classes.

I was willing to put a lot of money, that I admittedly didn't seem to have these days, on Baekhee's mother not knowing Baekhee was in this class.

A long time ago, Baekhee and I used to be friends.

That had changed when we had started here. I'd caught her cheating off me in an exam ...

I finished my laps first and stalked back into the school. I was freezing and it made me even more annoyed at the fact I was out there in the first place. It was November and the temperature was cold enough that the frost on the playing fields didn't start to melt until close to lunchtime.

If I ended up in hospital with a cold, I was going to make sure Atlantis was sued for this. At least then I'd be able to pay for my college fees.

Inside, in a building which didn't have heating, the rooms were just as cold. I detoured to my locker, changing my soaked sweater for an oversized hoodie I had left in there after an early morning study session.

I wringed my hair out, allowing it to drip on the floor, and then checked my appearance in the mirror I hung on the back of my door. I didn't have panda eyes, but it wasn't great.

I ran a finger under my eyeline, smudging it slightly, and then I ran my hands through my hair, ruffling it at the roots. If I was going to have to go back to class like this, I was going to rock it.

Annoyingly, my pants were soaked, and I didn't have spare pair of them in the locker. I only put my gym clothes in there on the days I had gym. If I wanted dry clothes, I needed to go back to the dorm, and given I was sure Chanheon ssaem would just send us back out there, I decided to suck it up.

I was, of course, going to complain to my mother later. With any luck, she'd realize what a colossal waste of time this was and cancel this stupid partnership. Or at least let me return to the academics before I fell too far down the ranks.

I returned to the class still managing to beat the rest of my group.

Ugh.

Not only did I have to participate in this, I had to do it with Lucinda, Baekhee and Miyeon. Miyeon, at least, could dance. I'd caught her and her street dance crew busking in Hongdae a few times and she was good. Eunbyeol was also on my team and a reasonable dancer. Her strength lay in singing. She could hit some high notes!

I was the only one in the classroom apart from Chanheon ssaem. He was at the front, reading over some notes, refusing to look at me. There was no doubt he knew I was there.

Eunbyeol, Miyeon, Lucinda and Baekhee joined the class moments after me. While everyone was as drenched as I was, only without the good hair and dry sweater, they all looked reasonable ... apart from Baekhee. She honestly looked like she was going to throw up or pass out—or both. I rolled my eyes, having no time for her. She'd burnt that bridge a long time ago.

"Where is everyone?" Eunbyeol hissed.

"Didn't you notice the other classrooms?" Miyeon asked her. "It looks like everyone has broken up into their groups to practice."

"Practice what?"

Before Miyeon could answer, Chanheon ssaem

finally stood and walked over. Thankfully, Lucinda remained quiet. I swear, if she had opened her mouth, I was going to gag her: I was not going back out in the rain again.

He walked over to Eunbyeol, handing her an envelope, but his attention was on Lucinda. "I hope that will serve to teach you a lesson," he said as Eunbyeol took the envelope. "You have five weeks." He left us alone in the classroom.

As soon as the door was closed behind him, I reached over and took the envelope from Eunbyeol as she was taking too long to open it herself. The front was addressed to our group: Team Yellow. I turned it over and tore it open, tugging a piece of paper out. "4-Minute, Crazy."

I guess that was the song we're going to perform. I was curious if the other groups had the same song or not. I stared at the song. 4-Minute had two rappers. While I could sing, what I was secretly good at was rapping.

My mother would have killed me if she knew how much I loved K-pop and not the classical music she insisted I listen to, but I loved the attitude some of the girls in the girl groups gave: 4Minute, 2NE1, EXID …

"I don't understand," Lucinda said, interrupting my thoughts with her stupidity.

"4Minute is a group, idiot," I informed her. "This is the song Ro Chanheon expects us to learn."

"I've never heard of it," she shrugged.

"Have you been living under a rock?"

"New York," Lucinda sniped, sarcastically. "This may come as a surprise to you, but I don't know all the groups yet."

"I'll find the video," Eunbyeol offered, helpfully. She pulled out her phone and loaded up the video.

I reached for it, already knowing I could handle Jiyoon's part. "Just to be clear, I will be taking Jiyoon's part," I told the American. "Lucinda, your rapping is acceptable. You might be able to pull off Hyuna's lines."

"Fine," she shrugged.

I arched an eyebrow, wondering why that had been so easy. Lucinda was irritating and the type of person who would have argued with me just for the sake of it. I paused, waiting for some form of disagreement, but when it didn't come, I handed the phone back to Eunbyeol.

I made us watch the video a few times and then, seeing as no one else was going to take charge, assigned a member of 4-Minute to each of us. Eunbyeol was our strongest vocalist, and Miyeon wasn't far behind. Baekhee … well … she could sing too.

Seeing as we had a classroom now, it made more sense to learn the dance now, as I told the others. I wasn't a bad dancer, but I wasn't great at teaching. I turned to the other Koreans, seeing as Lucinda had never even heard of 4Minute. "Which of you knows the choreography?"

Baekhee took a step back, lowering her head as she moved behind Lucinda. No surprises there.

"I do," Miyeon and Eunbyeol both said at once.

I looked at them both expectantly. "Why are we still waiting?"

Eunbyeol turned to Miyeon. "You teach it."

Miyeon gave her a wary look, but she nodded. "Jump in if you need to." She turned to the rest of us. "Right, line up."

Bakehee's hand slowly raised into the air. "I can't dance."

"I don't think anyone here is surprised by that statement," I declared.

"It's OK," Miyeon assured her. "Of all the girl group dances, it's probably one of the easier ones. The main thing is to have some confidence and be sexy."

I snorted at that. Baekhee was not a sexy girl.

Lucinda arched an eyebrow at me. "There's no need to be nasty," she told me, before turning to Baekhee. "Don't worry; I'll go through the moves with you as many times as it takes."

"You know we have five weeks to learn this, right?" I asked.

Lucinda spun back to me. "You're not helping."

"On the count of four, I want you to move your feet like this," Miyeon declared very loudly.

I rolled my eyes at them all. I had homework to do, and I had no intention of staying here all night. I took my position and mimicked Miyeon.

Z

We were there until long past dinner. Baekhee sucked royally. It took her four times as long as anyone to get each step, and once Miyeon tried to combine them, she would make a mistake and get it wrong.

It was the same for the rest of the week.

By the time Friday evening came around, I was glad to go home. Honestly, if I had been depending on this class to get into Atlantis, I would have murdered her by now. She was dragging everyone down.

Just before midnight, I declared I'd had enough.

While Lucinda decided waste her time with continuing to try to teach someone who couldn't be taught, I went back to my room and gathered my things for the weekend.

My mother was waiting for me, Vivaldi playing in the background. She took one look at me and narrowed her eyes. "Didn't you shower today?"

"I came straight from practice," I explained. "I am going to shower when we get home."

Other than that, the car ride was spent in silence. I spent it watching the rain lashing against the windshield as the wipers fought to keep it clear. Something felt off, and I couldn't work out what it was, but I didn't want to bring it up. Mother was in an irritable mood.

I went straight to my bedroom, freezing in horror when I walked in. Most of my furniture and belongings were gone. "Mom!" I yelled. "We've been robbed!"

My mother appeared in the doorway. "No, Yerin. Our belongings have been taken away to attempt to pay for some of the debt your imbecilic father left us."

"You can't call him that!"

"I can call him whatever I want as I divorce him."

My mouth fell open. "You can't do that," I whispered.

Mother took a few steps towards me. "Yerin, I can and will do anything I deem absolutely necessary to protect myself. The only reason we are still in this house is because the lawyers are arguing who this house belongs to."

I shook my head. "That's not a reason to divorce someone. You're supposed to stay by him during the hard times."

"These aren't hard times," Mother snapped. "These are times of survival. His actions must have consequences."

"Divorce?" I asked again. "That is completely unreasonable! He's not even here to clear things up—"

"He's in America!" Mother yelled. "He ran off to America to avoid being arrested for fraud. Your father stole money from the Academy and us. I am doing everything I can to protect us, Yerin! Why do you think I let Atlantis partner with SLA? We need the money. And right now, with your grades, that partnership is the only future you have!"

I pushed past her, my vision blurred with tears, running down the stairs and out into the drive. I wasn't sure where I was going once I got onto the street, but I knew right then I couldn't stay in that house. My father wasn't a criminal. And how could he be in America? He wouldn't just leave without talking to me first. He couldn't leave without me.

I wandered without seeing, without feeling. It was cold and it was raining still. I had no coat on and I was still wearing my slippers, but I just felt numb.

I walked up the street instead of down this time. I'm not sure why I went that way, but I found myself in a small playground. There was a climbing frame with a tunnel, and I went and crawled into it, dripping water everywhere.

Curled up, with my arms around me, I sobbed into my knees. How could she do that?

Divorce?

How could *he* do that?

"Yerin?" the voice was soft, but it made me jump.

I looked up, finding Seungjin at the entrance,

watching me, eyes full of concern.

There were two things I didn't want right now: pity, and a gorgeous boy seeing me like this. "Go away!"

"No," he said, softly, crawling in the tunnel with me. I started to shuffle away, but a hand shot out wrapping around my wrist.

"I don't want you to see me like this," I told him.

"You don't want me to see you like this, or you don't want an idol to see you like this?" he asked.

"Does it have to be one or the other?" I asked, trying to wriggle free.

"I know it's tough, but if you want to talk to someone about your parents' divorce—"

I stopped trying to get away from him, and instead turned in the small space and shoved him. "My parents aren't getting divorced."

"OK," he said, letting me go.

"My dad is in America for work," I told him.

"Then why are you out here crying?" he asked, softly.

"Because …" I slumped forward onto my knees, allowing my weight to settle heavily on the floor of the metal tunnel. I didn't give him an answer, instead listening to the rain as it fell, making chinking sounds all around us. Seungjin didn't try to move, and neither did I as I sat there, tears streaming down my face. I had no words and no energy.

"My brother is in China," Seungjin said, when I had eventually stopped crying. "He didn't tell me he was leaving. I'm not sure he's even coming back."

I looked up at him in surprise. The press had reported Atlantis opening a Chinese office in Shanghai, with Lee Sejin heading out there to oversee it while a mysterious long-lost sister of Seungjin's was taking over the Seoul office. "I'm sorry," I told him.

"Why?" he asked. "It's not like you chased him off." He laughed bitterly. "I'm certain it was Holly who did it."

"Why would she do that?"

He shrugged. "I don't know, but everything was fine until she showed up."

A gust of wind shot through the wind tunnel, and I was suddenly reminded that I was soaked through and cold. From nowhere I started shivering, my teeth chattering.

"You should go home."

"I don't want to."

Seungjin pulled a face. "Then go back to school."

I slowly shook my head. "I don't want to do that, either."

He licked his lower lip. "Do you want to come back to my house?"

I could feel my eyes practically bulge out of my head. "What?"

"It's late. It's really late," he pointed out. "You can't stay here all night. We have a guest room."

It was late. I hadn't left the school until after midnight. It must easily have been two or three in the morning. "Why are you out so late?" I asked, suspiciously.

"I'd had food delivered. I was at the gate accepting the delivery when I saw you walk past." He shrugged. "You aren't wearing shoes or a coat, so I followed."

"Oh," I mouthed.

"Come back to my house. You can have a shower

and I'll order more food."

I glanced past him at the rain. It was sill pouring, and the longer I sat, the colder I was getting. My house was an empty shell I didn't want to return to. "OK."

Seungjin slid out of the tunnel, into the rain. I realized, as he stood up, he wasn't wearing a jacket either, although he did manage to get shoes on before he followed me. He held out his hand and I took it, expecting him to help me out, but he stared at me in horror. "Yerin, you're freezing."

"I'm OK," I lied. Now my hand was in his, I was even more aware of how cold I was.

"I bet corpses are warmer than you," he scoffed.

"Your flirting needs work."

All of a sudden, I was tugged out of the tunnel, straight into the rain—and Seungjin's arms. "You'll know when I'm flirting," he murmured.

I stared up at him, my heart pounding. All of a sudden, I wasn't quite so cold anymore.

I also really wanted Seungjin to kiss me.

I have no idea where that idea came from, but it was then all I could think about. A shiver ran down my spine and the gaze which had been locked on me was suddenly broken as Seungjin stepped back. "Come on," he said, tugging me towards the park's gate.

We ran across the grass. I don't know why, really. I hadn't dried off in that climbing frame and I couldn't get any wetter. But I followed Seungjin out of the play area, trying not to slip on the puddle covered grass in my thin slippers. On the road we slowed slightly as we avoided the water running down the side of the road like a small river.

Then, he pulled me towards a gate in a tall stone

wall. After typing in a code and letting me through, he leaned down to pick up a small black carrier bag. He really had ordered food …

We walked across the lawn, and I looked around the grounds in awe. It was immaculate. I thought my mother had gardening standards, but it was nothing compared to this place. He even had a fountain with a trident in it—the logo of Atlantis Entertainment—although that didn't surprise me.

Inside was a welcome warm haven. I stood in the foyer dripping water everywhere. In the light, I could see just how filthy I was. "This way," Seungjin said, taking my hand once more and leading me down a hallway.

We passed several doors until he paused outside of one. "This is my entertainment room," he said. "When you're showered, if you want something to eat, come in here." He carried on down the hallway and stopped at another door. "This is a guest room. You can stay here tonight." He pushed the door open and we stepped inside. "You can shower in there." He pointed to a door across the way. "I'll leave some clothes on the bed for you to change into."

And then he left, shutting the door behind him.

제9장

Z

Seungjin

I paid for the delivery of pizza and jogged back to the house. This time I'd had the sense to use a coat, umbrella, and Sejin's running shoes. After shedding all the unnecessary items, I took the pizza box back to my entertainment room.

I stood outside and took a deep breath before walking in. This was the first time a female, other than my mom or grandmother, had been in there. I couldn't understand why my heart was beating so fast either. It had only been a light jog between the house and the gate; I was used to performing or practicing for hours.

After another deep breath, I walked in. Yerin was already in there and I swear the sight of her took away that breath I had just inhaled.

I had left her an oversized sweater and a pair of sweatpants, not having any girl's clothes in the house (aside from my grandmother's and I was not waking her up to explain that one …).

They drowned her.

Yerin was at least twenty centimeters shorter than

me. She'd had to roll both sweatpant legs and the sleeves of the sweater several times. Her long black hair hung down her back, the damp ends curling slightly, somehow making her look even smaller.

She was looking at the photographs of me at various stages of my short-lived Bright Boys career which hung on the wall, but she turned when she saw heard the door click.

This was the first time I'd ever seen her without makeup. Her skin was flawless and pale, unlike mine. It made her look younger and more vulnerable and I had another urge to wrap her in my arms. It was also good to see her without the mascara streaked cheeks, even if her eyes were still a little red.

"I got pizza."

Yerin walked over, and it took me a moment to realize the reason she was clutching at her clothing was because she was shy? Yerin ...? Shy?

Then again, this might also be her first time alone in a guy's house.

I moved over to the side of the room with my widescreen TV and beanbags, kicking two into the middle of the space, but leaving a respectful distance between the two as I put the pizza in the middle.

I turned, finding her lingering on the edge of the rug. "Do you want a drink?" I had a small fridge which I walked over to and opened, showing her that it was filled with soda, banana milk, and water.

"You have banana milk?" she asked, her eyes lighting up.

I grabbed a bottle, along with a Sprite for myself, and joined her back at the beanbags, taking the one she had left free. I reached out, handing her the bottle.

While she jabbed it with a straw, I flipped the pizza box open. I'd had no idea what she ate, but I figured you couldn't go wrong with chicken. Judging from the way she snatched up a slice and devoured it, I was confident I'd made the right decision.

"Do you feel any better?" I asked her.

She nodded, then indicated to the photographs. "Do you miss it?"

I glanced over my shoulder, my gaze settling on a photograph of me doing a body roll on our debut stage. "It's like someone cut off my leg," I admitted.

"I think you'll get it back," she said, softly, making me look back to her. "You were born to be on the stage."

"And if I don't?"

She shrugged. "I guess you make a new future for yourself."

"You know you're not bad yourself, right?" I'd watched her in class. She was rough around the edges, but although Lucinda and Miyeon were better dancers, she was the one who always caught my attention.

"I want to go to Harvard," she admitted.

"You can still enjoy performing."

She shook her head, picking a piece of chicken off the pizza. "Why? It's not what I want to do."

"Fun?" I offered. "And if it's not what you want to do, and it's not fun, why are you doing it?"

"My mother wants me to. And it's not that I don't enjoy it, but it's pointless. More than pointless, it's a distraction. My test scores are lower than normal." She ate the piece of chicken and chewed thoughtfully. "The only positive is Baekhee is spending even less time studying than I am, so her test scores have slipped too.

Thankfully, while my scores might have slipped, the ranking hasn't changed."

"Baekhee is the one that can't dance, right?" I asked. In all honesty, I hadn't bothered to learn many names in my class. I hadn't seen the point.

"The one who is going to destroy my grade for this class." She glowered at her pizza. "I don't see why this needs to be graded."

"Because it counts for us." I was talking about me and the other members of Bright Boys.

"But it doesn't count for me," Yerin objected, angrily. "I'm stuck doing a class which isn't going to help me get into college. If I don't get into Harvard, then what do I do?"

I shrugged. "You make a new future for yourself?"

She looked up at me, staring with those eyes that were slowly losing the red tinge. She didn't say anything, but her expression was startled. She probably wasn't expecting me to use her own words on her.

We sat in silence, eating the rest of the pizza. It didn't take long.

I picked up the empty box, setting it beside the trashcan. "What's it like?" I looked back and found Yerin standing in front of my photographs, staring up at them.

"The best feeling in the world," I admitted, joining her.

"Really?" she asked, looking up at me, slightly skeptical.

She had a slight pout to her lips. I wanted to kiss them.

What the … yeah, who was I kidding? I'd wanted

to kiss her since I saw her in my sweats.

"Then kiss me," she said in a breathy whisper.

"Did I say that out loud?" I asked, embarrassed.

"No," she told me, stepping closer. "You didn't need to."

Yerin was bossy and confident. She was pretty and smart. A lethal package rolled into one. A lethal package that was sure to be my undoing.

I kissed her anyway.

I'd never had a girlfriend before. Before I'd signed with Atlantis, I'd either been too young to be interested in girls, or I had been too busy dancing. Then, I was in Atlantis and the contract told me I couldn't date. Mom had always told me not to kiss girls you never intended on dating and I agreed with her.

So why was I kissing Yerin?

My hand slipped up, cupping the back of her neck as she gripped the front of my sweater like it was the only thing saving her from falling off a cliff.

But what was saving me from falling off that cliff?

I wasn't even clinging on. I was diving headfirst off it.

And yet it was Yerin who broke the kiss first.

"I'm sorry, you're not allowed."

"Don't apologize," I told her, firmly. My hand was still on the base of her neck, playing with the hair which had almost dried out. "I wouldn't have done it if I didn't want to. Besides," I added with a shrug. "I'm not in Bright Boys anymore."

Her palms smoothed out the front of my sweater. Or maybe she was feeling the muscle underneath … "It's late. I should probably go home."

I glanced out the window. It was still dark and it

was still raining. "I thought you were staying here."

"I don't know if that's a good idea."

"It was just a kiss," I told her before I could think my words through.

Yerin abruptly stepped back. "I know."

"No," I said, shaking my head. "I don't mean it's *just* a kiss. I mean, I don't expect any more from you."

"I know," she agreed again.

With a growl, I reached for her hand, stopping her from walking away. "Yerin, I like you," I blurted out, surprising even myself at that one. But it was true. "When I say it's just a kiss, I don't want you to think that I expect more from you. But, yeah … I like you."

She stared at me, and then she flicked her hair over her shoulder. "Of course you do. Who wouldn't?"

I had to smile at that.

"But I should still go home. It's going to be less awkward if I can slip in before my mother wakes up and not have to explain wearing a guy's clothes."

I suppose that made sense. "Then I will walk you home."

Z

Our first evaluation was looming and I was ready to kill TK.

It wasn't just the evaluation that was looming, either: Hyunseo had finally had a date set for his hearing and it was the day after our first evaluation next week. Min Gukyung *still* hadn't dropped the charges, and I couldn't do anything with TK either.

If that wasn't enough to want to kill TK, he wasn't making it any easier himself.

I already hated him, and I was finding it a struggle on a daily basis to listen to Ryan and not beat the crap out of TK.

If Team Yellow, Yerin's team, had Baekhee, we had TK.

It was like watching a baby gazelle with three left feet. He was tall and lanky and had no hand-feet coordination at all. He could sing. He could sing very well—I would give him that. He even had the ability to sing and move at the same time, which was not something a lot of people had naturally. Most had to work on that skill.

But he could not dance.

It wasn't that he couldn't remember the moves, because he could—so long as it didn't require the feet moving at the same time as his arms.

The second that happened, anyone around him was in danger of being punched.

In this instance, it was Jaehoon who got on the wrong end of the blow.

"Are you blind?" he yelled at him.

Yes, we were all following Ryan's instruction of not singling him out and doing anything to him, but that didn't mean any of us liked him. And he wasn't helping the situation.

"I'm sorry!" he cried, jumping out of the way and hanging his head.

"It's Ko Ko Bop," Sungil snapped. "You're supposed to make it look sexy. I've seen sexier roadkill."

Harsh but true. There were certain parts of the song where he honestly looked like a headless chicken wafting its wings about.

The guy was a dork. An uncoordinated dork that

had somehow been gifted with an ability to sing.

"Why are you even here?" Sungil asked. "Surely you know idols have a certain image you don't fulfil?"

It wasn't that he was unattractive. He was good looking enough, but that didn't save him from his dorkiness.

"I'm sorry," he apologized.

"Let's just go from the top," King muttered.

He was irritated and I couldn't blame him. He, Jaehoon, and I, had a lot riding on this. Sungil ... I wasn't even sure why he was here considering his father had yanked him out of Atlantis before the ink had even dried on his contract ... but even he was trying.

King and I had spent hours re-choreographing a routine for eight people to fit five, and the only one who still didn't get it was that idiot.

If I failed this because of him, I was going to ignore Ryan and punch him.

King walked over to the music player and stared EXO's song again.

This time, for the first time all week, TK accomplished it without going wrong. He still looked as awkward as a scarecrow in the wind, but that part was his problem. We wrapped up soon after that. It was late and we had our evaluation the following day.

However, I had to make a detour before heading back to the room. "I'll see you there," I told Jaehoon. I had left my bag in the classroom. Intentionally.

Jaehoon waved me off. They were all too exhausted, or worrying too much, to care. Although I was just as tired, I found myself jogging to the homeroom. Partly because it was after curfew and I didn't want to get caught, but also because there was something more important than a bag in there.

I carefully pushed open the door, stepped into the dark room, and pushed it closed. It had barely clicked into place before arms were wrapping around my waist. "Yerin!" I hissed, surprised.

I twisted in her arms and found her staring up at me, her eyes glinting in the little light that was coming in through the windows. "I was cold."

It was mid-November and outside was getting into negative temperatures and it wasn't much warmer in a classroom with no heating. I'd seen shows on TV (on the rare occasion I watched it) to know the rest of the world had heating in classrooms, but it was something that South Korea didn't do as standard. This school had a small heater at the front of the room by Nam Ssaem, but it wouldn't have been on at this time of night.

"I can warm you up," I teased her.

She stood on her toes and kissed me. She tasted of oranges.

Kissing in a classroom wasn't the most romantic of things I could think of, but we were restricted on where we could be.

"How did your practice go?" I asked her, eventually. Her arms were still wrapped around me.

Yerin looked away. "Baekhee is going to screw this up for me."

I reached for her chin, gently pulling her face so I could see it. "Why is it an issue? It doesn't count for you."

Yerin wriggled free of my grip, walking over to the window. She folded her arms, staring outside. "Mother sent divorce papers to my father. She said I'm going to need to get a scholarship if I want to go to Harvard, but my academic ranking dropped below Ha Baekhee. I won't get a scholarship, but I wouldn't get one anyway: I'm not a scholarship kid."

"Is being a scholarship kid that bad if you get to go to Harvard?" I asked, joining her.

She gave me a look of disgust. "I am not a scholarship kid."

I held my hands up. "Yerin, I don't care. It's not my future. But you're the one who said it was yours."

"I am not a scholarship kid," she said, yet again, as though repeating it could change something. "But that's not even the problem. I got a rejection letter: my grades weren't good enough. I didn't even get an interview."

"Then what are you going to do?"

She shrugged. "The opportunity to be an idol is right in front of me."

"Yerin, it's not an easy option, you know. It's hard work," I told her, irritated. There were so many people who figured we had it easy, but it was late nights, constant practicing and evaluations, watching what you ate, being judged for your appearance as much as your talent … If your company didn't put money into your promotions, you wouldn't do well, and then you wouldn't earn money, but if you weren't popular enough, your company wouldn't keep promoting you. The pros outweighed the cons—they always would. But it certainly didn't mean it was an easy life.

"I should have known I couldn't talk to you about this!" she snapped.

I stared at her, wide-eyed. What on earth …?
"You're not talking to me," I told her. "You're making

repetitive statements about you not being a scholarship kid. Do you really want to be an idol?"

"What do you care?" Yerin muttered, storming for the door.

I watched her go, confused. It was no secret that Yerin was the Queen Bee at this school, and with it could come a very … temperamental and fiery personality, but I had no idea what had just happened.

I walked over to my desk and picked up the bag I had left, slinging it over my shoulder.

Girls were crazy. No wonder Atlantis didn't want us dating any.

제10 장

Seungjin

There were only two male groups in our class, and the other group, Team Green, had just performed their version of Wanna One's IPU. Badly.

A small part of me felt bad for them. It wasn't easy to put on a performance and then be judged for it. And the comments the three judges were giving were harsh—they weren't holding back. Some of the members of that group had looked like they were going to cry.

But a larger part felt relieved. Each year had its own performance classes and that meant more competition. I hadn't gotten any information out of Dad about Holly's plans, and I refused to call her and ask her. But the less people I had as competition, the better.

I uttered a silent prayer to the Goddess of Fate and Destiny that luck would be on our side today. This was the equivalent of a midterm and this evaluation would apparently be taken into consideration at the final performance. We were expected to do well now, and we were expected to improve in the final.

My group, Team Blue, took up our positions. Ro Chanheon hit play.

And for the first time, our performance was good.

Hell, it was almost perfect.

We hit all the notes, cues, and beats, and even TK didn't mess up. The performance was being filmed and I was looking forward to watching it back later, but I was certain it couldn't have gone any better.

The song ended and we were rewarded by a round of applause from the class. I allowed myself to relax, sending the goddess a follow-up thank you. Then I joined the others in a line in front of the judges.

I waited, satisfied with our performance, while the three judges had a quick deliberation. The three were made up of familiar faces from Atlantis. Alongside Ro Chanheon were Sa Hyseun, the female vocal trainer, and Ruzt, an idol rapper signed to Atlantis.

I was expecting to hear praises.

And then Ro Chanheon opened his mouth. "Three of you are former rookies at Atlantis," he said. I stared at him, confused, but nodded. "And you," he pointed at Sungil. "You were a trainee there." Sungil nodded. "Then why the hell was that performance so bad? If EXO had seen it, *they* would have been embarrassed at that attempt of copying their song."

My mouth fell open. Ro Chanheon was supposed to be my ally. He had never had a bad word for me when I had been a trainee. What was this? And, more to the point, where was this coming from? Our performance had been good—great, in fact! Chanheon knew why we were back here. Did he need a reminder?

"We're not rookies anymore," I pointed out, irritated. "We're not because that jerk's brother," I jabbed a finger in TK's direction, "Ruined everything for us. You're still at Atlantis. I know you know this. So why would you put him in a group with us? He wants to destroy us like he has Hyunseo."

Chanheon looked at me like I had accused him of being a demon.

If the shoe fit …

"How dare you?" Chanheon cried.

"Seungjin, let it go," King muttered at me, under his breath.

Something in me snapped. I was done with this. I was done with trying to prove myself again! I had done nothing wrong and once again I was facing criticism. I spun around and glowered at King. "Don't you dare stick up for him," I growled at him. Knowing I needed to get out of there before I said something I regretted, I stormed out of the room.

It wasn't until a while later, when I was lying on my back on the roof of the school, that I regretted my actions.

My go-to place, the dorm room, didn't have a shelter. The school roof did. If it wasn't for the fact it was, once again, raining heavily, I would have gone back to my room. Instead, I stared up at the shelter, too irritated to move despite the fact I was cold. It was already dark. I'd been up here for a while, but I couldn't shake the anger.

I was angry.

I was always angry these days.

I was tired of being angry.

But I couldn't stop *being* angry.

I'd never used to be this angry. What now felt like a lifetime ago, I had been a class clown. I wasn't the academic type: that was why I liked to dance. But it meant I had been the first to goof off in class.

Now …? Now I couldn't remember the last time I had laughed.

I hated feeling this way.

The problem was, I didn't know how to make it stop.

I knew it was stupid.

I was still blaming TK.

It wasn't TK's fault—it had never been TK's fault. It had been his brother's fault, and it had been Hyunseo's fault, and even though I knew that, it was Hyunseo who was always absolved of the blame.

Hell, TK had been working his butt off for the performance assignment, and I had ignored it. Considering he had no formal idol training, he wasn't bad.

As much as I was angry at Ro Chanheon, he had spoken the truth … our team had been very good, but considering we were all at the same level, when we had one person who had never even been a trainee in the group putting on a performance as good as those who had, we had done badly.

In the back of my mind a voice was trying to tell me that if we had spent more time working together than arguing with each other, the performance might have been better.

"Shut up," I told it.

And I was angry at myself.

My phone vibrated in my pocket. I pulled it out, ready to dismiss another message, but I realized it was from Yerin. **Where are you?**

School roof, I texted back.

I wasn't surprised when a door opened. Yerin was already lying down beside me before it closed. "You missed my evaluation."

I turned my head and found her staring up at the roof. "I was going to punch someone."

"I want to punch someone too. Baekhee messed up, *again*, and then Lucinda dropped her honorifics with Ro Chanheon."

"I bet that went well," I muttered.

"They're doing a hundred laps between them."

"Why aren't you there?" If I knew Chanheon, he had assigned that punishment to all of them.

"He said a hundred laps had to be run; he didn't say by who," she explained as though she knew my thoughts. "And I still wouldn't run any for Baekhee. She's messed up my chances."

I rolled onto my side, propping myself up with an elbow as I looked at her with narrowed eyes. "Messed up what chances?"

"All of them," Yerin replied, refusing to look at me. "Mom told me last night. She's got enough of the results in to know I've dropped a place in the rankings *again*. Baekhee overtook me. I'm never going to America now. I don't have enough money for college. Father ..." she sniffed. "I had an account set aside for college and Father took that."

"I'm sorry," I muttered. I reached out for one of the hands she had folded over her chest and took it, allowing my thumb to trace patterns on the back of her hand.

"Life sucks, Seungjin."

"Yeah, it does," I agreed.

She finally looked at me then. "Why are you so angry?"

"I'm not angry," I protested.

She snorted. "You practically growled that at me. And you stormed out of the evaluation."

"I left that evaluation because if I stayed any longer, I was either going to say something that would upset Chanheon, or I was going to punch TK."

"Because you're angry," she pointed out.

I sat up, letting go of her hand, and scowled. "OK, yes, I'm angry. Wouldn't you be?"

She lay there, pursing her lips as she considered the question. "I guess I would have been."

"Would have?" I repeated in disbelief.

She nodded. "I still would be. I just don't like seeing you angry," she added, reaching up taking my hand back.

"I don't like being angry."

"What would stop you from being angry?" she asked.

A million things.

But right in that moment ... only one.

I leaned over, placing a hand on either side of Yerin's shoulders. "You," I whispered, before claiming her lips with mine. She tasted of oranges again. I had no idea what lip balm she used, but I loved it. Almost as much as I loved kissing her.

I closed my eyes and lowered myself so that my forearms were bearing my weight, but enough for me to be brushed up against her. With each movement of our lips against each other, the anger in me seemed to dissipate. All I could hear was my heart beating in my chest, the rain falling upon the tin roof above us, and the glorious little moans Yerin would occasionally make.

Z

"Are you feeling better?" Yerin muttered.

It was late. We were still on the roof. Every time I'd tried to stop kissing her so we could go back to the dorms, I'd changed my mind and kissed her again.

There were people in life who carried a stress ball in their pockets. Yerin was my stress ball and I wanted to keep her with me all the time.

I was back on my side, one arm propping up my head as the other was reached over to Yerin, playing with her hair.

Every time I kissed her, time stopped.

It didn't, of course, but my thoughts stopped. Everything that ran through my mind went on pause and all I could think about was her.

Which didn't help when I stopped kissing her.

Because now, new thoughts were creeping in.

The ones that were pointing out that I was still under an Atlantis contract; the same Atlantis contract which forbade dating. The thoughts that were telling me, despite how wrong things seemed to be going, I was still desperate to be back on the stage as an idol again, and I was going to accomplish that.

And then where would Yerin and I be?

"Seungjin?"

I slowly nodded, wrapping a lock of her dark hair around my finger.

"Thank you."

I looked at her and cocked my head. "For what?"

"You made me feel better too." She gave me a smile and then wriggled out from underneath me. "It's long past curfew. We should go back."

We darted back to stairs. Out of our little bubble, it was cold. It had been cold on the roof, but wrapped up around Yerin, I had barely noticed it. Judging from the way Yerin was shivering, I had a feeling she was the same.

We stepped out into the corridor, heading back to the dorm. I reached out to take her hand, when I heard voices. Instinctively, I wrapped my arms around Yerin and pulled her to the wall. The school had several guards. Mostly, they were based at the dorms overnight, but they still patrolled the school. If we got caught, we were in trouble.

"I recognize those voices," Yerin hissed at me.

I listened.

"You can't call me that, King."

"It's Lucinda and King," Yerin said.

I frowned. What were they doing out at this time of night? When I walked around the corner, it was obvious. King's hand was in Lucinda's hair and he was leaning into her ...

"Are you kidding me?" I blurted out, angrily.

The pair leaped apart.

"What are you two doing here?" King asked us.

The anger I had finally gotten out of me was back in a snap. I stormed up to King, glowering down at the younger man. "Are you kidding me? We've been sent back to this hell hole to clean up our images and you're here fooling around with a fan?"

"What about you?" Lucinda snapped at me.

"You're out with Yerin. What's your story?"

"Seungjin and I are just friends," Yerin snorted from behind me. I half-turned to her, surprised. She was my friend. It was just strange to think of her that way. She had always just been Yerin …

"That's more than what me and King are," Lucinda retorted.

My attention was on King at that statement. He looked hurt at her words.

There was definitely something going on between them. I'd thought so for months—I was willing to bet that her dating Sungil wasn't entirely correct either. It made no sense.

I'd seen the way King had been looking at her. "If you go around touching fans like that, you're going to get into even more trouble than you're already in."

King rounded on me, his eyes flashing dangerously. "Don't you dare accuse me of touching fans inappropriately."

I shrugged. "I never said that, but if the shoe fits…"

"What is going on here?"

The four of us froze. I recognized Ro Chanheon in an instant. "Nothing sir," we all replied, almost in unison.

"Curfew was more than thirty minutes ago. Would any of you care to explain why you're not in your rooms?"

"We were just returning from cleaning the classrooms," Lucinda hurriedly supplied. "Sir."

"Really?" Chanheon asked, looking at the rest of us. "Which classrooms were you cleaning?" There was something about the tone of his voice which made me think we were doomed.

I wasn't the only one.

"Aw hell," Lucinda muttered under her breath.

"I want you all to report to the front of the school at 5 am sharp," he instructed us. "Dress warm."

"Is that not outside of curfew?"

Yerin was right: that girl couldn't help herself. She really needed to learn when to just shut up.

"I am going to enjoy this," Ro Chanheon informed us.

Whatever 'this' was, I wasn't looking forward to it.

"Get back to your dorms. Now."

We did as instructed. Lucinda stormed off ahead. King was trailing just behind her. Outside, it had finally stopped raining.

"Why are you angry at that?" Yerin asked, quietly.

We were on the path between the school and the dorm. Chanheon wasn't with us, and Lucinda and King were far enough away from us that we could talk. "Who wouldn't be angry at being punished? If it wasn't for those two, we'd be in our rooms now and—"

"I'm not talking about that," she told me. "I'm talking about the fact you're angry King was kissing Lucinda. Do you like Lucinda, or something?"

I pulled a face. "No."

"Then why does it matter if he was making out with her?"

"Because she's a fan and he's not supposed to be doing that."

Yerin stopped suddenly. I had to turn around and walk back to her. "What?" I demanded.

"Then what am I?"

"You said it yourself: you're a friend." She stared at me like I had just told her I had kicked a puppy or committed some other heinous crime. "What?"

"Nothing," she snapped, before flipping her hair over her shoulder and storming past me.

"What the …?" I hurried after her. "Why are you getting mad? You're the one that said that!"

Yerin stopped suddenly again, only this time, I had to avoid walking into her as she whirled around. "I said that for their benefit, jerk," she spat. Then, leaving me staring after her, she took off at a run to the dorm.

"What just happened?" I demanded to the night air.

Girls.

They made no damn sense!

제11 장

Yerin

My alarm went off and I slammed my hand down on it. Seeing as it was my phone, it didn't do much good. Muttering curses under my breath, I picked it up and cancelled it.

It was four in the morning and I'd not slept. At all. I'd been tossing and turning all night, and for once, it wasn't Kareun's snoring that had kept me awake. Although she had been doing her best impression of a bus on the other side of the room.

Kareun was someone who could sleep through a fire alarm (and would have done on two occasions if I hadn't awoken her for the drill). As such, I had no issue with turning the light on to get ready.

One of the few benefits left to my mother being the principal was that I only had to share a room with Kareun. I got dressed in clothing I knew I would be warm in, but I could move in: if there was one thing that I'd learned about Chanheon, it was that he saw exercise as punishment. I was not going to ruin a good pair of shoes over Lucinda Williams.

Once dressed, I moved into the small area that could almost be considered a kitchen—if it had an oven and a full-sized refrigerator. Normally, I had breakfast in the cafeteria. It was too early for it to be open, but I had a small hotplate in the room and got some porridge warming while I fixed my hair into a high ponytail.

After picking at the porridge that I was hungry enough to eat, but too upset to want to, I went into the bathroom to brush my teeth and stared at my reflection. I'd had no sleep and I looked like it: my face was puffy, and my eyes were ringed in red.

Seungjin.

He'd never called me his girlfriend, but I had assumed after all the kissing, that was what we were. I'd only called him a friend because I knew he wasn't supposed to have a girlfriend.

Except for me, of course.

But if he'd never called me that, and he was happy to class me as a friend, what was I really?

I sighed and hung my head.

I was an idiot.

Of course I wasn't a girlfriend.

How could I be?

But that didn't mean it didn't upset me. I was Cha Yerin! I was the best-looking girl in the school. My mother was the principal. Up until recently, I had been one of the highest ranked academically.

Who wouldn't want to date me?

… Seungjin, apparently.

I switched the lights off before I left, and then went down to bottom of the steps outside of the dorms. I purposely went to one side, avoiding the others who were already there waiting, and pulled out my phone.

Until Ro Chanheon arrived in his car, I listened to my music, ignoring everything else.

When he did pull up in his small car, after keeping us waiting, I put my phone away and stood.

Chanheon wound down the window. "Get in."

"I'm sitting in the front," I declared. I was not getting squished in the back with Seungjin ... I was not getting squished in the back at all!

"Yerin, you're the shortest one here," Lucinda said, rolling her eyes at me. "Let Seungjin sit in the front."

"I am sitting in the front," I repeated. I didn't care if Seungjin was the tallest.

Beside Lucinda, Seungjin let out a sigh. "Let her sit in the front. We won't be in here long." He moved to the car and got into the back, sliding over to squeeze in behind Chanheon.

A moment of guilt flashed through me, but I set it aside and got in the car.

However long Seungjin had expected us to be in the car, he had probably grossly underestimated it. The journey, which had lasted longer than an hour and had taken us out of the city, had been spent in awkward silence.

While Lucinda didn't seem to have any clue where we were heading, I did. I just couldn't work out why Ro Chanheon was taking us up Bukhansan, the mountain which sat to the north of Seoul. There was nothing up it. Just a few houses and a National Park, and I swear I was not leaving the car if he insisted on us going for a hike.

Chanheon drove us almost all the way up a long and winding road, the surface of which was gradually changing from asphalt to dirt and gravel. Finally, we dove through a gate and the car came to a stop in front of one of the few traditional houses up Bukhansan. One look at it told me there was either a generator or no electricity at all.

Marvelous.

I got out of the car, the others falling out behind me, complaining of stiff and cramped muscles. At the top of the mountain, it was freezing. I'd dressed for warmth and had brought my coat, but the wind whipped around me, making me squeak in surprise.

"Follow me," Chanheon declared before walking off. I followed him, glowering at the back of his head. It was too early and too cold for him to be this relaxed. He led us around the back of the one-story building and pointed to a fallen tree that was about half the length of the house. "That needs chopping up into firewood."

The four of us looked at the tree, then back to Chanheon. "We'll never get that done before class," Seungjin pointed out.

Chanheon shrugged. "You will be here for however long it takes."

"Are you expecting me to chop a tree up?" I asked, ready to walk out of there. The area was filthy and damp. The tree was covered in green moss which looked like it was going to stain my clothes if I got near it. I folded my arms and glowered at our teacher. "Do you know how expensive this coat is?"

"Take the coat off," Chanheon shrugged at me. And at that, he walked off, disappearing back around to the other side of the building.

I stormed after him. "Wait, does my mother know where we are?" Chanheon ignored me.

I glowered at the space he had been in. There was no way my mother knew I was here. I pulled out my phone, ready to call her ... only there was no signal. Of course there wasn't—we were up a mountain.

I shoved the phone, and my hands, back into my pockets and stalked over to the others. They were standing around the fallen tree, looking like they were actually considering doing as Chanheon had told them.

I looked at the small collection of tools: a two person saw and two axes.

Ha! Even if there was a chainsaw, I was not doing this.

And that's exactly what I told them.

"Just shut up and grab the other end of the saw," Lucinda told me. She picked up the two-man saw and held it out to me.

I folded my arms, tilted my head at her, and tapped my toe on the ground.

"I can't do this by myself," Lucinda told me.

Let me go cry a river.

"I'll saw with Luna," King sighed.

"Of course you will," Seungjin muttered, staring pointedly at King while Lucinda proceeded to tell King her name was Lucinda.

Actually, that was a good point. Why was he calling her Luna anyway?

"What does that mean?" King demanded.

"Any excuse to work with your girlfriend, right?"

"She's not my girlfriend!"

"He's not my boyfriend," Lucinda added

I rolled my eyes. "Will you two just get a room."

"I sincerely hope you break all your nails today."

"Go to hell!" I yelled at Lucinda.

"You're here. I must already be in it."

I took a step towards her, fighting with myself not to rip her hair out. I hated her. She was acting like she was a somebody when reality, she was a nobody. A nobody sent here to make my life miserable. I wasn't going to admit it, but she was right: I was in hell.

King held his hands up. "If it's such an issue, Luna and I will use the ax," King told Seungjin. "You two can saw."

"I've told you; my name is Lucinda!"

I laughed, bitterly, but this was almost entertaining. "Great, now we're in the middle of a lover's quarrel."

"Then why don't you and Seungjin explain why you two were wandering the halls after curfew too?"

"That's a good point," King chimed in.

"Don't deflect your relationship onto us," Seungjin said, shaking his head.

I folded my arms and pointedly refused to look at Seungjin. If that was the way he was playing this, I was done. He was not worth how upset this was making me. I was Cha Yerin, and I was not going to be made miserable by a boy.

"What are you doing?" King asked, bringing my attention back to the scene in front of me. Specifically, Lucinda, who had decided she wanted to chop up the tree by herself and had apparently gotten her ax stuck in it.

Idiot.

"What I can to get home," she grunted, sounding as irritated as I felt.

"Let me," King muttered, before attempting to pull it free. It took some effort, and then it was in his hands. He turned back to me and Seungjin. "Yerin and Luna—Lucinda—need to use the saw."

I snorted. "I'm not using anything." To make my point, just in case they thought I wasn't being serious, I moved over to the tree stump, found the cleanest, non-green part of it I could, and perched on the edge of it, folding my arms. "You all might be used to manual labor, but I'm not."

"What does that even mean?" Lucinda demanded. "Other than you saying you're lazy."

It was a good job I wasn't near her or I probably would have slapped her. "I'm saying that my mother pays for people to do that work for me, so why should I do it? You, on the other hand, are probably used to working manual labor considering your background."

"My background being I'm American? Or a dancer?"

"All the scholarship kids have crappy jobs like that," I pointed out.

"Yerin, I have never had a job. Instead of working, I went dancing. I practiced at least eight hours every day during the week before and after school, and more over the weekends when I wasn't in competitions. Dancing isn't a cheap hobby. There are registration fees, competition fees, I pay the dance school fees, and I have different competition outfits."

I stared at her in disbelief. I knew she could dance, but until then, I hadn't really thought about it. "You're a dancer." The more I thought about it, the more I realized she might have a point. Dancing was an expensive hobby.

"I am not here on a scholarship. The fees I'm paying—my parents are paying—are similar to what the fees were for the private school I attended in New York. State, not city, because there is a difference," she added, like I cared.

I pursed my lips. "Then what do your parents do?" I'd asked her this before and never gotten a straight answer.

"Why does it matter? Will knowing their occupation suddenly make me eligible to be your friend?"

"Yes," I shrugged. How could she not see that a person's family was something important to consider when choosing a friend. I wouldn't trust the family of someone poor to come into my house. As my mother always told me, your friends are a reflection of you.

"How about we just suck it up, get this tree chopped up, and then we can go back to school where we only have to talk to each other in our performance classes?"

"I don't do manual labor," I told her again.

I didn't.

At least, not with the chopping.

It was late morning and I was cold, tired, and hungry. To try to distract myself, I started moving the pieces of wood they had cut up and adding them to a pile that had already been started behind the house.

I felt a little more human after Chanheon had cooked us beef stew for lunch. Which also irritated me—just how long did he really intend for us to stay out here?

After we had washed up, we returned back to the stupid tree, led by Chanheon. He eyed our progress with disapproval. "You still have a lot to do. You want to be quick, otherwise you'll be cutting in the dark. It might be faster if all four of you helped."

I swear the last part was aimed at me. "How long do we have to stay out here?" I demanded. Enough was enough.

"How long does it take to chop up a tree?" Chanheon shrugged, before disappearing around to the front of the house.

"I really don't like him," Seungjin muttered under his breath.

"He has a point," Lucinda said, giving me a pointed look.

I glowered back. "I don't do manual labor," I told her through gritted teeth.

"So I've heard."

"You two get started," Seungjin told them. "Yerin and I will be right there." Before I could protest, he was leading me away from the tree and out of earshot.

"What?" I demanded.

"Why are you in such a bitchy mood?"

"I'm always in a bitchy mood," I shot back at him. "I'm a bitch."

"You're crazy," he muttered, rolling his eyes. "But you're not a bitch. At least, not normally with me."

I shrugged at him, wrapping my arms around myself to keep warm.

"What's wrong, Yerin? Is this about what you said last night?"

"Nope," I said, shortly.

Seungjin folded his arms and stared at me.

"What?" I demanded.

"We're not going anywhere until you tell me what's wrong."

I gave him a hollow laugh. "Get comfortable."

For a ridiculous length of time, we just glowered at each other. It was incredibly petty and childish, but I had nothing more to say to him.

Or at least, I didn't think I did, but seeing as he just kept staring expectantly at me, as though it wasn't obvious, I figured I would spell it out to him.

"What are we?"

He seemed surprised that I broke first, but he recovered quickly. "Friends."

"Then why do you expect more from this conversation?"

"Why are you upset about that?"

"Because I like you, idiot," I snapped at him. "And I *thought* you liked me."

"I do," he said, slowly. "But I can't date."

"That means you're just going to waste my time, stringing me along so you have someone to make out with?" I demanded.

"No!" he objected, thankfully looking offended at that. Though it seemed to irritate me more. "I can't date, Yerin. I can't risk what I am barely holding onto."

"THEN STOP KISSING ME!" I yelled at him. "Because if you really thought that, you wouldn't be taking that risk!"

He looked shocked. "What?"

"You heard me," I told him, marching up to him. "If you were really that worried, you wouldn't be creeping around and finding secret spots and times for us to make out. You just wouldn't do it at all." I jabbed at his chest, feeling a sliver of satisfaction when he winced. "That's why you're getting so annoyed at King and Lucinda. It's not that they're dating; it's that they're managing to get away with it and you're too scared."

"I'm not scared," he snapped.

I stared at him, tilting my head as I slowly shook it. "If that's the case," I said, quietly. "You're just an ass." I walked away from him. "I'm done with this place."

"Then why don't you stop being such a lazy, spoiled, prissy queen, and help out. Then maybe we'd get things done quicker."

When I turned back, he was already marching back to join the others.

I watched him go. I knew I was being precious about it. I didn't like chores. I wasn't sure how many people did. I also did have a maid who would do that for us—or at least we used to have one. She'd gone about a month ago, with Mother lying to say she wasn't up to the job and would be replaced, and then not replacing her.

But it was like doing this was finally accepting that things were changing and there was nothing I could do to stop it.

I was Cha Yerin, daughter of the principal of the Seoul Leadership Academy: the *QUEEN* of SLA.

I had tried so hard to keep up the façade, like my mother was doing.

Because the moment I let it slip, I knew I wouldn't be the Queen anymore.

With the back of my icy hand, I brushed away a tear that was threatening to fall, and then slowly, reluctantly, made my way back to the others.

제12 장

Seungjin

It was almost dark, and I really didn't want to be out here anymore. From the corner of my eyes I could see the looks Yerin kept sending my way, and I didn't like it. Why couldn't she understand that I couldn't date her? It wasn't like I hadn't told her that. And even if I hadn't, *everyone* knew idols didn't date!

In the last hour, King and Lucinda had made good progress on attacking the trunk. They weren't finished and because the sun was setting and I had a chill I couldn't shake, I picked up an ax and turned my attention to the tree.

I allowed myself to get lost in the work, enjoying the warmth it generated, but also how the monotony was something I could get lost in …

Until I caught a glare from Yerin.

And then it sent a pang of guilt through me.

Guilt and … disappointment.

The thing was, I actually liked her.

"We need to stop now. I can't see anything and it's cold." I turned, finding Yerin giving me a look of contempt. Wonderful.

Thankfully, despite the look Lucinda was giving me, the others agreed. We walked around to the front of the building as a group, taking our time in the dim light. I was looking forward to going back to the dorm and curling up in my bed. My body ached. Although I was used to being active and dancing, chopping wood had used muscles in my back and shoulder that didn't normally get a workout and I was eager to get back and relax.

I looked for the car, ready to call dibs on the front seat—Yerin was definitely going in the back this time—and then I realized I couldn't see it. I stopped abruptly, looking around.

"What's the matter, Seungjin?" Lucinda asked me.

"Where is the car?" I asked, slowly. Was I going blind?

"Where's what …?" Lucinda trailed off. I turned back to them as confused as Lucinda sounded. "Where's the car?" she repeated. "Where's Ro Chanheon?"

I looked around, trying to understand what was being asked. The words made sense, but why would a teacher leave us up the side of a mountain?

"Did he forget us?" Yerin asked. At least I wasn't the only one who had thought that.

"How do you 'forget' four students?" Lucinda asked, looking at her like I was an idiot.

"Maybe he has gone to get food?" King suggested.

The grounds illuminated slightly as the moon came out from behind the clouds. I looked around again, but it was obvious there was no car there. Even one as small as Ro Chanheon's couldn't be hidden that easily.

There had to be a reasonable explanation. Maybe he had simply moved it out of the grounds and onto the street? I jogged over to the gates and tried to open them. They wouldn't move. "I think they're locked," he told them, confused. Why would someone lock us in here?

"This is ridiculous teacher behavior," Yerin declared. "And when my mother finds out, Ro Chanheon will not be employed at Seoul Leadership Academy anymore." She pulled her phone out of her pocket and unlocked it before trying to call her mother. After several attempts, she held it up in the air, cursing it. "Why is there no signal?"

"Probably because we're in the middle of the boonies," Lucinda snorted.

What the hell were the boonies??

"Countryside; the middle of nowhere," she clarified. "Now what?"

"What about you three?" Yerin asked. "Where are your phones?"

"In my room, charging," Lucinda replied.

Yerin looked at King who shrugged. "I don't have one," he told her.

"Who doesn't have a phone?" she snorted.

"A lot of trainees, actually," King pointed out.

Yerin rolled her eyes. "Seungjin has a phone." She whirled around and looked at me. "Where is your phone?"

In one place that wouldn't be of any use tonight. "The dorm." It wasn't that I had forgotten it, so much as Chanheon would probably have confiscated it, and

I'd only just gotten it back. I had no idea what to do. I looked at King, hoping he did.

"As irritating as Chanheon is, he would have done this intentionally, not accidentally. He's probably still trying to teach us a lesson," he offered, as though that was enough.

"What is it with Koreans and weird lessons and punishments?" Lucinda huffed, walking off, King close behind her.

I had no intention of following, until Yerin did.

"What are you doing?" Yerin asked.

"If he has done this intentionally, he's probably left us a note somewhere," Lucinda explained. "Use the light on your phone to see if you can see anything."

Yerin did as she said, turning the flashlight on. I was surprised to see a note stuck to the door.

As I said, if you hadn't finished by the time the sun set, you would stay here.

"That's it?" Yerin said, tearing the note from the door and turning it over. The back was blank.

"Hold up," Lucinda said. "I'm a little slow at reading."

"It said if we hadn't finished then we would stay here," King supplied.

"Until when?" she asked.

"It didn't say."

"I am not going to become a mountain woman," Yerin declared. The idea of Yerin becoming a mountain woman had my lips curving up and I had to turn my head before she saw and bit it off.

"You wouldn't survive as a mountain woman," Lucinda informed her.

"OK," I said, once I'd made sure the smile was

completely gone from my face. "Ro Chanheon is not going to leave us here forever. He is probably going to leave us here overnight." Being abandoned up a mountain did seem extreme, even for him, but here we were.

"Can teachers really do this?" Lucinda asked in surprise.

"Oh. My. God!" Yerin exclaimed in exasperation. "You're not in Oz anymore. Get over it already."

"Kansas," Lucinda said with a sigh. "We're not in Kansas anymore."

"We have two options," King said, interrupting them. "We can either spend the night here, or we can make our way back to the school by ourselves."

"It took us over an hour to drive here," Lucinda pointed out. "It will take most of the night to walk back."

She wasn't wrong.

"We don't have to walk all the way back," Yerin said, her eyes lighting up. She held her phone up. "We only have to go as far down as we need to find civilization and signal."

"Then let's go," Lucinda agreed.

Yerin turned towards the gate, the light from her phone's torch leading the way. Back at the gate, King and I shook it a few more time, but it wasn't opening. He really had locked us in. Ignoring the fact that he had left us up a mountain, it probably was the safe option.

It didn't help us get out of here. "We're going to have to climb over the wall," I realized, stepping back to look at it. I was over one hundred and eighty centimeters. The gate and the wall either side had to be at least 200 centimeters. "Do you girls want to stay here?" I offered.

I had been thinking they wouldn't want to attempt to climb over, especially Yerin who hadn't wanted to help out all day, but she and Lucinda shook their heads quickly. "This is the perfect setting for a horror movie," Lucinda told me.

"I don't think there are ax murderers walking around out here," King laughed.

Lucinda shared a smile with him. "I don't know: there are two axes over there and if Yerin continues to be annoying, there might be."

I burst out laughing. It earned me a smack in the gut from Yerin. "And you're supposed to be on my side."

"I'm sorry," I told her.

I wasn't.

Yerin let out a grunt of exasperation and stormed off towards the wall. She turned back at us and pulled a face. "Someone is going to need to give me a hand up."

"Don't break a nail, will you," Lucinda snorted.

"Let me go over first, and I can help you both down on the other side," King told her. "Seungjin can help you both up." King looked at the wall, and then at me. "Do you think you can get up by yourself?"

King was short. He was taller than the girls, but he was still short. Of the four of us, there was only one of us that wouldn't have a problem getting over that wall. "I'm not the one who needs to worry about that."

That was all it took for King to take a running leap at the wall and haul himself up and over. "OK," he called.

I walked over to the wall and crouched down, holding my hands out. Lucinda went first, stepping into my hand and I quickly boosted her up. As soon as she was on the other side, I turned to Yerin. "Your turn."

She walked over, biting her lip. "You're not going to drop me, are you?"

I was going to give her a snappy retort, but in the end, I just shook my head. She stepped up and was soon on the other side. Once clear, I reached up, hoisted myself up then dropped onto the soft ground beside the others.

The walk down the road was creepy. There was no person or house in site, so the only light was coming from the moon through a filter of branches and evergreen trees. I didn't like it. I had grown up in the center of Seoul and I was used to noise.

"How on earth did Chanheon find this place?" I muttered, peering between the trees. I was half expecting a wolf or something to stare back at me.

The next thing I knew, I was being laughed at.

"What's so funny, Lucinda?" Yerin demanded.

"Look at us," Lucinda said, still laughing as she gestured to the four of us. "We are four kids who grew up in households with money in the city. We are the four worst people to put alone in the countryside. If this was a post-apocalyptic movie where all technology suddenly died, we'd be useless. We'd be the first to die."

I looked at the four of us again. Aside from Yerin who was wearing what looked like a ski jacket, the rest of us weren't in clothes suitable for the negative temperatures we were walking in. Even the grip on my running shoes wasn't the best thing for the slippery gravel road beneath us.

Much as I didn't want to admit it, Lucinda was right. I wasn't designed for camping, much less fending for myself. Hell, if all the adults suddenly disappeared from the world, I wouldn't know what to do: I didn't even know how to cook. Even in the dorms, Ryan or Jaehoon had taken care of that.

The next thing I knew, Yerin was on the ground, shrieking in pain.

"Are you OK?" Lucinda asked in alarm. She crouched down beside her, trying to see if she was hurt.

"My phone!" Yerin yelled.

"Your phone isn't as important as your leg," Lucinda informed her.

Yerin batted Lucinda's hands away. "It is when we need it to call for help!"

"Hell," I muttered under my breath, scanning the ground around us, trying to catch a glimpse of the case glinting back at us in the moonlight. Only, there was no moonlight. There also wasn't any light from the phone itself. Yerin had been using the torch to help guide us, so even if it had fallen torch down, it would still have had a glow to it on the ground.

"Everybody just stay still," I said. My eyes caught a brief glimpse of something. "I think I see it!" The next thing I knew, I was feeling something get crushed beneath my feet.

"Please tell me that wasn't my phone," Yerin muttered.

I closed my eyes, wincing, as I crouched down. I lifted my right foot, just enough to slide her phone out from it.

"Great!" Yerin cried in irritation before collapsing backwards on the ground.

I picked the phone up and examined it. It was dead. Great.

"It was an accident. This didn't happen intentionally," Lucinda pointed out, jumping to my defense.

"We're still screwed," Yerin snapped, angrily.

"We are not screwed," Lucinda told her, firmly. "We just need to walk a little further." She stood and then offered her hand to Yerin.

Muttering things under her breath, which I was sure was aimed at me, Yerin allowed Lucinda to help her up. She took a step towards me to get the phone back, but then crumbled to the ground again yelling out in pain.

"What's the matter?"

"My ankle!" she winced.

I thrust the phone into my pocket then dropped down beside Yerin. "Let me look." She didn't fight me as I gently ran my hand over her ankle, prodding it, carefully as I tried to feel for swelling. She winced. "I'm going to move this a little more," I warned her. "Be honest and let me know how much it hurts."

I'd barely turned it before she was punching my shoulder, yelling in pain. "Ow!"

"Enough," Lucinda snapped. "He's trying to see if it's broken, sprained or twisted. He's not trying to pull your foot off. Unless you've got the most ridiculously low pain-threshold, suck it up and let us know how it really hurts."

"It hurts!" Yerin objected, she turned to me, staring up at me with tears in her eyes. Another shot of guilt for Seungjin …

I lowered the foot but left my hand on her. "I don't think it's broken, but I don't think you should be walking on it."

"What do we do then?" Lucinda asked, looking down the road. "Do we split up?"

"There's no way that Chanheon would have left us without the intention of coming back first thing tomorrow," King pointed out. "If we try to carry Yerin down the mountain in no light, we run the risk of hurting ourselves. The safest option is to go back to the house."

"How do we get back over the wall?" Yerin asked.

King shrugged. "We'll figure that out when we get there."

Still feeling guilty about the phone, still crouching beside her, I turned my back to her. "I'll carry you," I told her, softly.

"So long as you do a better job than you did with my phone," she grumbled.

I waited until I was standing, my hands holding her legs firmly as her arms wrapped around my neck. "You remember that it was you that dropped your own phone, right?" I asked her.

"Whatever," she muttered.

Taking care so I *didn't* drop her, we walked back up the hill. Yerin wasn't heavy at all, but the weight of her on my back was almost comforting. Her earlier words kept playing in my head, as they had done on and off all evening.

What she had said was bothering me; about how, if I was that worried about being caught then I wouldn't have done anything to start with ...

That wasn't right. The only reason we were hiding was so the world wouldn't find out. Just because I didn't want to get caught didn't mean I didn't like her.

Yerin was annoying. She was barely speaking to

me, but her words were irritating me.

We arrived back at the house and the four of us stared up at the wall. It had been easy enough to get over without carrying Yerin. Lucinda and King were trying to come up with a plan to get her back over.

"Hold tight," I told Yerin. Before she could object, I charged at the wall, letting go of my grip on her at the last moment as I leaped up and grabbed the top of the wall to the soundtrack of her screams in my ears.

"Shut up!" I hissed as I pulled myself up.

On the top of the wall, I gripped her legs again, readjusting her on my back. "Give me a warning before you do something like that," Yerin hollered in my ear as she smacked the back of my head.

"I did," I snapped at her. "I told you to hold on. Now, hold on, again."

I dropped off the wall on the other side.

Once more, I was rewarded with a smack to the back of my head. I refrained from dropping Yerin to the ground.

"Are you OK?" Lucinda called over the wall.

"Yes, we're fine. We're going inside," I shouted back.

"Are we?" Yerin demanded.

"The other option is I leave you outside in the cold," I told her. I was still tempted, but I continued to carry her over to the old house. She was muttering something, but I couldn't make it out as I opened the door the note had been pinned to and walked in.

제13 장

Seungjin

There were only small windows in the room, but as the moon had disappeared behind the clouds, they weren't doing much good anyway. I allowed myself a moment to let my eyes adjust to the near darkness. "I wish I had a light," I muttered.

"We had one, until someone destroyed it."

"I didn't do it intentionally," I retorted through gritted teeth.

The clouds shifted allowing a little more moonlight to illuminate the room. I spotted a pile of bedding in the corner and moved over to it. With Yerin still on my back, I plucked the top blanket off, spread it on the floor, and then finally crouched down to let Yerin off.

Strangely, I missed the warmth once she was gone.

Seeing as she was shivering, I figured she did too. I moved back to the pile of blankets and picked up another, using it to drape over Yerin's shoulders. "Thank you," she said, surprised.

I nodded, then moved back to the side of the room, wondering if Chanheon would have had the sense to leave a first aid kit.

He'd done one better.

I found a box of candles and matches.

There weren't many, but they made all the difference in the small room. They also allowed me to find a first aid kit. Armed with light and bandages, I moved back to Yerin. "I'm going to take your shoe off before your foot swells," I told her.

She nodded. The only sound from her was a whimper as I pulled her running shoe off. "It hurts," she told me.

"I think it's only a sprained ankle," I assured her. I'd sprained mine several times before. They were painful and uncomfortable, but quite quick to heal provided they were treated correctly. In this case, it needed a compression, ice, and elevation. I had two of the three handled. The third ... it was a good job it was a cold night.

"Thank you," Yerin said, quietly, as I stuffed a rolled-up bandage on the floor. Underneath her.

"Are you warm enough?" I asked her.

She nodded, refusing to look at me.

"Is this how it's going to be now?"

"What?"

"Acting like we broke up when we didn't even date."

She finally looked at me then, her eyes lined with incredulity. "Exactly."

I threw my hands in the air. "Yerin, I can't date."

"So you keep saying," she shrugged.

"Because it's the truth!" I snapped.

She folded her arms and glowered up at me. No wonder the other students at school were scared of her. Her stare was intimidating.

But I wasn't the other students. "What do you want to hear from me?"

"Honestly, nothing."

"I'm beginning to think the rules are there just so we can keep our sanity," I told her.

"Your sanity?" she repeated, laughing dryly. "Seungjin, have you ever just stepped back and looked at yourself? The person affecting your sanity is you!"

"What does that mean?" I demanded.

She arched an eyebrow at me. "You're all over the place. I'm not even sure if you know what you want anymore."

"Excuse me?"

"Your group gets disbanded because one of its members gets into a fight with a member of the public," she continued, ignoring me. "So you all get sent back to a school which literally changes its curriculum and mission statement *for you*, and you spend half that time fighting with a guy who can do nothing to help you get back to being an idol, but could completely destroy you if it ever got out how you treat him."

"How I treat him?" It was my turn to repeat her. "Are we forgetting who orchestrated the little incident in the cafeteria?"

"Which you were all for," she said, matter-of-factly, and with no shame. "You get angry at Atlantis who are trying to help you. You get angry at the teachers who were sent over to help you, and then you get angry at me because you don't know what you want."

"I know exactly what I want," I scoffed. "And I'm

angry because people are working against me to stop it all from happening." I folded my arms. "And if we want to talk about turning the mirror on ourselves, maybe you should look at yourself, because you might be the queen at SLA, but you might as well change your name to Maleficent. And you also don't know what you want, so don't pretend you've got your life on track."

"Maleficent?" she repeated, shocked.

"Yerin, you're a bitch," I informed her. "You think I've been mean to TK, but at least I have a reason, whether or not you think it's acceptable. You, however, are mean to everyone. You claim the thing in the cafeteria was to help me, but I know you enjoyed it. You're a bitch to Baekhee, and I have no idea why. Yes, the girl is fat, but that's not something you need to call her out on in front of everyone. And … and more than that, you're an elitist snob. How many times tonight alone have you told Lucinda you can't be friends with her—not because you have nothing in common, which you probably do have—but because you don't know what her parents do? Is that why you want to date me? Because I'm an idol? Or because my dad owns Atlantis?"

The words were out of me before I could stop them. They were mean and cutting, and yes, they were true, but just like Yerin didn't need to call out Baekhee, I didn't need to say them.

I also hated the way she looked at me afterwards; like I had ripped her heart out.

"Go to hell, Lee Seungjin," she told me, coldly.

I turned around and walked out of the room.

Outside, the anger left me.

Anger.

Again …

I was beginning to think I needed to see someone about that.

With a sigh, I leaned back against the closed door. "For what it's worth, Yerin," I muttered to no one. "I'm sorry."

Maybe, in the long run, this was for the best. I *couldn't* date. If she hated me, she'd move on quicker.

I glanced out across the grounds, my eyes picking up on something on the ground. I cocked my head and squinted, trying to work out what it was …

Lucinda was lying on top of King …

"What are you two doing?" I yelled.

Those two were a thing. They had to be.

I watched as Lucinda scrambled up off King. "We're coming!" he yelled back at me.

Cold and irritated, I stepped back inside.

Of course, I regretted that when I looked over and saw Yerin hastily wiping her cheeks as though she had been crying. I sighed. "Yerin—"

"Don't." I wasn't the only one who was angry.

Before I could apologize, Lucinda was pushing open the door behind me. She moved over towards Yerin. "How is your ankle?"

"It hurts. I'm cold. I'm hungry." Her response was clipped.

Lucinda frowned, sticking her hands into her coat pockets and pulled out something. The next thing I knew, she was throwing me something. I caught it and arched an eyebrow. "You have food?" The kimbap was no longer triangular, but I didn't care. I was starving. I tore off the wrapper and ate it quickly.

"That's it," Lucinda said, peering around the

room. "Did Chanheon leave anything for us? Have you looked in the other rooms? Is there any food in them?"

"I was binding up Yerin's ankle."

"I'm going to check them out," Lucinda declared, carefully picking up one of the candles and taking it outside with her.

"I'll come with you," King said, following her.

I waited for the two to leave before I sat down in front of Yerin. She was still refusing to look at me, the kimbap only nibbled at. I knew she had to be hungry. "I'm sorry," I told her, meaning it.

"Mmmm."

"You're right. I am angry all the time, and mostly it's at things I can't change." I shivered, rubbing my hands over my arms and shoulders. It was going to be a cold night, and not just because of the temperature. I sucked in a deep breath. "And more importantly, I'm sorry about what I said before. It was rude and it was mean."

"The reason I don't like Baekhee is because our first year at SLA, I caught her cheating. She stole my mother's keys while she was at my house and broke into her office to take a copy of the final exam answers." She looked up at me. "And the only reason it never went public was because I didn't have any evidence."

I rubbed at the back of my head. OK … that sounded like a reasonable explanation to not like her …

"And before you say anything else, she then spread rumors that *I* had cheated on that exam. No, I don't like her, and yes, I will take every opportunity to hurt her like she hurt me."

I sucked in another deep breath. "And Lucinda?"

"Lucinda … TK … they're all the same: they're

sucking up money from the school when the school needs it. Instead of bringing in kids who don't pay for anything, they could keep classes small, and reinvest in our education."

"It's called philanthropy," I told her, dryly. "You know; doing good for others when you have the money and position to do some good."

"Sometimes charity needs to start at home!" she snapped at me.

I arched an eyebrow. That was the first time I'd ever heard Yerin even hint that help was needed. "What happened?" I asked, gently.

She shook her head. "I'm not telling you," she snorted. "I've not even told Kareun what's happening, so what makes you think I'd share that with you, when you've made it perfectly clear that I mean nothing to you."

"Isn't it obvious that you do mean something to me?" I asked, almost surprised at my own words.

No, not surprised at them.

Just surprised I was saying them out loud.

"No, Seungjin, it's not," she informed me. "Unless I'm someone you can take your anger out on."

"I deserve that," I agreed.

She snorted again. "You deserve more than that."

"That's true." I shifted my weight so that I was on my knees in front of her. "Cha Yerin, I am truly sorry for what I said to you. I do consider you to be my friend."

Not just a friend, but I could hardly say that to her now.

"If that's what you consider me to be, then fine," she huffed, although she didn't look happy. "But that's it. We're not something else."

Not being something else was better than being nothing at all.

"I'm hungry," Yerin grumbled.

I stood. I wanted to say more to her; to apologize again … to try to put into words all the things I wanted—needed—to say to her, but now wasn't the time. I sniffed at the air. "I think they might have found something to eat. I'll go check. Stay here where it's warm."

"I'm not planning on going anywhere," she said, pointing at her ankle.

I stepped back outside. The outdoor oven Chanheon had cooked the stew on earlier was lit and something was bubbling away on the top of it. My attention, however, was on King and Lucinda.

I *swear* something was going on between those to. I waited for King to walk off, leaving Lucinda alone. "Are you dating King?"

"No," she replied.

"And what about me?" I don't know why I asked that. Someone had mentioned it once, and there had been the note—although the handwriting had been too scruffy to match Lucinda's still-learning meticulously-neat Hangeul.

Lucinda smiled at me. "Wouldn't you know if we were dating?"

"No, that's not what I meant. Kareun said you liked me."

"We had fun at karaoke, but the most I liked you was as a friend."

"Liked?" So she *had* liked me?

"I know you think you have your reasons, but the

way you've been treating TK is cruel."

Ah ... the other kind of 'liked'. I sighed, tired of justifying myself over this. "His brother—"

"His *brother*," she cut me off before I could explain. "Exactly: his brother, has done questionable things. Not TK. TK's actually a nice person. He has his faults, like we all do, but he helped out with Baekhee when he didn't need to."

I cocked my head as I gave her a look of incredulity. "You don't know what happened. You weren't there."

"From all accounts, neither were you."

And just like that, I remembered what day it was. It had been late when we had returned to the dorm the night before, and really early when we had left this morning that I'd not had chance to talk to Jaehoon. I also didn't have my phone with me ...

I turned and kicked at something that was on the small porch. It soared through the air, hitting the side of the wooden house with a bang that sounded much louder in the still, quiet air. Nearly as loud as my cursing.

"What's the matter?" King demanded, appearing from nowhere.

"It's Hyunseo's court date and we're stuck up a mountain," I yelled, furious at the fact that I not only had forgotten about it, but I had no way of knowing what had happened. There was a part of me that was convinced Chanheon had done this intentionally.

"He's going to be fine, hyung," King told me.

I stared at him in disbelief, wondering when he had turned psychic. Much as I wanted to believe that, at no point until now had anyone indicated he was going to be 'OK'. "Is he, though? You read the news stories.

No one believed in him. No one believed in us. That's why Holly disbanded us."

It was Lucinda who responded. "From what you've said, she sent you back to SLA. I don't think she would have done that if she didn't think you were worth the second chance she's giving you."

I couldn't keep myself from rolling my eyes at that. "What would you know?"

Lucinda shrugged. "I know very little. This ... *life* of yours is ... crazy. It's crazy and it's competitive, and people either seem to love you or hate you to the extreme. You keep acting like it's not fair that you were disbanded, and that you have to start again, but the fact you *can* start again shows someone at Atlantis has faith in you."

I stared at her in disbelief. Her words were eerily echoing what Yerin had said.

She stared back, suspiciously "What?"

"Do you really think that?" I asked.

"It's not like there have been many other groups who have been through the same scandal as you guys have, but your company still has your back."

"They sent us back to school," I pointed out.

"They could have just sent you home," she returned. "If they weren't on your side, they wouldn't have kept you at Atlantis. I mean, I know you have rules and everything, but when it comes to someone breaking the law—"

"Ya!" I objected, angrily

Lucinda held a hand up at me. "I didn't say he was guilty or not, but the fact is, Hyunseo was arrested, and it seems like the only reason others weren't was because Hyunseo kept quiet. Either way, there is a court case. If

Atlantis really wanted to get you gone, they didn't need to look far for an excuse. Instead, they kept you. I'd take that as a win."

She'd been dishing up bowls of rice as she had been speaking. Full, she picked up two spoons, stuck them in and started walking towards the room Yerin was in. "TK had nothing to do with this. The ones bringing him into it are you, and honestly, it makes you look like jerks."

I couldn't wait to get out of here.

제14 장

Yerin

My mother didn't come with me to the hospital. Instead Nam Woosung, our homeroom teacher, accompanied me. "Are you OK, Yerin?" he asked me as I sat on the bed, waiting for the x-ray to come back.

"What teacher abandons students up a mountain?" I huffed. "I have four weeks before the performance evaluation."

Nam ssaem gave me a half shrug. "Regardless of whether or not I feel the punishment was appropriate, your mother and the board do, Yerin, and I think …"

I didn't hear what he thought. I looked over to the door, expecting to see the doctor but finding Seungjin.

"I'll go see if the doctor has any news," Nam ssaem said, walking past Seungjin and closing the door behind him.

"What are you doing here?" I asked.

"How's your ankle?"

I narrowed my eyes at him. "What are you doing

here?" I asked, again.

Seungjin walked hesitantly to the bed, like he expected me to throw something at him. Which, had there been anything within arm's reach, I possibly would have done. When he got close enough, he held out a bag he'd been carrying that I hadn't noticed. "Here."

I took the bag from him and pulled something out: a new phone. "What's this for?"

"To replace the one that I broke. I took it to the store this morning and they said it was beyond repair," he explained.

"Oh," I muttered. I had been missing my phone. When we'd returned to school, I'd tried walking back to the dorm so we could shower and change into our uniform before class, but I hadn't gotten very far before Nam ssaem had seen us and insisted on taking me to hospital. "Thank you." I set the bag on the small table beside my bed. "Shouldn't you be in class?"

"Some things are more important."

"Like what?"

He stood awkwardly by the side of my bed. "Like you."

I was still annoyed and upset with him, but it didn't stop my heart fluttering. Curse it. "Oh."

"I meant what I said last night," he told me.

I arched an eyebrow. "Which part?"

He shifted his weight, wincing. "The part about being friends."

"Seungjin," I sighed, settling back into the pillows. "A guy and a girl can't just be friends."

"We can be."

He looked so sincere, that I stupidly believed him.

"OK," I conceded. "We can be friends."

With a smile, Seungjin took the seat beside the bed. "Good. And I want you to know that if you ever need anyone to talk to, I can be that person."

Before I could tell him there would never be a day that I would spill my secrets to anyone, much less him, the door opened, and Nam Woosung and the doctor walked back in.

The doctor walked up to the edge of the bed and nodded his greeting at both of us. "The x-rays have come back clear and I can confirm you haven't broken it. Keep the compression bandage on it, and take it easy for the next few days, and you should be back to normal by the weekend."

Normal … I wasn't even sure what that was anymore.

Z

Thanks to being on a mountain, and being in the hospital, I had missed a day and a half of classes. I was already stressing about that when Ruzt announced the change in evaluation plans. As well as our group performances, we were expected to perform a solo piece in whatever our strength lay: singers would sing, rappers would rap, and dancers would dance.

And, because Baekhee had dropped out of our group, Ruzt was suggesting we take the opportunity change our group performance choice to something which would suit us all, implying that the rap parts we'd assigned ourselves for the 4Minute song didn't play to our strengths.

As well as three weeks from this evaluation, we

were three weeks from finals.

I did not have time for this, and yet here I was, late in the evening, arguing over song choices.

"This is ridiculous," Miyeon sighed. "Instead of finding a song that plays to one person's strength, we should find one that works for all of us."

"Or everyone who actually wants to be an idol," Lucinda shrugged. "I know I'm an OK rapper, but I don't want to do this for a career. So who here does?"

No one put their hand up.

"Then why are we arguing?" she laughed. "Look, let's just pick a song that's straightforward and do it well, rather than try to pick out something one of us is going to struggle on and do it badly?"

I wanted to disagree on principle, but she had a point.

"I don't know K-pop, but I would say, let's pick a song by a four-member group which has two rappers and two singers and then we don't have to worry about reworking parts," she shrugged. "Any suggestions?"

"Blackpink, 2NE1, Mamamoo, Stellar, EXID," Eunbyeol started to list.

Miyeon held a hand up. "We have to do two. I suggest EXID and Cupcake."

"Cupcake have five members," I pointed out.

"But Cupcake's 'Could This Be Love?' would work well vocally, for all of us."

"I don't even care anymore," I muttered. "Whatever." I limped to the door. "I have to study. Eunbyeol can tell me what you've chosen and I'll learn the lyrics."

"Yerin!" Lucinda cried in exasperation. "We need to practice."

I shot her a look. "I thought you said you didn't want to be an idol? Besides," I pointed at my bandaged ankle, "How am I going to dance with this?"

At that, I walked out of the practice room, pulling my phone out of my pocket. My mother had sent me a text message demanding I go to her office. Wonderful. No doubt she had the end of week rankings and I had slipped once more, rather than being concerned that I had been abandoned up a mountain and ended up in the hospital.

"Everything OK?" Seungjin asked, falling into step beside me.

"Shouldn't you be practicing?" I asked him.

He gave me a sideways glance. "Shouldn't you?"

"I have other homework to do," I told him. "I still care about my grades."

"How is your ankle feeling this evening?"

I stopped and looked up at him. "What is this?"

He grinned. "A conversation between two friends."

"Well, from one friend to another *friend*, you might want to go practice some more, because your last evaluation didn't go so well."

He leaned forward, grinning. "Want to help me practice?"

"Nope," I informed him before limping away. Much as I wanted some sass in my walk, the sprained ankle meant the best I could do was flip my hair over my shoulder.

I rounded the corner and flopped against a wall.

"What are you doing, Yerin?" I asked myself. That was straight-up flirting. We'd already established that he and I wouldn't be a 'he and I'.

"Is something going on between you and Seungjin?"

I nearly jumped out of my skin as Kareun appeared beside me, hands on hips, staring at me like I murdered babies in my spare time. "No," I told her.

Her eyes narrowed. "It didn't look like it to me. That looked like a flirting."

At least it wasn't me seeing things. "Seungjin and I are just friends," I told her.

"Since when?" she demanded. "When did you become friends with a member of Bright Boys?"

I had somehow forgotten she was a Dazzle. "We live near each other," I shrugged. "It's nothing more than that."

"It better hadn't be, Yerin," she said, taking a step towards me. "You don't date idols."

I held my hands up and fixed her a look. "I'm not dating an idol," I told her, firmly.

"Good," she muttered. "Because I would ruin you."

"Excuse me?" I asked, blinking. As a fan of Bright Boys, she took the term to the extreme, even back when they had been a group. She was one of those fans who clearly expected the members to stay single for them. But I was surprised to find her threatening her best friend.

"You heard me," she shrugged. And then she walked off.

I watched her leave, shaking my head in amazement, simply because I couldn't work out just how serious she was being. Unfortunately, knowing her as well as I did, I was sure she would carry out that threat.

Now I was starting to understand just why Seungjin had been adamant there was nothing going to happen between us.

Only, he *was* flirting with me.

This whole thing made my head hurt. I had enough to worry about with finals and this stupid performance evaluation.

My phone beeped at me: it was my mother. Again.

With a sigh, I continued my slow walk down to her office and entered. The look she gave me told me I was not going to enjoy this conversation.

"Your grades and rank have slipped again, Yerin," she told me. "I wouldn't mind if your performance marks were better, but they're abysmal. I read Ro Chanheon's feedback, and frankly, I'm disappointed. You're supposed to be setting an example for the other students."

"Mother," I said, trying to keep calm. "I cannot focus on my academics and my performance classes."

"If you want to succeed, you will."

I fell silent. There was no way anything I was going to say would be heard.

Mother tilted her head. "You do want to succeed, don't you?"

"Of course!"

"Then why are you acting like such a disappointment?"

I could feel my bottom lip start to quiver and I had to clear my throat and straighten my back. "I don't want to be an idol, Mother. I want to go to America for college."

"Your father signed the divorce papers this morning," she announced, like she was offering a guest tea or coffee to drink.

My mouth fell open. "What?" I'm not sure how vocal my question was, but it had my mother rolling her eyes at me nonetheless.

"Don't act so surprised, Yerin," she said, coldly. "I told you it was going to happen. Your father has agreed to stay in America and cut off all contact with you."

"He agreed?" I blurted out. "What about what I want?"

"Stop acting like a child," she snapped at me. "It is in your own best interest."

"If you were that worried about my interests, you wouldn't have divorced him to start with!" I cried.

"This was the only way I would agree to not to go to the police about the missing Academy money. A divorce is a much cleaner story than a criminal offense. Or do you want your father in jail?"

I didn't want either.

"Now, I've given it some thought, and I think your best option for the future is to sign with Atlantis. It will look good for the school if you can accomplish that, however I still expect you to improve your grades for the finals. How you end this year will dictate how your next year will go, and the reputation of Seoul Leadership Academy and myself, are dependent on it. With regards to your father, we are keeping up the story that he is working in America."

"You're going to pretend to stay married to him?"

Mother nodded. "Of course. I don't want my name to be associated with that topic. I have my reputation to protect and maintain."

"Then why can't you just stay married to him?" I

asked in disbelief. "I know he's done some bad things, but you're supposed to stick by him!"

My mother licked her lips as they settled into a thin line. "I think for the time being, while you are preparing for your final examinations, you should stay at the school on the weekends. Given your grades, I think you should return to your room now and start studying."

I left her office feeling like I was having an out of body experience.

My father had gone without saying goodbye.

My mother had banished him under threat of sending him to jail.

We were to pretend that everything was normal.

Everything was falling down around me, and it was like I was off to one side, watching it all unravel rather than experiencing it. Even my ankle didn't seem to hurt as I walked down the corridor, not really seeing where I was going, and then I walked into someone.

Snapped back to the present, I found Baekhee in front of me, apologizing profusely.

I looked around. Others were there, watching.

My hand shot out, grabbing at the front of her shirt, shoving her backwards into a locker, hard. "You need to watch where you're going!" I yelled at her.

A hand wrapped around my wrist. "Let go of Ha Baekhee, Yerin," Seungjin said, calmly.

I rounded on him. "Or what?"

"Or I will make you," Lucinda announced, appearing from nowhere.

"Am I supposed to be scared of you?" I sneered.

"Yerin, let go of Baekhee," Seungjin repeated, calmly.

"Or what?" I snapped at him.

"So that we can go get some bubble tea."

I blinked. "What?"

The hand that was wrapped around me released me, only so he could hold it out to me. "Bubble tea."

I took his hand, confused. The out of body feeling returned as we walked down the corridor, hand in hand.

Seungjin led me out of the school and off the grounds. Silently, compliantly, I followed. It was a good thing my mother's news had shocked me to the point my ankle didn't hurt. He led me to the back of a nearby coffee shop to a couch hidden away in the back behind giant potted plants and left me while he went to order drinks.

Alone, the tears that I had been desperately trying to fight back broke free.

I felt like I had been caught up in a tornado and sucked off the ground. Hell, I could have been in Oz and it would have made more sense than my life right now.

Seungjin returned carrying a tray with two steaming mugs on them. He took one look at me and set them down on the coffee table in front of me, before moving and sitting beside me on the couch. Without a word, his arm reached out around me, pulling me to him.

I didn't have the energy to fight him. More than that, I was craving his touch—anyone's touch—just something to make me feel.

My heart hurt.

My soul felt like a crack had appeared in it.

I sobbed into Seungjin's jacket while he rubbed

reassuring circles over my arm, making appropriate hushing noises.

In front of me, the two drinks slowly stopped steaming.

Finally, I felt like there was nothing left to cry. I tried to sit up, but Seungjin just clung to me. "What if someone sees us?" I asked.

"No one is coming back here," he assured me.

I had no idea how he was so confident, but I didn't care to ask.

"What happened, Yerin?" he asked me, softly. "You seemed OK when I saw you earlier, and then you just flipped out on Baekhee."

"Can you keep a secret?" I asked. I looked up and found him nodding at me. "My father's not in America for work," I admitted, lowering my gaze, too ashamed to look at him any longer. "He and my mother got divorced. Only, I have to pretend everything's OK and that's not what happened."

"I'm sorry," he muttered, resuming the rubbing of my arm.

"I don't know how to look at anyone anymore."

Seungjin stopped rubbing my arm and pushed me up off him, almost holding me upright as he gently gripped my shoulders. "You can start by looking at me. I don't care that your parents are divorced. I care that you're hurting over it, but their divorce has nothing to do with you."

"People are going to talk," I mumbled, still not looking him in the eye.

"How are they going to find out?"

"How won't they?" I asked.

"If you're pretending everything is OK, then how

will people find out?" he asked again. "No one knows about my parents."

I finally looked at him then, my mouth dropping open. "Your parents are divorced?"

"Last summer," he nodded.

"What happened?" I asked, my eyes wide. Seungjin was an idol, and his father even more famous than he was. How did no one know about it?

Seungjin sucked in a deep breath and leaned back. "My dad had an affair."

Apparently, my eyes could get wider. "What?"

"Twenty-five years ago, or so. He cheated on my mom."

"Then why get divorced last year?"

"Because two years ago was when dad found out he had a daughter with that woman. They were both living in America. Last year, he made her move out to Seoul. That was too much for my mom and they divorced. Thankfully, she was living in Daegu when my half-sister moved here."

"How on earth does no one know about this?" I asked in amazement.

"Mom had never been one for the fame. She was—still is—a doctor. She put in a transfer and if anyone asks, and they usually don't, I tell them she's working at a hospital there."

"Do you get to see much of her?" I asked, curious.

Seungjin shrugged. "Not really, but most idols don't seem their parents often, even if they live in Seoul."

That was true. I knew a lot of trainees and idols could go years without seeing their family. Seeing as how I had always been at school, and father had always been at work, I hadn't really seen much of him anyway.

"We're not that much different," I realized.

"Not really," Seungjin agreed, reaching for his cup. He took a sip and winced. "These have gone cold. I'm going to get a fresh one. They didn't have bubble tea, so I got you a hot chocolate before. Is that OK, or do you want something else?"

"That's OK," I said. "Thank you."

Seungjin stood, then glanced back at me. "Um, Yerin?" I looked up at him, questioningly. "You, um, might want to go to the bathroom," he said, gesturing to his face.

My hands flew to my cheeks as he disappeared. *My makeup!*

Mortified, I moved to the bathroom, wincing as the feeling seemed to return to my aching ankle, and cringing the moment I saw my reflection.

If life didn't stop making me cry, I was going to have to invest in waterproof makeup.

I cleaned up my face as best I could, which involved removing more of it than I liked. This was no good: I was going to have to abandon that hot chocolate and get back to the dorm to fix this. I'd come out without anything other than the coat on my back and I didn't have any makeup in my pockets.

The question was, how could I get out of here without Seungjin seeing me?

I opened the door and stepped out—straight into Seungjin.

I let out a squeal and tried to duck back into the bathroom, but he grabbed my wrist. "Where are you going?"

My free hand shot up to try to cover my face. "I need to go back to the dorm."

"Yerin," he said, softly. His other hand wrapped around my other wrist, tugging my hand away from my face. "I've seen you without any makeup at all, remember?"

"Yes, but—"

"And you're still the prettiest girl here."

I lowered my hands, but not before I flipped my hair over my shoulder. "You know, you're right. I am."

Makeup was the least of my problems.

제15 장

Seungjin

December

"I have a crush on Cha Yerin."

There. I said it out loud.

I was in an empty classroom, waiting for practice and I couldn't get her out of my head. I'd heard that when you have a song stuck in your head, if you listen to it once, it would get it out. I was hoping a similar thing would work when you had a girl stuck in your head.

I can report, it doesn't.

All it did was send weird fluttery sensations through me.

That one, I wasn't going to admit out loud.

We had come to a weird truce. Weird, because we weren't really arguing. But it was a kind of truce, none the less.

We had spent the last three weekends together at my house. The first two were spent studying. Yerin hadn't told her friends her mother wanted her to stay at school (nor had she told them they were divorcing), and I'd offered to let her come to mine to study. She'd stayed in the guest room.

The more time I'd spent with her, the more I knew I shouldn't. She was beautiful and smart, determined and strong. She was also incredibly pig-headed, but most of the time, I found the stubbornness endearing.

And then I'd find myself using words like endearing …

She'd made it clear that we would only be friends. I'd made it clear that we could only be friends.

And then there would be times when I'd look up and watch her chew the lid of her pen while working out a problem, and I wanted to revoke my decision.

I'd catch her watching me, and I was sure that she felt the same way too.

The thing was, ever since Bright Boys had disbanded, Ro Chanheon, my former Atlantis ally, was now a foe, not a friend. All he did was ride my ass and tell me, and my team, that we weren't good enough to be idols again.

With Sejin in China and no word from him, and a half-sister who was preoccupied with another group, there was no one in my corner at Atlantis.

Holly had gotten her wish. Since Hyunseo's case had wrapped up, the press had lost all interest in us. We could walk the streets, and no one would spring a camera on us.

No one outside cared either.

So why should I?

The door opened and Yerin walked in.

Her hair was on top of her head in a high ponytail,

and she was wearing leggings and an oversized sweater (mine, for the record), and she looked incredible.

I pushed myself away from the wall, strode over, cupped her face, and kissed her.

To hell with it.

She kissed me back, her hands on my hips.

Her lips were soft, but her kisses were hard.

I wasn't the only one that wanted this.

She clung to me as we kissed, allowing me to deepen it, a soft groan reaching my ears.

Finally, I pulled away. "I would like for today to be our first day," I told her, breathless.

Her breath hitched. "Seungjin."

"Yes?"

"Seungjin."

"Yes?" I responded, more irritated as she poked at my side.

My eyes shot open and I found Jaehoon's face at an angle, peering at me in both bewilderment and revulsion. "You're drooling."

I sat up, wiping my face. My cheek was sticky.

Nice.

Which was when it hit me that it had been a dream.

Disappointment settled over me.

Jaehoon was a good-looking guy, but he wasn't my type at all.

I pulled a face at him. "What do you want?"

"I think the question is, what do you want?" he returned, quirking an eyebrow. "Or *who* do you want?"

I shoved him away as I got to my feet. "Shut up," I grumbled, looking towards the door. "Where are the others?" I wasn't expecting Yerin. Not yet, at least. We had a Team Blue practice. Our final one before the evaluation tomorrow.

"On their way," Jaehoon shrugged as he jumped onto the table I'd been sitting at. "Are you going to tell me who you were dreaming about?"

I shot him a look. "You," I informed him, deadpan.

Jaehoon considered it, and then nodded. "I can't say I'm surprised. I dream about me too."

"Do we need to leave you two love birds alone?" Sungil asked from the doorway, his serious expression on his face as usual.

"Don't worry, you and King will always be my OTP," Jaehoon informed him, blowing him a kiss. "I've told you this before."

King appeared beside Sungil and arched an eyebrow. "You and your 'one true pairing'," he sighed.

I watched them quietly, feeling slightly jealous. I'd never had a friendship like that with anyone. These guys had known each other from a young age, and despite Jaehoon debuting in an idol group, King doing his own thing as a solo artist, and Sungil doing neither, they still had a strong friendship.

The closest I had become with someone in Bright Boys was Jaehoon, and that was only because he was closest in age. I knew our friendship was nothing in comparison to the one he had with King and Sungil.

"Can we just practice?" TK sighed as he slipped into the room past King and Sungil.

As well as EXO's Ko Ko Bop, we had been told to perform a second with only two weeks to master it. We'd chosen H3RO's Who Is Your Hero? and it still wasn't as good as Ko Ko Bop. Considering we had just over 12 hours to be ready for it, I was worried.

This was everything.

We practiced for hours. We all had sweat pouring from us—even with the windows wide open and the almost arctic wind howling in around us. We practiced one dance, my phone propped up to record it, and then we'd gather around, watching and critiquing each other. Ro Chanheon was a stickler for the details, and we had to be perfect.

"Guys, we agreed we wouldn't be here all night," King muttered wearily, hours later. It was already long past curfew.

Normally, I'd protest. At Atlantis, we'd practiced later and longer, but I had agreed to meet with Yerin this evening too. I scooped up my phone and checked the time. There wasn't much time to run through things again.

"I think I'm going to stay a little longer," TK said.

I looked over at him and sighed. Even though Hyunseo's court case had been settled and he'd been cleared of the charges, I still didn't like TK. I hadn't kept that a secret. Neither had Sungil.

But to give him credit, TK really had sucked it up and worked hard. "We're done with the group practice," I told him. I could hardly tell him to go to bed when I wasn't going to. I walked to the door, pausing as I got close to him. He flinched slightly, but I ignored it. "If you do what you did just now in the evaluation tomorrow, you'll do OK."

I could see the surprise on his face, but I didn't stick around for his response. Instead, I left the classroom and ran back across the grounds. It had started snowing, settling on the ground. I wasn't surprised to see several foot tracks in the snow. I expected there would be more heading back to the dorm later.

Yerin had taken the keys from her mother and unlocked a storage room in the dorm's basement. With it being too cold and wet to practice on the roof, we'd needed to find another location, and with so many students practicing for the evaluation, she'd come up with the idea of going to the dorms instead.

Not only were we closer to the snacks, but we could stay out later, practicing, than we could in the school. Until the last week, the teachers and security were sending students back to their rooms if they had been caught out after hours (although no other students had been sent up Bukhansan) and giving them a detention. This last week, they were clearly turning a blind eye. If students weren't practicing, they were still awake in their dorm rooms, studying for the exams that were also taking place.

I raided the vending machines on the way to the basement, grumbling at myself about that. We were still expected to study.

I was possibly on track for passing … I didn't care. The more I'd practiced, the more I'd danced and sung, the more I knew I was going to be an idol again.

I pushed open the storage room door, surprised to find Yerin already there. Although her hair was pulled back into a high ponytail like in my dream, she was wearing her school uniform still, her bare legs sticking out from under a thick coat. It wasn't much warmer down here.

She was in the middle of rapping her part of our

duet and although she saw me, she didn't stop. I leaned back against the wall and watched her, eating an apple. She was … incredible.

As well as giving us a second group song to master, Ro Chanheon had announced we would also need to perform a solo piece in our area of strength *and* perform a duet. He'd picked the names, supposedly at random, and I had been paired with Yerin.

I wasn't complaining about that. I was happy for any time I could spend with her. Most of the time.

Sometimes, I just wanted to reach out and kiss her.

Much like I wanted to now.

She finished her verse off and then killed the music. We had chosen to cover a song by Tablo ft Taeyang called Tomorrow. We'd struggled to find a duet that was a female rapper and a male vocalist that would fit to our strengths, and instead decided we'd use one with a male vocalist and a male rapper.

Yerin walked over, pulling the apple from my hand and taking a large bite from it.

"I brought one for you," I told her, pulling a second out of my pocket.

Yerin shrugged, continuing to eat the apple. "I have ramyun," she said, pointing over to the convenience store pots that she'd already set cooking.

"You are a wonderful person," I responded, my stomach grumbling at the sight of them. As I walked past her, I placed a kiss on her cheek. It wasn't until I got to the two pots on top of a shelf that I realized what I'd done. I quickly cleared my throat as I turned back to her. "Any preference?"

She slowly shook her head as she stared at me

with wide eyes, and then nodded. "I want the spicy one."

I grabbed the cheese flavored ramyun pot, pulled back the foil lid that had been kept on to help the ramyun cook, and then broke my wooden chop sticks in two so I could dig in.

The cold room had made them cool enough to eat and it didn't take me long to devour them. All the dancing and singing constantly kept me hungry as I burned off crazy amounts of calories. Yerin finally joined me, picking up her pot and eating her noodles at a slightly more refined speed than I had.

I put my empty pot on the side, ready to take with us when we left, and waited for Yerin to finish eating. She had lost a lot of weight in the last few weeks. She hadn't been heavy to start with, but whether it was all the physical activity, the stress of exams, or the stress of what was going on with her parents, I wasn't sure.

"Have you heard from your father?" I asked her, carefully.

She shook her head.

"I haven't heard from Sejin, either," I told her.

"What about your sister?"

"Half-sister," I corrected her. I'd finally told her the truth about who Holly was. She had been shocked, and I was sure she hadn't believed me—until my father had announced it to the world.

At the same time, he had announced that some crazy lunatic sasaeng had broken into H3RO's apartment at the dorm and tried to attack one of their members, Kyun. What the press didn't know was that Holly had been there at the time. Not just there but *living* there.

That made no sense to me.

I knew that my dad had set her up with an apartment not far from our home, so why was she living with them? I knew the previous manager had, but he was a guy. Holly living there was very inappropriate. I could understand why they'd not shared that piece of information with the press.

"And no. I don't want to talk to her anyway."

"She's going to be one of the judges tomorrow," Yerin pointed out, like I didn't know that fact.

"Which is exactly why I don't want to talk to her," I snorted. With the announcement that Holly was joining Atlantis officially as the Vice Chairwoman, and she would be stepping back on H3RO's management duties now they had all resigned with the company, I had realized that she was the reason Sejin was in China. She had pushed him out of the company he had been running and sent him to Shanghai.

If I saw her, I was going to yell at her. And that would probably be the least of it.

I knew enough to know that she was going to have a say in my career, and there was nothing I could do to stop that, so I at least had to pretend I was OK with how things were—at least until the contract had been signed.

Just a couple more days of pretending.

"Let's get this done," Yerin sighed, setting her empty pot beside mine. "I still have exams to study for."

I shook my head in amazement. How she was still managing to keep on top her studies was incredible. She was incredible.

I turned on the music before I could do something stupid.

Like kiss her.

Focus, Seungjin!

Tomorrow was a slow song, with lyrics about the loss of losing someone you loved—a breakup. In one of our performance classes, Sa Hyesun had said to draw as much of your own experiences into what you were singing when it came to ballads and slower songs.

I had never experienced a breakup. Yerin was the closest to what I could have classed as having a girlfriend and they didn't quite meet the requirements for this song, especially as she was still right by me. Instead, I found myself thinking about Sejin.

I missed my brother. I missed him more when he didn't answer my calls or make the effort to return them. Even the KaKao chat messages were no longer just 'seen'. The last message I had received from him was **Focus on school.** That was it.

I was choosing to believe it was because he wanted me to pass the audition, not because he didn't think I could and that was my only path now.

Choosing to do what he said, I focused on the last practice session we would have. Or, I tried. Our choreography made that difficult. Given that it was a slow song with heartfelt lyrics, being close during the dancing was a given. It had also helped Yerin: her ankle had remained strapped up since the morning after our night on the mountain.

By the time we called it, at nearly four in the morning, I was reconsidering my earlier thoughts at being happy to spend time with her. It was a fine line between enjoyment and torture, and we were dancing on top of it.

"Thank you," I told her, as we walked up the

stairs to avoid the elevator and the cameras in it. Four in the morning was a bit much to expect security to turn a blind eye to.

"For what?" she asked.

"For working so hard. I know you're still working on getting to an American college, but you're still working at our practices like getting a contract with Atlantis is just as important to you as it is to me."

She chewed at her lip, giving me a brief nod of acknowledgement.

I meant it. We had spent hours in that storage room when she could have been studying. I wasn't even sure she was putting in as much effort for her team's performance.

We reached her floor and she opened the door. Then she turned back to me. "It's important to me because it's important to you," she said, softly, before disappearing into her floor's hallway.

I caught the door before it slammed shut and woke everyone up but didn't follow. Instead, I grinned to myself. The stupid smile stayed on my face, even as I crashed onto my bed.

She hadn't said it in so many words, but Cha Yerin still liked me.

제16 장

Yerin

The evaluations had taken place in the auditorium. It had started off well. The first performance, the cover of DDD by EXID was the one which I was most worried about. The choreography for the dance wasn't as technical or complicated as the dancing that accompanied songs by boy groups, but it was difficult enough when we were all wearing four-inch heels, and my ankle was still bound up underneath the skintight wet-look skinny jeans I was wearing.

I had been worried I would fall and mess things up, but I hadn't. I hadn't even messed up my lines. Everyone in the group had given a perfect performance. I didn't like half of Team Yellow, but I couldn't help but grin at all of them as we walked over to take our positions for the second group performance.

And that was when it went wrong.

Seungjin had been right. I was still determined to go to America and study. I'd been researching the possibilities now my father was now living out there. Harvard might have been off the table, but there were other colleges.

Other colleges closer to my father and further away from my mother.

After announcing that she and my father were divorcing, she had barely spoken to me unless it was to chastise me for my slipping grades, stressing that I should focus on signing with Atlantis.

The more she said that, the more I wanted to do the opposite. Most nights I was getting only two or three hours sleep as I made sure to study while practicing.

It wasn't that I didn't want to pass. I still wanted to do my best. I would at least allow my mother the ability to say I had turned down that opportunity. Plus, no one wanted to look stupid on a stage in front of some important and influential people in the industry.

That had been the plan, at least.

And then, midway through my part in the Cupcake number I forgot my lines.

What was worse, I froze.

The number one rule is to keep on going, but the part of my brain which formed words failed me. I only just kept my feet moving, but my body and my arms seemed to be controlled by someone else too.

When the words did return, it was three lines later and I was out of time. I knew it as I sang them, but I couldn't stop myself. It threw Miyeon off too.

My solo performance was better. Just rapping, with no dancing to worry about, I picked up my mic, walked to the center of the stage and gave the panel of judges my version of Jessi's Gucci.

Ironically, at that point, while I was wearing the Gucci heeled pumps I had bought before all of my credit cards had been cancelled, I didn't not feel Gucci. I felt like a fraud.

Alone, without anyone else on the stage, I realized what it was that had put me off really committing to signing with Atlantis: I wasn't a rapper.

Yes, I could rap, but these weren't my lyrics. They were Jessi's. So many rappers took an active part in writing the lyrics to the rap line, and I wouldn't do that. In a group, I had others to work with. Alone, it was just me.

I wasn't bad. I just wasn't authentic.

I walked off the stage once I had finished wrapped up in a blanket of thick feelings. I was ready to walk away and quit, and then I found Seungjin waiting for me.

"You were brilliant," he told me.

"Thank you," I muttered, paying lip service to his compliment. I didn't feel brilliant. I also couldn't walk out of there. It wasn't my dream, but it was his. I had one more performance. I'd spent so long pretending everything was daisies and rainbows in my life that another hour wasn't going to hurt me.

Seungjin cocked his head, and then pulled me to one side. "What's the matter, Yerin?" He peered down at me, then bent his long legs so his head was just in front of mine. "You killed Gucci. They'll remember that, and not the Cupcake number. All you have to do is make sure the last performance is the best because that's the one they'll remember. And you've got me for this one: I won't let you fail."

His words made me feel guilty but determined.

I wasn't going to let him down.

"How is your ankle holding up?" he asked,

pointing to the hidden injury. "I checked the order. We're first up with the duets and we're not getting feedback until tomorrow, so we can head back to the dorms straight after and ice it."

"That sounds wonderful," I told him. The ice, not the going first. The ankle was sore, and while being the first to perform wasn't my preference, I was appreciating the idea of getting my shoes off.

"Lee Seungjin, Cha Yerin," someone called.

"Hwaiting!" Seungjin said to me.

"Hwaiting!" I returned.

We walked onto the stage, taking my position to the side and I sucked in a deep breath while waiting for the music to start. From the center, Seungjin looked over at me and gave me one of his rare smiles.

The opening bars started, and our performance began. For the first few bars, it was just him singing, and then, from the other side of the stage, it was me rapping. Seungjin had choreographed it so our dance was separate but in sync as we each performed the first half of the song.

By the middle, we were dancing together. Drawing inspiration from some of BTS and Seventeen's slower numbers, the dance was more masculine, but it fit the song.

The actual music video to the song was simple: Tablo and Taeyang alone in the middle of a desert. At some point, that was what our performance seemed like to me: just us two.

I wasn't perfect. I'd messed up some of my lyrics but covered them with an ad-lib and I was confident it came across as intentional. Seungjin was flawless. It took everything in me to focus on my own part and not just him. He was someone who deserved to be on a stage. If he didn't get back in Atlantis after this, something was wrong in the world.

The song was supposed to end with me slowly walking away from Seungjin.

I almost dropped my mic when he reached out for my hand, tugging me back to him. I somehow managed to spin into him using the weight of my good leg, but it didn't stop me crashing into him.

He held me there as I stared wide-eyed up at him, half-wondering what he was doing, half-wanting him to kiss me.

The music stopped.

Seungjin didn't let me go.

I didn't move.

"Thank you," a voice boomed through the speakers.

The spell was broken and Seungjin let go of me, walking off the stage. I followed after him, pointing out to myself that the reason why my heart was beating so wildly was because of the performance, not because of Seungjin's presence.

He'd already disappeared when I made it to the corridor. At that point, I no longer cared. I was exhausted and I could practically hear my bed calling for me. Sure, the polite thing to do was probably stay and cheer my classmates on, but I wanted to get out of the heels before my ankle buckled under me.

I gathered my belongings from one of the classrooms I'd left them in, making sure to swap the pumps for a pair of more comfortable running shoes, and then walked back to the dorm. It had snowed a little more, but the paths were clear enough.

I knew I had the room to myself for a while. Kareun was second to last with the duets. I stripped off the outfit I had performed in and pulled a thick, comfortable robe on while I wiped all the makeup from my face. Once it was clear, I had a hot shower, spent mainly on one leg, and then I dried off so I could pull on my most comfortable pair of sweats.

I put a facemask on and then settled down at my desk: I still had one last exam to study for.

I'd barely gone over my notes when there was a knock at the door. Despite everything, the last person I expected to be there was Seungjin. He was still in the clothes he had performed in, complete with the makeup, but holding a black carrier bag. "I got ..." he trailed off as he stared at me.

"What?" I asked, frowning. The action made my facemask shift. I let out a shriek as I darted into the bathroom to remove it. It had a picture of a tiger on it! I quickly rubbed the leftover moisturizer into my face, wondering if the sink would open wide enough to swallow me.

It didn't.

Instead, I had to leave the bathroom and found Seungjin making himself comfortable at my desk. He looked up at me as I got close, and smirked.

"Don't say a word," I threatened him, still feeling embarrassed. "And make yourself at home," I added, pointedly.

"I will," he agreed.

"Boys aren't allowed on this floor," I told him, suddenly realizing it was just me and him in my room.

Seungjin looked around my room with a frown. "I can see why: then we'd find out you have better rooms. I have to share with King and Jaehoon!"

"My mother is the principal," I reminded him. I folded my arms. "Why are you here?"

As though I reminded him, Seungjin turned to me, and then, slowly, walked up to me. As he got closer, I started moving backwards, until suddenly, his hand shot forward, reaching for my head. At the same moment as the back of my legs hit the mattress of my bed, his hand stopped my head from whacking the base of Kareun's above mine.

Of course, it brought us closer again. Neither of us moved. "What are you doing here?" I whispered.

Seungjin raised the black plastic bag he was still holding. "I figured you wouldn't have cooled down."

"I'm fine," I assured him, although his proximity was certainly raising my body temperature a few degrees again.

Seungjin rolled his eyes. "Lie down."

"What?" I shrieked at him.

My objection made him wince. "I bought cooling packs for your ankle, Yerin," he cried. Once more, I waited for the floor to swallow me whole as I slid down onto my bed. Seungjin crouched down on the floor beside the bed. "I'm going to pull that trouser leg up," he warned me. Then he did just that, revealing just a little more than my ankle.

I could see his cheeks pinken slightly and he kept his attention fixed firmly on the task at hand. He pulled a gel icepack from the bag, activated it, and then wrapped it around my ankle.

I flopped back onto my bed and stared up at the slats above me. My life had turned surreal at some point.

"It's not as swollen as I expected it to be," he said.

"Does it hurt?"

"It aches, but it doesn't really hurt."

"You were amazing today, Yerin," he told me, softly. I turned my head and found him watching me.

"Do you get any sneak peaks on the results, seeing that your half-sister is in charge?"

Seungjin snorted derisively. "As if that was going to happen!"

"I saw your performance; they'd be crazy not to accept you back, either," I assured him. Saw it? I couldn't take my eyes off him.

"What is going on in here?" Kareun demanded.

Seungjin leaped away from me in an action which was more graceful than I could have managed, as I sat upright. "Seungjin was just helping with my ankle," I hurried to tell her, pointing at the icepack.

"Are you here to help me too, oppa?" Kareun asked, ignoring me and looking at Seungjin with big doe-eyes.

"What do you need help with?" he asked, warily.

She gave him a flirty giggle. I knew that move: I'd seen it before. "I have sore lips," she told him.

My mouth dropped open as I failed to hide my shock at her brazenness.

Even Seungjin seemed surprised, but he recovered quickly, pulling a chapstick from his pocket and tossing it too her. "That should help," he responded, smoothly. He turned to pick up the plastic bag, shooting me a discreet look, then stood. Politely, he bobbed his head at the both of us. "I should leave," he said before hurrying towards the door.

Kareun watched him leave, and then turned back to me, her eyes narrowed. "What. Was. That?" she demanded.

"You know he's my performance partner, Kareun," I groaned as I pulled the icepack off my ankle and swung my legs off the side of the bed.

"I saw your duet. That was something."

I ignored her, moving back to my desk. Once seated, the icepack went back on my ankle as I stretched my leg out in front of me. "I've told you, there's nothing going on between us."

Kareun moved over to my side, giving me a smile that was anything but happy. If anything, she looked like a snake, ready to pounce. "Seungjin is this close," she held up her hand, millimeters between her finger and thumb. "Literally, *this* close to re-debuting. If you stop that happening, I promise, I will make you suffer."

I stared up at her. "That's a really interesting choice of words for your *friend*," I pointed out. "There's nothing happening between us, but if there was, would you really make me suffer?"

She gave me a look and I had a flash of fear run through me. The girl in front of me had been my best friend for over a decade, but right then, I wasn't sure if I knew her anymore.

"If Seungjin was to date, the last person it should be is you," she informed me. "It should be me. I care about him more."

"Sure," I agreed.

"Anyway," she shrugged. "I just wanted you to know." Before I could say anything, she had spun around and kicked my ankle. "Oops," she said insincerely as I yelped in pain.

"Kareun!"

"Just know, it will be worse if you do end up

dating him," she looked back at me.

I clutched at my ankle, fighting back the tears.

Z

It was lunchtime and I was ready to drop. I had stayed up all night studying for the last exam, which thankfully, I think I had aced. Now I wanted to sleep.

Only, after lunch, we each had a twenty-minute slot with the coaches from Atlantis for our evaluation feedback.

I'd made my decision as I walked into the exam: I was going to America. I enjoyed rapping and performing, but Kareun was a reason as to why I didn't want to go to Atlantis. That and the fact that I missed my father. I didn't see him much, but Christmas was always our time. I also didn't like the way he had been sent away.

Seeing as he wasn't replying to my KaKao messages or text messages (I was assuming he had a new phone), I emailed him. I sat nibbling at a sandwich while I typed out the email on my phone, telling him I would book the flight tonight. It was two days until Christmas, and we only had three days off because of the weekend. I would have to miss the first day of school after Christmas, but I didn't want to wait until the end of January for the end of our school year.

With the message sent, it was time to head to the auditorium. I threw what was left of my sandwich in the trash and walked over to the school. Most of my class were already there. The corridor was busy because the other years had also been given the opportunity to audition too: I saw Seungjin with Dongyeol and Ryan and they were in the year above us.

Nam Woosung finally called my name and I walked into the auditorium. The judges table was in the same place as it had been for the evaluations, but there was a chair on the other side of it. All four judges watched as I walked down to it. I bowed respectfully at them, and then waited for them to tell me I could sit.

Once Ro Chanheon gave me the go ahead and I sat, Holly gave me a welcoming smile. "Hello, Cha Yerin. I understand your mother is the principal here."

It wasn't a question, but I nodded anyway.

"You're rough around the edges," Hyesun declared. "Your singing needs a lot of work, but you're pretty."

I didn't miss Holly's reaction to that; closing her eyes and wincing.

"Your singing isn't your strength," Ruzt said, before Holly could. "Your rapping is."

"It's not that much better," Hyesun disagreed.

"Which, respectfully, is why you're here to judge on vocals, and I am here to judge on rapping." Ruzt looked back to me. "It's not the best rapping I've seen over my time here, but there's something raw there that can be worked with."

"He's not the only one who thinks that," Holly agreed. She flicked through a notebook, stopping on a certain page. "I have a couple of female trainees at Atlantis I would like to debut, and I would like you to join them."

I folded my arms and glared suspiciously at her. "Are you just saying that because my mother is the principal?"

Holly met my stare. "Trust me when I say the last

thing I care about is nepotism. If I offer someone something, it's because I think they can do the job well. In this case, I think you would make a good addition to a girl group I have in mind."

"I only did this class because my mother wanted me to."

"And if you didn't enjoy it, that's fine, but if you're interested in becoming an idol because *you* want to become an idol, I'm giving you that opportunity." Holly pushed a large envelope towards me.

I stayed sitting.

Ro Chanheon's eyes narrowed. "Regardless of whether you choose to become an idol or not, you will show Vice Chairwoman Lee the respect she deserves. Otherwise, you will spend longer than a night up a mountain."

"Excuse me?" Holly asked, arching an eyebrow. "A mountain?"

"Just disciplining my students."

Holly's mouth settled into a thin line as she glanced at me, then back at Chanheon—he was going to get a telling off when I left the room. She looked back at me. "Read the contract over. Think about it over Christmas. If you're interested, return it to me at Atlantis."

I stood, taking the contract and shoved it in my bag. I walked out of the room and pulled out my phone. I had no interest in Atlantis. What I wanted was to go to America.

My father still hadn't replied. I frowned, then, impulsively, bought a plane ticket on the emergency credit card my parents seemed to have forgotten about.

제17 장

Seungjin

I paced back and forth as slowly the other former members of Bright Boys filed into the auditorium. Despite the fact I had my cell phone on me, and I knew a few of them had phones again, none of the them messaged me with their outcome. I had no idea if that was a good or a bad sign, but it had my stomach churning.

Eventually, there was only one other person left: Lucinda. *That* couldn't be a good sign …

I didn't get nervous before going on stage, but when Nam Woosung called my name, for a moment, I thought I was going to be sick. I walked into the auditorium and took a seat. "Well?"

My question, and lack of manners, was directed at the one person behind the table: Holly. She pushed a thick envelope towards me without saying a word, but instead, arching an eyebrow.

I leaned forward and took it.

PROJECT: ZODIAC.

"What's this?" I asked her.

"I have spent weeks putting this plan together," Holly told me. "That's it."

"Zodiac?"

She nodded.

"That's not Bright Boys."

"I would have thought when I disbanded Bright Boys it would have been obvious that you were never going back into Bright Boys," she told me. "Bright Boys doesn't exist anymore, Seungjin. And it's never going to. I know Hyunseo was cleared, but the damage done to Bright Boys was irreparable."

"Then what was all this?" I exclaimed, jumping to my feet as I waved at the auditorium.

"Sit down, Seungjin" she said, before sighing. "I said Bright Boys was irreparable, not you. If you're set on being back in Bright Boys: leave. If you still want to be an idol with Atlantis, sit down, shut up, and listen to my plan."

I sat down, clutching at the envelope. "Well?"

"I am creating a new group. As you may have gathered from that," she pointed at the envelope which was crumpling in my fist, "The group will be called Zodiac."

"And you want me to be part of it? I though you said I was only in Bright Boys because my dad let me in?"

Holly's mouth settled into a thin line. "Do all the men in my family have selective hearing?" she asked me. "If you'd care to remember correctly, I had said a lot of people in Atlantis—and outside of it—had said they thought you had gotten where you had because of your dad." She reached for a notebook and leafed through it. "I watched your debut stages, and I could see you had talent back then. You're a brilliant dancer, Seungjin. But, honestly, your vocal skills were lacking compared to other members. Being back here at SLA, your vocals have become stronger."

"You did think I got in because of my dad!" I glowered at her.

"You know what, I don't know. All I know is, if anyone asks me now, I'll be happy to say that you got into Zodiac on your own merit."

I sat back, staring at her, before staring at the envelope.

"The other teachers had to leave; we misjudged how long this would take. However, the feedback you have received is excellent. All of them have commented on how they have watched you improve over the weeks, and all of us, myself included," she stressed, "Thought that duet you did with Cha Yerin was beautiful. In fact, I almost questioned whether putting you back in a group was the best option for you. However, I know *you* want to be in a group."

I continued to stare at her. "Do you really mean that?"

"Yes," she said, firmly.

My throat suddenly felt like it was closing in on me as tears threatened to break free: a combination of relief, and just happiness at hearing that from her. "When do I get to redebut?"

Holly sucked in a long breath, and I knew that I wasn't going to like the answer. "Actually, this is a long game." She folded her arms and leaned forward on the table. "First things first: Zodiac ... you are the *only* person, outside of a select few at Atlantis, who knows about that name, and I need it to stay like that. Do you understand?"

I slowly nodded.

"Your debut date is going to depend on how hard you all work."

"Who …?" I frowned. "Who made it?"

Holly shook her head. "Until individuals hand me a signed contract, I'm not going to say because I don't know myself. If you're in, come to Atlantis December 26th, and meet the others. We'll all know then."

"OK …" I shared a room with two people who would be able to give me an answer in about half an hour …

"Seungjin, if this progresses how I want it to, it's going to move very quickly. You need to be committed, and more than that, you are going to need to listen to me. I get that you don't like me, but this affects more than just you," she said. "If you can't do that, don't sign up for this. I can have you debut as a solo artist; we can wait for another group for you to debut in. Or, if it's what you want, I will keep my promise and release you from Atlantis altogether."

Silently, I stood. I opened the envelope and pulled the contract out, keeping hold of that while I set the envelope on the table in front of her. When she shot me a questioning look, I shrugged. "I share a room with other people."

At that, I walked out of the room. The door we exited wasn't the same as the one we entered, but I was surprised that there was no one there. Instead of heading straight back to the dorm, I went into a nearby classroom so that I could read through the contract.

It wasn't different to the previous one, until you got to the details. Most contracts were for seven years.

This one ... this was a pre-debut contract. I'd never even heard of one of these before! It stipulated that I would be a member of an unnamed group. And that was it. The details were vague.

Then, on the last page: a post it with a hand written note "Trust me. Please."

I nearly ripped the paper up—this wasn't what Holly had just told me!

Instead, I took a deep breath and forced myself to stay calm. She had said I would be in a group, in 'Zodiac', and while this wasn't what the paperwork said, she had also said I was the only one who knew this ...

I had two days until I found out the answers for certain, and I shared a room with Jaehoon and King who might be able to offer a little more insight in the meantime. I gathered up the contract, stuffed it in my back pocket, and hurried back to the dorm.

My room was empty.

I got on well enough with Jaehoon, but I wasn't really close to either him or King, despite sharing a room with them.

Yet, I did expect them to be in our room.

I flopped down on my bed and read through the vague contract again. *Trust me.*

It was hard to do that.

And why weren't my roommates here? Had they been given different news?

I pulled my phone out of my pocket, needing a distraction, and sent a message to Yerin: **What happened? Did you get in?**

It took ages for the reply. **Sorry, waiting for a taxi.**

I frowned. She wasn't answering the question.

What was with all the vagueness? **To where? Home? Atlantis?**

Yerin: **The airport. I'm going to California.**

She was leaving now?! My concerns about Atlantis were shoved to the side. **When are you coming back?!?!?!** When I didn't get a response, I leaped off my bed, grabbed my coat, and ran out of the door, still clutching onto the contract. I hammered at the elevator button, and when it didn't seem to move from the ground floor, headed for the stairs, taking them two at a time.

Outside it was dark and cold, but it wasn't snowing. I charged along the path to the front gate, trying not to slip on the areas which were freezing over again. "Yerin!" I yelled. I could see her getting into a taxi, but she didn't hear me. By the time I got to the gate, she was gone.

My reaction was impulsive, waving down the next taxi and instructing it to take me to the airport in Incheon. It was just under an hour's drive to the airport, and I was nearly there when Yerin responded.

Yerin: **I'm only going for Christmas and a few days after. I'm missing a few days of school to see my father. What's my mother going to do? Expel me? Calm down, Seungjin—I'm coming back.**

I ran my hands through my hair, wondering why I had overreacted like that.

Seeing as I was almost there, I decided to keep going. I had the opportunity to see her off, and I might as well take it.

The taxi pulled up and I hurriedly paid him so I could get in and find Yerin. She was easier to find than I imagined, joining a line with four sparkly purple suitcases.

Four.

For a few days.

"Don't they have restrictions on how many suitcases you can take?" I asked her, after cutting under a rope so I could join her.

She jumped, dropping her passport. I crouched down and scooped it up to hand it back to her. "What are you doing here?" she asked, eyes wide.

"I figured someone should wait with you until your flight," I lied. No need to tell her about my panicked moment about her leaving for good.

The startled expression softened. "Oh … thank you."

We stood in silence as she worked her way to the front of the line. I waited to one side, watching as she argued with the desk clerk about how many cases she was checking, and eventually presenting a credit card. There was a limit on the cases then …

Once she was checked in and had the boarding pass in her hands, she walked back to me. "I have a few hours."

"Want to get something to eat?" I suggested, hoping she would say yes: I was starving!

She nodded, looking around. "There's not much to choose from out here."

"Burger?" I suggested, pointing to a Burger King.

"Sure," she shrugged. A short while later, we were sitting at a small table, eating a hot burger. "What happened with your evaluation?"

"I got back in, I think," I sighed. I pulled the very rumpled contract from my pocket and pushed it over to her.

"Seungjin," she scolded me. "You just got ketchup on it. What on earth are you doing with this?"

I shrugged. "Your burger wrapper is probably worth more."

She gave me a disapproving scowl as she picked up a napkin and wiped her hands. She picked it up and skimmed through it. "Trust me?"

"My sister."

She nodded, setting it back down. "I don't know if this is something you want to hear, but I do think she's trying to do right by you, you know."

"The contract is vague."

"It's an entertainment company. Considering how much that industry is worth, I would think there's a very good reason it's vague, Seungjin. It's different from mine."

I nearly choked on a fry. "You mean you got in?" I thought her lack of answer on that question was because she hadn't.

"Of course," she said, flipping her hair over her shoulder. "I'm Cha Yerin. They'd be a fool to turn me down."

"You accepted?" I asked, slowly.

"I said I wouldn't, but I haven't formally rejected the offer," she replied. "I was told to wait until after Christmas to give them an answer, but I will turn it down."

I was disappointed and I wasn't sure why.

I'd lost my appetite, but she carried on eating. "Are you going to accept your offer?" she asked.

"Yes," I replied.

She nodded, giving me a bright smile. "I'm glad. If anyone deserves it, you do. Don't tell Kareun, but you were always my favorite."

"I was?" I grinned.

"I know you're going to do bigger and better things, but I was always a Dazzle," she told me.

"Where in California are you going?" I asked, changing the subject before I said anything embarrassing—like declaring she was my favorite too. Favorite what, I wasn't sure … but she was it.

It hit me then.

I might have well as been slapped in the face with fresh noodles. I had fallen for Yerin. I mean, I knew it anyway … I just wasn't …

I was screwed.

"He's in Los Angeles," Yerin replied, oblivious to my internal monologue. One of the biggest smiles spread across her face as she spoke about her father. "It's only for a couple of days, but I can't wait to see him." Her phone beeped at her. "I don't even care what I do while I'm there." She picked up the phone. "I should probably move through to security …"

Yerin's smile dropped from her face quicker than she was reading the message. Her complexion went ghostly as tears started building up in the corner of her eyes. "Yerin?"

"He told me not to come," she whispered.

I barely heard her over the noise of the airport. In fact, I was sure I was mistaken as to what I'd heard. I reached over and pulled the phone out of her hands to read the message on the screen.

Why would you do that? Did your mother put you up to this? I have nothing left to give. Stay where you are, Yerin. There's nowhere for you to stay. I don't want you to see me like this.

I read the message again, blowing out a long breath. "Yerin?" I looked up and found her with her head bowed, mostly hidden behind a curtain of hair, tears dripping into her lap below.

I swore softly, reaching out for her. Just as my hand settled on hers, she stood abruptly, jerking her hand out of me reach. "Don't!" she screeched. The next thing I knew, she was running off, into the terminal.

I swooped down to grab her abandoned bag, and then I charged after her, yelling apologies over my shoulder as I avoided colliding with people. I managed to keep my eyes on her until she ran into a bathroom.

I couldn't follow her in there.

Instead, I paced back and forth outside, waiting for her to come out. After nearly forty minutes or watching dozens of women going in and out, but Yerin never reappearing, I was going crazy with worry.

I was going to get in so much trouble …

I waited for the area to go as quiet as possible, and then walked in.

I was promptly smacked around the head by a halmeoni … or more specifically, her umbrella, and ushered (if that was the right word when she was beating me with the umbrella) back out. "OK!" I protested, trying to avoid the smacks. "I'm sorry! It was a mistake!"

"Disgusting pervert," the old woman muttered, moving away.

I rubbed at the side of my head, glowering after her. I hoisted Yerin's bag back up over my shoulder and turned back, trying to work out how I was going to get in the ladies' bathroom, when Yerin appeared.

Without stopping to think about what I was

doing, I marched over, wrapped my arms around her, and pulled her to me. She didn't fight me, but equally, she didn't hug me back. More importantly, she didn't seem to be crying anymore.

"Excuse me!" a woman said in irritation.

I looked up, realized we were blocking the entrance to the bathroom, and then let go of Yerin. I reached for her hand and led her out of the way.

She followed after me, her eyes on the ground in front of her. "Are you OK?" I asked her.

"No."

That was obvious. "Didn't your father know you were coming?"

She shook her head.

"Would passenger Cha Yerin please report to gate 14 for boarding."

I glanced up at the ceiling, as though I could see the owner of the voice broadcasting the announcement over the loud speaker. "What do you want to do?" I asked her, softly.

"I can't go to California," she muttered, tears threatening to spill.

I nodded. "You wait here, and I'll go talk to the airline and see if we can get your luggage off the plane." She nodded numbly. "Stay here."

She looked up at me, miserable. "It's not like I have anywhere else to go."

I resisted the urge of holding her again, and instead moved over the airline helpdesk. Despite explaining the situation, they couldn't do much other than call the gate and tell them to leave, along with Yerin's suitcases. I wasn't surprised, and I wasn't expecting a different outcome, but I had hoped I might have been able to get her luggage for her.

Disappointed, I walked back to where I had left Yerin, and momentarily panicked when I discovered she wasn't there. I spun around, spotting her on one of those seats which wrapped around a potted tree. Relief filled me as I walked over and sat down next to her. "I couldn't get your bags back," I told her, apologetically. "They are currently on their way to America. The airline person said they would send them to SLA when they arrived back at Incheon."

Yerin didn't say anything. Instead, she sighed and leaned towards me, resting her head on my shoulder. I reached my arm around her, holding her as we sat in silence. I wasn't sure what to say to her and I figured it might be easier for her if I waited for her to say something.

Only, the first thing I heard from her after a long time had passed, was a snore. I glanced down. She'd brought her legs up beside her as she leaned into me, but it didn't look comfortable. Gently, I lowered her head so she could use my thigh as a pillow.

It was garnering some interesting looks. I reached into my pocket and pulled out the black facemask I always carried with me, wishing I had a cap with me. All I had was my coat, so I pulled my hood up.

I sat there for hours. My leg went to sleep, and I was desperate for the bathroom, but I felt like, at that moment, the only thing I could do for Yerin was watch over her as she found some peace in whatever dreamworld she had entered. I couldn't get her parents back together and I couldn't get her father to accept her, but I could do that.

Eventually, she stirred, rubbing sleepily at her

eyes. "Oh," she muttered, sitting upright. "I was hoping it had all been a dream."

"I'm sorry."

As though realizing I was there, she blinked, looking at me in alarm. "You're here."

I nodded. "I wasn't just going to abandon you in an airport."

"My dad did," she muttered, miserably, tears threatening to fall again.

"I think we should leave here now," I told her, gently. "It's not the best place to spend Christmas."

"Is it Christmas?" She looked around, though I'm not sure what for. "What time is it?"

"Some time around four." I stood, shaking out my leg as pins and needles hit me, along with the overwhelming need for the bathroom. "I'm going to be right back," I informed her, darting over to the bathroom as quickly as I could with the limp caused by my sleeping foot.

I didn't like what I saw when I returned. Yerin was curled up on the chair, staring off into space, looking miserable and ill. It was like all the energy had left her. Even her hair seemed flat and limp. I rejoined her, forcing myself to be perky. "Right, let's head back to SLA."

"What's wrong with you?" she asked, suspiciously.

"Nothing," I responded, brightly.

Lies. I was exhausted, hungry, and, having spent the night in a check-in lounge, cold.

"But I don't think we should stay here, Yerin."

Yerin shook her head. "I can't go back to school."

"Then go home. It's Christmas."

She shook her head again, the tears back. "It's not home."

I sucked in a deep breath. "Then come back to mine," I offered before I could stop myself. But saying it out loud made it seem like a great idea. "I have that guest room, remember? We don't celebrate Christmas so it's not like the family will be around."

"I don't know," she said, slowly.

"The other option is getting a hotel room," I shrugged.

Yerin's eyes went wide. "What?"

"No, not like that," I said, hurriedly, although … I shook my head. "I'm not leaving you alone in an airport."

제18 장

Yerin

I don't know why I accepted. It was wholly inappropriate to stay at a boy's house, regardless of the situation, but the other option for me at this point would be staying at the airport.

My mother was going to kill me. My father didn't want me. I hadn't spoken to Kareun since she had 'accidentally' kicked my ankle. The last thing I wanted was to be stuck in a room with her, having to answer questions as to why I hadn't gone home seeing as exams were finished with. She had an excuse: she was from Jeju.

So here I was, once more in the guest room at Seungjin's house. I sat on the bed and looked around, lost. I had nothing with me short of what had been in my carry-on, and aside from my iPhone and iPad, the only other things had been a limited supply of makeup. Thank goodness there was a change of underwear in there.

But things like my toothbrush and nightwear—that was all somewhere over the Pacific Ocean.

There was a soft knock at the door, and I walked over to answer it. It was Seungjin. "I wasn't sure if you'd be asleep," he said.

I'd slept all night in his lap—my face flushed at that memory—so I was no longer tired. He was the one who had been up all night. "I'm not tired."

He held out a pile of clothing. "It's all going to drown you, but I don't have a sister …" he frowned. "I don't have a sister who ever lived here to borrow clothes from. I thought you might want to change. There's spare toiletries in the bathroom too."

"Thank you." I took the clothes from him and he backed out, closing the door behind him.

The amazing thing about a hot shower is how it can make you feel human no matter how crappy life is. It was like the hug I needed. And so were Seungjin's clothes: sweats and a sweater that smelled of him. If I couldn't have his arms around me, this was next best thing.

My stomach growled at me. It had been hours since I'd eaten last: a burger that I'd thrown back up in the end. I left the room, looking for the kitchen.

My family was … had been wealthy. Our house was in the same neighborhood. But Seungjin's home was deceptively enormous. I wandered the hallways, staring at the artwork lining the walls. I didn't know much about art but was willing to bet they were all originals.

Eventually, I found the kitchen. It was large and immaculate. It also wasn't empty. An elderly woman was supervising someone, who was clearly the housekeeper, as she made breakfast. The smell made my stomach grumble and my mouth water.

The housekeeper spotted me first, her reaction causing the elderly woman to turn. "Who are you?" she demanded.

"Hello, I am Cha Yerin," I greeted her, politely. "I am a friend of Seungjin's."

She walked over, her gaze skimming over me as she did. "Why are you wearing my grandson's clothes?"

"I … uh … I'm …"

"She's staying with me today, halmeoni," Seungjin answered for me, breezing into the kitchen behind me.

"And that requires her wearing your clothing?" Seungjin's grandmother folded her arms, giving me an unimpressed look.

"Yes," Seungjin responded with a shrug.

She rounded on her grandson with a glower. "I already had one gold digger in this family. I will not have another."

"Relax, halmeoni," Seungjin said as he walked to the kitchen counter and peered at the cooking food. "We're just friends."

"Friends who wear each other's clothes."

Seungjin glanced over his shoulder. "I've never worn Yerin's clothes. Yerin isn't Holly—or Holly's mother. She's a friend. She's spending Christmas day with me."

"We don't celebrate Christmas."

"Exactly," Seungjin leaned over and lifted a spoon out of a pan, blowing at the food in the spoon.

"Sit down and eat it at the table!" his grandmother barked. She turned to me. "I assume you're joining us for breakfast."

It wasn't a question, but I gave her a polite,

hopeful smile.

Z

"Your grandmother hates me," I told Seungjin as we moved to his entertainment room after breakfast.

Seungjin nodded. "She hates everyone. Except Sejin."

"She doesn't like Holly."

Seungjin snorted. "That's an understatement. Holly is an illegitimate child conceived, not only out of wedlock, but with a woman he's never married. My dad didn't grow up with money—he made it all himself— but my grandmother is ruthless when it comes to those who seek to threaten it. Throw in the fact my mom and dad got divorced because of her, and she's never going to be Miss Popular around here."

"Is that why you don't like her?" I asked, curiously. "Your sister, I mean."

Seungjin slowly shook his head, sitting beside me on the couch. "I actually didn't care either way when it came to her originally. It was her mom and my dad who brought her into the world. It's not her fault."

"Is it because of Bright Boys?"

"She went to Atlantis knowing who I was, and she has done everything she can to help H3RO: a group she has *no* connection to. Meanwhile, at the first opportunity she got, she disbanded the group with her blood in it."

I bit my tongue from commenting further. I had been so angry and upset when Bright Boys had disbanded, but I'd met her since, and I thought she seemed decent enough. I'd trust her with my career.

"If you feel that way about her, I guess not signing with Atlantis would be the smarter move," I said quietly.

"She asked me to trust her, and part of me doesn't want to, but the other part of me says she can't screw me over twice," he told me.

"I meant me."

Seungjin's whole body turned to face me. "You?"

"I don't want to go back to SLA," I told him. "I can't keep looking my friends in the eye and worry about them finding out about my father."

"No one likes the D word, but it won't be as bad as you think."

I looked at him, sadly. "This coming from the guy who had spent the last two years telling the public your mom just works in another city?" I shook my head. "But it's not that. I'd rather they find out that than the truth."

"What's the truth?" Seungjin asked, confused.

I could feel my jaw starting to quiver and I couldn't stop myself from crying again. "That my father doesn't want me." The look of pity Seungjin gave me had me up on my feet walking away from him. "That. That look is exactly what I don't want anyone giving me. I don't want anyone's pity."

Arms wrapped around me, making me jump, as Seungjin pulled my back against his chest. "That look was of someone who wants to find your father and punch him. *That* was the look of someone who hates the fact that the person who is making you feel this way, has no idea what a fool he is being towards his own daughter." He stepped around so he was facing me, but his hands never left me. "That was the look of someone who wants to take away all the pain and doubt you're feeling and replace it with all the love and awe I feel for you."

I stared up at Seungjin, and for the first time, didn't feel like crying on him. I had no idea how he did it; part of me was irritated that I couldn't find that calming feeling by myself, but mainly I was grateful that somehow, Seungjin was my friend.

The irritation suddenly consumed me, pushing that gratitude to the side.

This … this wasn't me. I was Cha Yerin. I didn't need anyone to tell me how I was broken or how they could be the ones to help me.

I also shouldn't be letting anyone see me in this weak state.

"We should do something," I declared, changing the subject as quickly as possible.

"OK …" he looked around the room before looking back to me. "Do you want to go to Lotte World?"

I glanced down at Seungjin's sweats that I was comfortably wearing. "Something that doesn't involve leaving your place. You said you don't celebrate Christmas in this house. What do you normally do on Christmas day?"

"Last year I was training with Bright Boys. We had a comeback in the new year to prepare for." He glanced around the room again, before pointing to the far corner. "Do you want to sing?"

He was pointing at an area which had been set up with a karaoke machine. I suppose it wasn't that much different from going to a noraebang. "Sure."

Z

Considering how badly my Christmas had started, it had ended great. We spent the morning singing, had lunch, napped, spent the afternoon learning the dance routines of some of the newer K-pop songs which had been released, and then we watched movies while eating pizza until late in the evening.

I'd awoken early, staring at the ceiling in Seungjin's guestroom, trying to work out what I was going to do.

Today was the day I was supposed to return my contract to Atlantis.

If I was going to return it …

I rolled onto my side and turned the lamp on. The one thing I knew now, was that I didn't want to be in America. I didn't want to be in the same country as a person who didn't want to see me. My mother had also said being an idol would help the school.

It wasn't like I was auditioning. I'd already done that and passed. Holly had even said she had me in mind for a girl group that was about to debut, which meant there wouldn't be much time spent waiting for that opportunity.

And yesterday, I'd realized how much I'd enjoyed performing—even if it was with just Seungjin.

I got out of bed and dressed: my clothes had been laundered and returned to me. While I got ready, I kept thinking it over, but every time, I would come to the same conclusion. "Do it, Yerin. What have you got to lose?"

When I walked into the kitchen a while later, Seungjin was already in there, leaning against the counter. He was eating breakfast; a box of cereal in one hand, the other delving into it to eat the cereal by the fistful. He paused when he saw me. "You're up early."

"I wanted to go to Atlantis this morning."

Seungjin slowly set the box of cereal down. "Are you serious? What about America?"

"I passed the audition, didn't I?" I asked, flipping my hair over my shoulder. "I just need to go home and get my mother to sign the contract."

"Do you think she will?"

I shrugged. "She brought Atlantis to SLA."

"Let's go then," he said, pushing away from the counter. "Unless you want breakfast?"

I shook my head. For some reason, I was too nervous to eat.

I followed Seungjin out and we walked up to my house. Although it was early, my mother was up, doing yoga. While Seungjin waited in the entrance, I presented her with the contract.

"I was wondering why this took so long to get to me," she sniffed, continuing with her warrior pose.

Not, *where were you yesterday?* or *why is there a charge for more than a million won for a flight to Los Angeles?*

"I was thinking it over."

Mother finally relaxed and took the papers from me. "What is there to think about? I told you: this is good publicity for the Seoul Leadership Academy." She walked over to the sidebar and opened a drawer, producing a pen and an ink pad. She quickly signed the documents and then added her thumb print. Wiping the ink away with a handkerchief, she passed the contract back to me. "I assume you won't be in any of your classes this morning."

"I don't think I'll be in any more of my classes," I pointed out as I slipped the contract into my bag.

My mother gave me a sharp look. "Cha Yerin, you will still be expected to graduate. You still have a year of school left. I made an agreement with Atlantis Entertainment to that effect."

"I don't think you realize just how much work goes into being an idol," I told her.

"Nonsense," she sniffed. "You sing a song and pose for a few photographs."

Instead of arguing, I just nodded my head at her. I knew enough to know I was already looking at sixteen-hour days.

And it was still a better option than being in this house.

I walked back to Seungjin who was busy reading something on his phone. "Can we go?" I asked, quietly.

Z

As far as I could tell, Seungjin and I were the first ones at Atlantis. Holly's assistant, who recognized Seungjin straight away, told us that Holly hadn't arrived yet. We didn't have to wait long before she did arrive, accompanied by Jun, a member of H3RO. He was even more gorgeous in person.

It took everything in me not to stare at him like the closet fangirl I was, as he joked with Holly. When he saw me looking, he gave me a swoon-worthy grin.

"Of course," I heard Seungjin mutter under his breath. I turned and caught him rolling his eyes.

"Cha Yerin?" Holly asked, giving me a bright smile. "I'm happy to see you here. I wasn't sure I would." She looked to Seungjin. "I'm glad to see you too, Seungjin."

"Mmmm."

"They're going to be a while. Let's go get an iced americano from the cafeteria," Jun said as he clamped an arm around Seungjin's shoulders. He dragged him off before Seungjin could properly protest.

"If you ever read a bio with subtle next to his name, it's a lie," Holly told me. "But Jun's right. I would like to have a chat with you and make sure you're one hundred percent sure about this decision, and then take you to meet your manager and the other members of your group."

I followed her into her office and took a seat on one of the two couches, while she sat on the other one. Then, remembering the contract, quickly pulled it out of my bag and handed it to her.

Holly took it and set it beside her without even looking at it. "When we last spoke, you didn't seem interested in becoming an idol."

"I thought it over."

She studied me carefully, and then nodded. "One of the important things in this industry is timing. I have two talented girls ready to debut, but they need two other members for a group, rather than a duet. I want you to be one of them. If the second girl gets back to me today, I want to debut you at the end of February. That's nine weeks. Nine weeks to learn your choreography and lyrics for your debut song, as well as film your music video and record the single."

"OK."

"If you can't do that, we need to push the debut back, and the next opportunity will be May."

"OK," I said again.

"OK," she repeated, standing. "Let's go meet the

others."

I followed her out of the office and down the stairs to a floor that seemed to be room after room of dance studios. Holly finally pushed one of them open and a Sonamoo song burst out. I walked in just behind Holly and stood to one side.

Two girls were dancing while a woman stood recording them. The younger of the two was definitely the better dancer. She was cute, maybe my age, if not younger, with hair which sat just below her shoulders.

The other girl was stunning. She had long, sleek hair, similar to mine, and she was tall—almost dwarfing the smaller girl.

I also knew, in the way two lions would size each other up, she was the one who wanted to be in charge. I kept my fingers crossed she wasn't older than me, even though she looked it.

When they finally finished and the woman stopped the music, the two of them bowed respectfully at Holly as she gave them an enthusiastic round of applause. "You girls look amazing!" she exclaimed.

"Thank you," the smaller one said, shyly.

"I have the newest member to introduce to you," Holly told them, angling her body to the side so she could see all of us. "This is Cha Yerin and she will be one of your rappers. Yerin, meet your group: Hoo Dasom." The older girl looked at me with suspicion. "And Pil Sojung." The younger girl gave me a wave. Holly indicated to the woman. "And this is your manager, Yan Kiae."

"Hello, Cha Yerin," Kiae greeted me.

A H3RO song started playing and Holly pulled her phone out of her pocket, answering it. "I'll be right there," she said, before hanging up. She looked at us all. "I'm sorry, I have to go. I'm not sure if and when the fourth member is coming, so please show Yerin around."

And then she disappeared.

The manager sighed. "You girls might as well head to the cafeteria and take a break. Let's meet back here in an hour."

And then it was just me, Dasom and Sojung.

They walked over to me. Dasom looked me up and down again. I folded my arms, cocked my hips, and stared back. "What year were you born?"

"2002," I replied.

Dasom put a hand on Sojung, giving her a friendly, but sympathetic smile. "Sorry So-So. It looks like you're still the maknae." She looked back to me, her smile evaporating. "2001," she snapped. "And while Sojung might be younger than you, she's been training here for four years already. I've been here six. If you're joining us and we're debuting soon, then you'd better do everything you can to make sure that happens, because if it doesn't then I *will* hurt you."

I glowered back, flipping my hair over my shoulder. "I must be good if they're ready to debut me," I sniped back. "Unnie."

I, Cha Yerin, was not about to let a girl who had been training for years without debuting, talk down to me. I didn't care how old she was.

제19 장

Seungjin

I sat staring at Jun-hyung. Something was up, and I couldn't work it out. "What did you do over Christmas?" I asked him, suspiciously.

Jun leaned forward resting his forearms on the table. "You, Seungjin, are far too young to know the answer to that. Besides … the answer isn't just a 'what'."

"You look happy."

"That's because I am happy. H3RO's happy. Holly is happy."

I pulled a face. "Why do you care if my sister is happy?"

"Because when Holly is happy, H3RO is happy."

"Are you drunk?" I asked him.

Jun laughed. "You'll understand one day."

I snorted at that. "If *Holly* keeps her promise and actually debuts me, then maybe I will."

"Seungjin? You're back?"

Jun and I both turned our heads to find the youngest member of Cupcake, Han Seorin standing by our table, running an apple around in her hands.

Strangely, her attention wasn't on either of us as she scanned the cafeteria.

"Hi, Seorin," I greeted her.

"Is uh … is Jaehoon here too?"

"How would I know?" I asked, narrowing my eyes. "Why do you want to know?"

She finally looked at me. "Oh, no reason!" she said, hurriedly. "It's good to see you." She bowed her head at Jun. "Sunbae."

I watched her walk away, tilting my head to the side. "That's a girl with a crush," Jun told me.

I looked at him and pulled a face. "Seorin and Jaehoon?" I watched Seorin walked out of the room, confused. "Those two were something years ago, but she saw sense and they broke up." I had never understood how Jaehoon had ended up dating Seorin. The girl was stunning and smart and sophisticated. Jaehoon was … savage, OK looking, and judging from the grades he'd been getting at SLA, not the brightest light stick at the concert.

"Maybe we should talk about Yerin and Seungjin?" Jun suggested, giving me a pointed look.

"Yeah, my love life is as thrilling as yours is," I muttered dryly. "And there is nothing going on between me and Yerin."

"Hmmm," Jun muttered, pursing his lips, thoughtfully. "And on that note, I think it's time to get you back to Holly."

Jun was weird.

He also left me to go back to Holly's office by myself—not that I needed a chaperone.

I was surprised to see so many faces in the small area outside, but before I could work out who was there, along with how many new faces there seemed to be, Holly reappeared.

"Because there's so many of you, we're going to use the conference room," she announced. "Follow me."

The last time I had been in the conference room, Sejin was yelling at us and sending us back to SLA as he suspended all activities for Bright Boys. We filed in, taking seat around the table, and I was finally able to see who was here.

Jaehoon, King, Joochan, and Ryan. That was it for Bright Boys? I turned to glower at Holly and call her out when two faces had me doing a double take. Twins. There were twins? They were identical.

"Thank you all for coming," Holly said, closing the door behind her. She moved over and took a seat at the table.

"Where are the rest of Bright Boys?" I demanded.

"Bright Boys no longer exists, Seungjin," she told me, patronizingly. "This is not Bright Boys 2.0."

"You promised—"

"I promised that I would do everything I could for you to debut again," she cut me off. "At no point did I promise a Bright Boys reboot. This ... this is going to be something completely different. If you're going to stop me from explaining everything, I'll ask for you to wait outside so I can spend ten minutes sharing the plan with everyone else, before I bring you back in and cancel all my afternoon meetings."

"Just shut up, Seungjin," Ryan hissed at me.

I shot him a look, but sat back in my chair, arms folded, glowering at the Vice Chairwoman.

She gave me a patronizing smile. "Thank you."

She turned to the table. "For anyone questioning the lack of respect, Seungjin is my younger brother."

"Half-brother," I muttered.

"And I also want to make it clear that Seungjin had to pass the same audition evaluation you all did, held to the same standards. Standards which will continue to apply to all of you as we head down this path."

I glowered at her, but a part of me was glad she had pointed that out. If I had to spend another four years telling everyone I was there because I had earned my place, and not because my dad owned Atlantis, I wasn't going to be happy.

Holly took a deep breath. "Let's start with introductions. I am Holly Lee and I am the Vice Chairwoman of Atlantis Entertainment. That is Lee Seungjin, Ryan Tseng, Kim Jaehoon, Yang Joochan, and Lee Minhyuk. Obviously, you guys know each other; the rest of you might recognize them as former members of Bright Boys ... and King."

"I'm still King," King told her.

"You're King of this group, but not King the solo artist," Holly said, frowning. "Stage names and whether you choose to have them and what they are, are down to you guys." She sighed. "And on this side of the table we have Kwang Insoo, Min Taekyung—"

"TK?" I spluttered, finally spotting him at the far end of the table. "You're letting *him* in this?"

"Seungjin!" Ryan hissed, punching my thigh under the table.

Holly licked her lips and then turned to me. "Min Taekyung is part of this group. Like you, he earned his place. If you don't like it, leave."

I glowered at her.

She stared back, refusing to back down. "I mean it Seungjin. If you don't like it, go. I will find something else for you. You've had this life before. You know how much time you're going to spend with each other."

I turned to look at TK. I hated the idea: the only reason we were here now was because of his brother. *Exactly: his brother.* I swear, it was like Lucinda was in the room with us. But it was one thing to be working with him for a school performance evaluation. It was a whole other thing to be in the same group as him for the next... who knows how long if we were successful.

He is not his brother.

He is not his brother.

He is not his brother.

"I'm staying," I muttered. There were enough people sat around the table that I figured I could avoid spending too much time with him. And people had to work with others they didn't like all the time, right. "I'm staying," I said again, directing my words at Holly.

"And then we have our twins, Hong Wonseok and Hong Wooseok—"

"I'm Wooseok," Wooseok said after Holly had introduced him as his brother. I don't think I was alone in looking between the two of them, trying to spot the differences. Honestly, the best I could do was Wonseok was wearing red and Wooseok was in black.

"I'm sorry," Holly, apologized. "I thought I had.... I'm sorry. I will work on this." She cleared her throat. "I do have one other confirmed member; Heiki Yokota. He's from Tokyo and will be arriving later this week."

"Is that all of us?" Ryan asked, politely. "Nine of

us?"

"Ten, including Yokota," Holly nodded. "For now, at least," she added, without elaborating further, much to my annoyance.

"Then, what's the plan? When do we debut?" Jaehoon asked.

Holly nodded. "I'm going to do something this company has not done before," she told us. "And I know you're going to have questions, but please wait until I'm finished, because I might answer some of them as I'm going." She waited for us all to nod our agreement. "OK, starting in February, I want to introduce you month by month, in smaller groups— pre-debut units. This will lead up to your group debut at the end of June. You're going to be the biggest group size-wise, and hopefully successfully too, that Atlantis has ever had, and I want to introduce you in small groups to allow the public to get to know you as individuals. I also want to give the group a bit of mystery. That's partly why the name of the group you're officially going to debut in will be kept a secret until the last moment."

I bit my lip, feeling, for the first time, excited. Begrudgingly, I had to admit, nothing like this had been tried before at Atlantis.

"Other companies have done something similar, and it's usually been done with some form of competition, pitching trainees against trainees," Holly continued. "I'm not doing that. Being an idol is enough stress to deal with. The fact is, you're all talented individuals. That being said, I am keeping a close eye on this group, and I will be discussing behavior and talent with your managers and coaches, and if necessary, we will make adjustments to the final line up."

It still sounded like a survival show to me—just with less cameras.

"Let me make it perfectly clear: Atlantis will not tolerate any violence or bullying. There are no second chances with that. Not only will you be out of this project, I will be kicking you out of Atlantis too." Holly purposefully met each one of our gazes. "I will not tolerate it. Aside from the fact it's disgusting behavior, as members of this group, you are representatives of Atlantis. More importantly, as idols, you're going to be role models to thousands. I don't expect you to be perfect, but I do expect you to be decent human beings. Understood?"

"Yes, buhoejangnim," we all agreed. I watched as Holly winced when we addressed her as Vice Chairwoman. Why would she wince? Didn't she like it?

"With that, I expect all of you still in school to attend morning classes when you can. I want you all graduating. I don't want any of you in the position, five or ten years down the line regretting the fact you never graduated. I also expect all of you to do a minimum of five hours voluntary work a week. The slight exception to that is the first unit, but I'll come to that in a moment. Is there anyone here who does not agree to these terms?"

No one said anything, but I put my hand up. "I'm not a high-ranking student."

Holly shrugged. "I don't want you all to be competing for the top spot in the school rankings. I just want you to graduate."

Was she going to have an answer for everything?

"I suppose I should tell you a little more about

the units," she said, smiling. "Wonso." We all stared at her, blankly. Still smiling, she reached into her back pocket and pulled out a flash card: **원소**.

Seeing it written in Hangeul didn't help either. It could have had the Romanization, wonso, there and I still would have been none the wiser.

She flipped it over. 1SO.

"Elements?" King asked, sounding as confused as I felt.

Holly nodded. "Exactly. We've stylized it a little to make the name stand out. There will be four units: Fire, Earth, Water, and Air."

I looked at Ryan. I couldn't help the grin. Holly had managed to surprise me.

"For now," Holly continued, "I only have Fire confirmed, as this is the only one with enough members. Which means this unit will be releasing the first single for this project at the end of February. Your song has been written and is ready for you to learn. Ro Chanheon has worked out the choreography. This group is going to have the hardest time in the sense you will have the shortest time to learn the choreography. This does not mean I think the guys in the final group will have the easiest time as they will be releasing their single a month before the group debuts. You're also all going up against established Atlantis groups during the unit period, as well as established groups outside of Atlantis. This isn't a race for a number one, but a mission to gain fans for your group debut."

"Who is in 1SO: Fire?" I asked.

The smile slipped slightly. "The groups have been chosen based on ..." she frowned. "I can't tell you. I have no idea how good you're all going to be at keeping secrets, and frankly, I'm going to treat you like JYP treats GOT7 and not tell you anything. But know this, the groups have been chosen specifically." She let out a long sigh. "And also, I'm still waiting on individuals to confirm they're signing with us so it might have to change last minute. But either way, it's nothing to do with talent or favoritism. You're all equal right now."

"But who is in the first unit?" I pressed, keeping my fingers crossed.

Holly nodded. "1SO: Fire will consist of Kwang Insoo, Lee Seungjin, Heiki Yokota, and Hong Wonseok. Any questions?"

"What about the rest of us?" Wooseok asked, sharing a look with his brother.

Holly, who had been holding her flashcard up, set it down on the table in front of her. "They're still dependent on other trainees. One of the groups only has one member in it at the moment, and I don't want to share who that is because I don't want anyone to think that is a reflection on that person. As soon as I have new members to add to a line up, I will call you to my office and let you know."

"What happens if they don't sign?" King asked.

"I have contingency plans in place," Holly assured him. "I have spent weeks working on this, and I plan on debuting a group in June. It's partly why I want to keep details secret in case things have to change. Please, just trust me." She smiled, reassuringly. "I have spoken enough now. Does anyone have any other questions?"

"Who is our manager?" King asked.

Holly laughed. "Managers. Plural. With so many of you, the group will have three when you debut, but each unit will have a manager dedicated to them. For today, I want you to focus on moving into the dorm and getting to know each other. Tomorrow, 1SO: Fire will come back here to meet their manager and hear their guide track."

With strict instruction that we were to now wear caps and masks whenever we were out in public, we were allowed to leave the conference room. An Atlantis assistant took us down to the underground parking lot and onto one of two minibuses. Those of us at SLA went there to gather our belongings. The new guys went straight to the dorms.

"What do you think?" Joochan asked as soon as the doors closed.

I fastened my seatbelt and turned to look at the others. "I'm trying not to get too excited," I admitted.

"The hell with that!" Ryan exclaimed, happily. "I think it sounds amazing and I can't wait to find out what my unit is going to be."

"If there is a unit," Jaehoon muttered. "You heard her; she only knows about 1SO: Fire."

"Guys, we've all got to stop being negative," Ryan said, firmly. "We survived Bright Boys disbanding, and we survived SLA. There's no point dwelling on the past: you can't change that. The future? That's ours to control."

"How much of it is in our control?" I asked.

Ryan leaned forward and smacked me upside the head. "Positive, Seungjin. You of all people should be positive. You're going to hear your song tomorrow!"

I sat back in my seat and closed my eyes.

Positivity.

After everything, it was hard to be positive.

But Ryan was right.

I had a debut unit, a new group to look forward to, and, finally … a future.

제20 장

Yerin

Mid-January

I was beginning to think I had made the wrong decision.

Within an hour of meeting Dasom, I hated her. She was mean and nasty; bitter at having been a trainee for so long, and even more resentful at the fact I had joined the group and wouldn't have to wait long before debuting.

Thankfully, she was acting the same to the fourth and final member of our group, but seeing as how that person was none other than Cho Miyeon who had been in Team Yellow with me, Lucinda, and Eunbyeol, it didn't exactly help me.

What was worse was that we were all sharing the same room too.

The dorms at Atlantis were nowhere near as nice as they were at SLA. Even if you ignored the fact that I'd had a nicer room to start with. This one was cramped, and because Dasom and Sojung had spent five years living in it, they had taken over it. When my cases arrived, having finally made it back from America, there was no room for them. I had the equivalent of a suitcase's space on a rack.

I'd had to push them under my bunk and go into them when I needed them. The only advantage was most of the time I was wearing leggings, a sports bra, and one of Seungjin's hoodies I had yet to return.

Despite the fact we had maybe four hours of sleep a night, I was wide awake, staring at the outline of the bunk above me—or what I could make out of it in the near darkness of the room. Dasom snored. It was like living under an underpass.

Most nights I'd sleep with my earphones in, drowning her out.

Tonight, I just couldn't sleep.

I hadn't gone into this blind, but being an idol was much, much harder than I expected it to be. As if to prove a point, the door opened, and someone switched the light on. "Wakey wakey!" a voice declared before shutting the door on our protests.

It was five in the morning and time for our morning run.

For the last two weeks, every day, we had been woken up at five and gone for a five-mile run along the Han river. It didn't matter if there was snow, rain, or simply freezing temperatures. As our fitness coach liked to point out, that was just motivation to move faster.

I rolled out of bed, avoiding Miyeon's feet as she swung over the opposite bunk and dropped down, and grabbed my clothes. With barely enough space in our room, I moved back onto my bunk to dress.

"Come on," Dasom grunted. Annoyingly, she

was a morning person. Unfortunately, she reserved the bubbly cheer and motivation for Sojung. As it was, she linked her arm through our maknae's and left the room without waiting for either of us.

Silently, I pulled my hair up into a high ponytail, before putting my mask and cap on. Although there was no conversation, Miyeon waited for me and we walked down to the dorm's back entrance together.

Outside, it was raining—that fine rain that soaked you within seconds of being out in it. Of course, that didn't stop our instructor. I didn't know his name—I just referred to him as The General. He led us down to the river, setting our pace.

Much as I hated running, I was better at it than the others, but I'd learned very quickly to let Sojung set the pace. The last time I'd set it, Dasom had tripped me.

I'd rather have been in a group with Kareun. At least Kareun was my friend as well as being a world-class bitch.

After our run, still wet-through, we went straight to the dorm's cafeteria. It wasn't as nice as the one at Atlantis, but that was a luxury for those groups who had debuted. It also only served low calorie options. I grabbed my meal and a bottle of milk and sat down at an empty table.

I was halfway through my sweet potato when Dasom walked past. "You know we're debuting in a few weeks?"

I looked up at her and arched an eyebrow. That still hadn't been confirmed. We were going to be given our song today. However, I failed to see the relevance. "Yes?"

"Then maybe you might want to reconsider all

those carbs: a moment on your lips and a lifetime on your hips."

I sighed. "I'm not fat, Dasom."

"No," she agreed. "Not until the camera adds ten kilograms." She walked off, joining Sojung at another table.

I stared at the remains of my tray.

"I was going to stay quiet, considering how many times I've heard you say something similar to Baekhee in the past, but I'm also not going to sit back and let my groupmate develop an eating disorder," Miyeon declared as she slipped into the seat opposite.

I looked at her in surprise. This was the first time she'd ever sat with me. "I've never said that!"

"I'm fairly certain I recall a conversation where Baekhee was referred to as an elephant," she said, dryly.

"That was Hyesun."

"And you agreed," Miyeon shot back.

"Only because Baekhee is fat!"

"We're not going to have this conversation, Yerin," Miyeon told me, firmly. "Now shut up and eat the rest of your breakfast. It's a long way until dinner and we have a full day of practice."

I ate because I was hungry, not because I was told to. When my plate was cleared, I went to return it to the hatch, walking past Dasom and her half of a sweet potato and cup of berries. I paused and looked down at her. "Unnie," I said, sweetly, "I think you're the one that needs to worry about your diet. I saw the figure on the scales. You're hovering near the top of the acceptable weight range of our contracts." Then, flicking my still wet hair over my shoulder, splashing her and Sojung, I sauntered away.

I hurried back to my room to change into some dry clothes before our rehearsal, hanging up my wet running outfit in the bathroom to dry. The others had done that before eating. I didn't care—I just wanted some space.

I hurried back downstairs to the bus stop outside the dorms. It was a short enough distance to be able to walk, but I had just dried off and wanted to stay that way a little longer. I was surprised to discover none of my other groupmates were there.

"The bus has just gone," Seungjin announced, appearing beside me. Like me, he was wearing a cap and mask.

Despite practicing in the same building, and sleeping in the same building, this was the first time I had seen him in over two weeks. I hadn't realized how much I had missed him until now. "Hi," I said, softly.

"Is that my sweater?" he asked, staring at the fabric which was poking out of my unzipped coat.

"Nope," I told him with a cheeky grin, before remembering I was wearing my own mask and he couldn't see it. I glanced around and pulled my mask down so that it hooked under my chin and sat down on the bus stop bench.

"You look like you've lost weight," he told me, doing the same.

"Idol life," I sighed. "And a five-mile run each morning."

"Ten for the boys," Seungjin agreed. "And two hours in the gym every evening. I've got abs."

"You've always had abs," I muttered. That earned me a look which had me staring at the passing traffic. "I saw your music videos."

"How are you finding it?"

I shrugged. That was a billion won question ... "I enjoy the rap lessons. I'm getting better at that."

"And the rest of it?"

"It's harder than I thought it would be," I admitted. "And lonelier."

Seungjin shifted, angling his body towards me. "How is your group? I heard they were planning on debuting a girl group soon. Is that you?"

"I assume so. It's me, two girls who have been trainees for a while, Hoo Dasom, Pil Sojung, and Cho Miyeon from SLA."

"You're debuting with Dasom?" he asked, surprised.

I turned to look at him. "If all goes to plan ... why?"

"I'm just surprised. She was supposed to debut with Cupcake but they held her back. I heard it was because she was ..."

"Because she was what?" I asked, narrowing my eyes.

"Not ready," he finished, lamely.

I rolled my eyes. "Of course."

"Just watch your back."

"Are you serious?" I asked, arching an eyebrow. "You can't leave it at that."

"It's rumors and I don't want to be the one to stir them up again."

"Seungjin!"

"Apparently, she was bullying one of the other trainees, OK?"

I sank back against the bus stop and sighed. "Of course."

"It's a rumor, Yerin. I wasn't there and I didn't see it happen."

"But watch my back?"

"Let's not talk about this," he suggested. "I'm sorry. I didn't want to upset you."

"I'm not upset," I assured him. I wasn't, but I was irritated. I forced myself to think of something happier. "What happened with you and your debut? Is it happening?"

Seungjin gave me an excited grin. "I have a unit debut in February."

"I can't wait!" I declared, happily. I was so please to hear that. "Is this your group? Do you have a name?"

"It's part of my group. 1SO: Fire. We're going to be filming the music video next week. But if things go to plan, we'll be debuting in June."

"All of Bright Boys?" I had my fingers crossed.

He shook his head, but he didn't look disappointed. "Yongsik just joined Onyx."

"Wait, what?" my mouth fell open. Since being at Atlantis, I had no idea what was going on in the outside world. Phones and internet had been restricted, and I was too busy trying to study when I could to even care about the news. But this was big. Onyx were a successful, established group.

"One of their members, Oh Bohyun, left and returned to China."

"But they were just about to start a world tour!"

Seungjin nodded. "Exactly. So they brought Yongsik in. Although he's going by CX now."

"Wow," I muttered, trying to process that. I was only just keeping up with the idea of debuting myself— the idea of being put into an established group just as they were going on tour was incredible. I couldn't do it. "And the others?"

"The only one we're unsure about is Dongyeol. His ankle is still in a cast."

I stared at him, allowing that to sink in, and then I threw myself at him. "Seungjin, I'm so pleased for you all!"

He hugged me back, tightly. "Thank you," he muttered, his mouth close to my ear.

I pulled away, aware I was grinning like an idiot. As a Dazzle, I wanted the members of Bright Boys to get a second chance. As Seungjin's friend, it was even more important to me. The news seemed to rejuvenate me, and I started to get to my feet, ready to hail the bus which was due any moment, but a hand held me back.

"I've missed you, Yerin."

I sat back down, nodding slowly. "Same."

Z

Our song was called Love Struck. It had a slightly rocky beat to it and was up tempo. The choreography was insane. The four of us were sat around a laptop, watching the choreography while listening to the guide track.

"What do you think?" Holly asked.

"I like it," Miyeon grinned.

"Is that our image? Rock?" Dasom asked, dubiously.

"This is the guide track, so it will change when you get in the studio to record it, depending on the producer. But I don't think it will change too much.

I didn't mind it. It sounded like a P!nk track and

I loved P!nk. It was also different to the songs the other girl groups were putting out. I had been half afraid this group would be a very sugar-sweet pop group, like Twice, Lovelyz or Oh My Girl. It wasn't that I disliked any of them, but I wasn't sure anyone but Sojung would be able to pull off that innocent look.

"You're going to be in the recording studio next week, so get your lyrics learned. The week after, you will be recording the music video and then you have three weeks to get the two combined and ready for your debut stage," Holly continued. "I'll leave you to it."

No sooner had she left, was she replaced by Ro Chanheon. I started at him in confusion. "I thought we had to learn our lyrics?"

Ro Chanheon's eyes narrowed. "We may be out of the Seoul Leadership Academy, but I will have you running laps around the building if I need to."

Thankfully, I had used the correct honorifics—I wasn't stupid like Lucinda—however, unlike Lucinda, I shut up.

"You're going to be expected to be learning and practicing both. Your individual singing lessons will be taking place this afternoon. This morning, you dance. This evening, you dance. I'm telling you now, if you want this debut to be successful—if you want this debut to happen at all—you will be becoming very familiar with this practice room."

I was under no illusion otherwise.

"As of tomorrow, I expect you all to be wearing heels. Heels no shorter than three inches. Because that's what you will be performing in and you will need to get used to the dance wearing them."

z

The first 'singing' lesson had been interesting. We had been given sheet music with the lyrics, and while the vocalists had notes to follow, both myself and Dasom just had lyrics. In a way, that filled me with relief; that I didn't have to worry about writing lyrics. Yet, as I read them through, I found myself wanting to change them. I waited until we had a break and approached the vocal coach.

"I was wondering, how fixed these lyrics are?"

He looked at me with an arched eyebrow. "You're wanting to change things already?"

"Only a little bit," I admitted.

The vocal coach shook his head. "That's not how this works. Someone has written this song for you. Unless you're invited to make changes, or collaborate, you keep them as they are. Don't try to run before you can walk."

I walked back to the others, snagging a bottle of water on my way. "What were you asking?" Dasom eyed me with suspicion.

"I was just wondering if we had any flexibility with the lyrics. The line I have about dancing in the street—I wanted to change it to dancing on a rooftop."

I was met with three confused looks and I lost any desire to explain that I had good memories of dancing on a rooftop, rather than a street. Not that I was going to share that piece of information.

Instead, I shrugged. "It just felt more natural."

"Do not screw this up for me," Dasom growled at me.

"Break's over," the vocal coach announced,

calling us back over.

I ground back my irritation and focused on learning the song. The more time I spent doing this, the more that I wanted it.

We stayed in the studio long past dinner and late into the night. The dry clothes I had changed in to had become damp with sweat the later in the day it had become.

And yet, I wasn't tired.

It was … exhilarating.

We still had hours of practicing before we reached the level of near perfection we needed, but it was like something had clicked inside of me. The idea of going to study in America seemed like such a distant memory to me.

It had finally stopped raining when we walked outside, late in the night, and we all walked back to the dorm together, exhausted. Sojung collapsed onto her bed and fell asleep in minutes, still wearing the clothes she had worn all day. Miyeon disappeared, muttering something under her breath I didn't really catch. Which left Dasom and I in an awkward silence.

"Do you want to shower first?" I offered. While it was the respectful thing to offer to my unnie, I was also trying to be nice.

Everything was starting to become real.

I had a group.

I had a song.

We were close to a debut date.

The last thing I wanted was to spend the next seven years with someone who didn't like me, especially considering how much time we were going to spend together.

Dasom narrowed her eyes. "I don't know what you're trying to do, but that won't work on me."

If she didn't know what I was doing (which, by the way, neither did I), how would she know it wouldn't work? "I'm not *trying* anything," I told her instead. "You clearly don't know me—"

"Oh, I know exactly who you are, Cha Yerin," she snarled. "And that's the problem." At that, she shoved me out of the way and marched into the bathroom, locking the door behind her.

제21 장

Seungjin

Late January

When Holly said to trust her, I hadn't. Not really. Not until a week ago, at least.

That was when everything seemed to move from zero to a hundred in the blink of an eye. Crazy didn't even begin to describe it.

1SO: Fire was appropriately named. We were on fire.

A week ago, the teasers had started appearing around Atlantis. It was subtle: fire beacons had been positioned on the street outside the Atlantis building. Two days ago, the giant screens on the front of the building had the videos edited so that the end of every clip went up in flames.

At first, I had been worried. Kota spoke almost no Korean, but thankfully there was a translator for the key meetings and practices, and for the rest, Insoo knew a little Japanese so we could get by. Kota was also an incredible vocalist. Even though he didn't know what he was singing half the time, he had spent hours with Insoo who had patiently pronounced each word for him.

For three hours every morning, Kota would have Korean lessons, and the rest of us would head to SLA. Those three hours were the only time I ever saw the other group members—and I had yet to see Yerin there.

I knew she was as busy as I was, but the last time I had seen her was for less than half an hour at a bus stop, then travelling the far too short distance to Atlantis.

I missed her.

"You've spaced out, hyung."

I glanced over at Wonseok. I could understand how someone would get him and his brother mixed up at first glance, but the moment you spent any amount of time with them, it was easy to tell them apart. Wooseok was the quieter one, happy to let his brother take the lead.

Wonseok was ...

"Do we need to call KARI?"

I arched an eyebrow. "What is KARI?"

"The Korea Aerospace Research Institute." Wonseok rolled his eyes. "I mean, I know I grew up on an island, but did you grow up under a rock?"

"I want to be *a* star, not *on* a star." I shot him a withering glare.

Wonseok looked up at me, opened his mouth, and closed it.

"What?" I demanded.

"Nuh-uh," he said, shaking his head. "I must not be disrespectful to my hyung."

"When has that stopped you?"

Very slowly, Wonseok gave me a grin. I knew I was going to regret giving him that pass. "I guess you are made up of as much hot air as a star …"

He was running away from me before I could put him in a headlock.

Wonseok was cheeky, and honestly, if it had been anyone else, I would have hated it, but with him, I liked his teasing.

But I was never going to tell him that.

Tomorrow, we were flying out to Jeju for a few days to film our music video. Because of that, we'd been given an early night … well, it was before midnight, which was earlier than normal!

I was too excited to sleep. Knowing Kota and Insoo had planned a quick study session before they went to sleep, and Wonseok was going to be up all night, watching dramas under his covers, I stopped in my room long enough to pick up a bag, and then went straight up to the roof.

It was icy cold, and would be colder up on the roof, but I had arranged to meet Yerin up there.

I was surprised to find her waiting. The roof had a covered area with summer outdoor furniture under it. Most of it was pushed back, hidden under tarpaulin to protect it from the elements, aside from a small metal love seat. Yerin was huddled up on the love seat, her legs up under her chin, staring out across the city.

Trying not to startle her, I settled down in the seat next to her. It was one of those seats where the chairs were next to each other but facing opposite directions. She gave me a soft smile as I sat down.

"You look …" she pulled her head of her knees and tilted it. "Happy."

"I am," I agreed. "Almost."

"Almost?"

I leaned forward, reaching for her chin, and kissed her. She kissed me back, a hand clutching at my forearm, and I teased at her lips with my tongue until she allowed me to deepen the kiss. She still tasted of oranges.

"What was that?" she asked as I slowly pulled away.

"Now I'm happy."

Her fingers ran over her lips as she frowned. "I thought we had an agreement."

"I want to amend that agreement," I told her. I reached up, this time, taking her hand and interlinking our fingers, before resting them on the chair arm between us. "I don't want to just be friends anymore."

"That's a little out of the blue, Seungjin."

"Not for me," I disagreed, running my thumb over the back of her hand. "I had come up here to ask you to wait for me—"

"You go to Jeju tomorrow, don't you?"

I shook my head and then nodded it. "Yes, but that's not what I mean. Things are about to get crazy for us. Even crazier than they are right now especially as we're both weeks away from debuting, but I want you to be my girlfriend. My actual girlfriend. Officially."

While the hand holding mine didn't let go, the other ran through her hair as she let out a long breath. "We're never going to see each other."

"We live in the same building. We work for the same company. We're debuting at the same time. Yerin, our paths are going to cross, and even if it's only a few moments here and there, we'll just have to make the most of them. The truth is, when I think about my debut stage, I think about you standing side stage, waiting for me."

"You'd be happy with moments?"

I shook my head. "No. But I'd be happier with moments than with nothing at all."

She stared at me, chewing her lip. "I thought I'd miss SLA, but the only thing I miss is not seeing you every day."

"Same," I admitted.

"Who wouldn't?" Yerin asked, reaching up to flip her hair over her shoulder.

I watched her with a smile: that, right there, was one of the things I missed about her. Her confidence. I wasn't going to bring up her father and America, but this had brought back one of the things I really liked about her.

She caught me staring at her, and her smile softened. "You make me feel a little less lonely doing this, even if I don't get to see you very often." The smile slipped from her face altogether. "But you're the one who told me we were just friends."

"You've never been *just* a friend." I got up. Still holding onto her hand, refusing to let go, I navigated around the chair so that I was in front of her, making sure her arm wasn't twisted in the process. "Until these last few weeks when I haven't seen you, I realized just how much I missed you. I missed talking to you every day. Be my girlfriend, Cha Yerin."

"Why does that sound like a proposal?"

"It's not a proposal, but a promise. A promise to be there for you."

She arched an eyebrow. "Even in Jeju?"

I sighed, disappointment flooding me. "You could just say no."

I started to let go of her hand and back away, but her grip tightened. "I'm teasing," she muttered as she pulled me to her. With one hand still interlinked with hers, the other supporting myself on the arm of the chair, she kissed me. Or maybe I kissed her … it didn't matter either way, because that kiss was our promise.

I didn't want to end the kiss, but I knew time was working against me. Our manager had said he would be checking in on us at midnight and it had been close when I had come up here. "I have something for you," I muttered as Yerin pouted at me. I leaned over the chair and grabbed my bag.

Refusing to let go of her hand, despite how awkward it was to open it with one hand, I tugged at the zipper. Yerin tried to help but I batted her hand away. "Here," I said, eventually pulling the first present out: a phone.

Yerin took it, arching an eyebrow. "You've already bought me a phone."

"Yes, but I know you had your phone taken from you. This is a spare so that we can keep in touch. It's got just my number in it, and it's not saved with a name."

"I knew this kind of thing would happened before I signed, but I feel like a spy or something."

"It's not worth being caught. My brother was very strict about that."

"What about your sister?"

I shrugged. "I know she wants to do well." I reached into the bag and pulled out another present. This one got a wide grin: a hoodie.

"Is this yours?" she asked, suspiciously.

"It's yours now," I corrected her. "To add to your collection."

"Exactly. So why do I need another?"

"Because when I'm not there, you can wear it and imagine I'm giving you a hug. It's not quite the same, but it's as close as I can get."

For a moment, I thought Yerin was going to cry. Then, abruptly, she stood up, almost making me fall over as the hoodie dropped to the ground. Before I could scoop it up, she had flung herself at me.

I'd never been one for any form of public displays of affection, even with the members of Bright Boys—despite the fact I knew fans liked it—and it wasn't the most public of places, but I finally let go of her hand so that I could wrap my arms around her. She seemed to fit against me like a piece of a jigsaw, nestling into my chest.

If kissing her was my favorite thing, holding her was second.

If anyone was ever going to make me choose between being an idol and being with her, I had no idea what I would choose.

For now, I was content holding her.

Which was when my own phone rang.

Unlike last time, we hadn't had our phones confiscated. However, our managers used them to keep track of us, and I fully expected them to check them on occasion … I'd bought myself a second phone when I'd bought one for Yerin, and done the same thing to that as I had for hers.

"Stay there," I instructed her as I moved away from her. It wasn't just a phone call, but a video call.

"Hello, hyungnim," I greeted him.

"Lee Seungjin, you are not in your room. Where are you?"

"On the roof," I replied, truthfully. "I needed some fresh air."

"It is midnight and you should be in bed. You have a wakeup call at four, and you will be filming all day tomorrow. Get down here, get a mask on, and go to sleep."

"Yes, hyungnim."

I hung up and then hurried over to Yerin. "Time for Cinderella to go?" she asked me.

I nodded. "If I don't, Oh Seokbeom will turn me into squashed pumpkin."

I wasn't about to go up against Oh Seokbeom. He had been our manager when I was in Bright Boys. I wasn't entirely sure what had happened, but he was the reason King had never debuted in the group. While we were still in this pre-debut stage, I was not going to do anything to risk it ...

Well ... except for date Yerin.

I was insane.

"I never asked. How are things with you? How is it going in your group?"

Her lips pressed into a thin line. "It's going."

I had been ready to head back to my room, but I stopped, folding my arms as I looked at her. "What does that mean?"

Yerin let out a long, weary sigh. "It's nothing. It's just an evaluation tomorrow."

"That's normal," I assured her, reaching out to cup her cheek. "You're going to be fine."

All of a sudden, the spark was back. Yerin's hair

was tossed over her shoulder and she fixed me a look. "Of course. I'm Cha Yerin."

"Yes, you are," I agreed.

Z

I had forgotten how bored I was with travel. We'd done a lot of it when in Bright Boys and airplanes and airports became very old, very quickly. I had expected that Wonseok would have been excited about it: he was young and hadn't traveled much.

Only, he had.

In fact, as he had listed the countries off that he and his twin had been to, he'd been to more than I knew existed.

"My dad owns hotels," he explained as the three of us stared at him in amazement (although Kota's confusion may have been from the lack of understanding). "All around the world," he added. He pointed at the resort as the minivan pulled in. "Including this one," he added, wryly.

"Huh?"

"Your dad owns an entertainment company, and mine owns the resort. Or twenty-six of them."

"You are rich?" Kota questioned.

"Yes," Wonseok admitted. "But I want to be Hong Wonseok, not Hong Wonseok: Hong Changseok's son."

"He was happy with you being an idol?" I asked, surprised. Sungil's father was rich—ridiculously rich—and he had dragged Sungil out of Atlantis because he didn't want his son being an idol.

"Of course," Wonseok nodded. "I've been lucky

because he has paid for all the dancing and singing lessons since we were in kindergarten. But I auditioned to get my place at Atlantis," he added, hurriedly.

I held my hands up. "No judgement from the son of the entertainment company's Chairman."

"What about you?" I asked Kota. "Where are you from?"

Strangely, we'd not had this conversation. Things had moved so fast, that short of names and ages, our conversations had been dominated by 1SO: Fire, the mystery group, and what we hoped would be in the future. We barely saw the other members: they were just as busy as we were, even though they had more time.

"I am from Tokyo. My mom is a teacher. My dad is ..." he frowned before saying something in Japanese.

Insoo leaned forward, saying something in Japanese before supplying the word in Korean. Dead.

Both Wonseok and I winced. "I'm sorry," I mumbled.

"My Korean is bad," he explained slowly. "I am learning, but I am bad. I will have less lessons when we get back."

"More lessons," Insoo corrected him, gently.

"Hyung, your Korean is good," Wonseok assured him. "When you get more confident, you'll have to teach me Japanese."

Kota frowned, and I could almost see him trying to work out what Wonseok was asking of him. Then he nodded, giving him a bright smile. "Yes."

"We have a tight deadline," Oh Seokbeom suddenly announced, looking at us in irritation. "Or do you plan on spending all day in the minibus?"

Almost in one single movement, the four of us

left the minibus and followed him down a path to a parking lot. There was no hotel room. Instead, we were ushered into a trailer for hair and makeup.

The concept of the video had never been shared with us. Until a couple of days ago, we hadn't even known it was being filmed in Jeju. Nonetheless, I couldn't stop my excitement from bubbling away.

Although I was doing a better job than Wonseok who was literally bouncing in his chair, much to the makeup artist's annoyance. I glanced past him at Insoo who was pouring over a piece of paper—lyrics, by the looks of things. Past him, Kota was busy asking the woman putting his makeup on the names of everything.

I sat back and allowed my hair stylist to style my hair, making it stick up in spikes with red gel that glinted in the right light. Our makeup was dark, with red highlights. With the dark clothes, I was almost convinced we were vampires or something similar. Only, we were filming our first set of scenes on the beach.

No. As I discovered when we walked down, we were on some dunes that seemed to spread for miles, and the videographer was filming with the sea behind us.

The first shots were of us lying down on the beach, like the points on the compass, our heads together in the center, as we were filmed from above by a drone. We shot the same thing for six takes, until we moved on to the solo shots. The four of us all had to lie there as the drone dropped lower.

With the sun above us, on a beach, it was going to look warm on the video. That was also the specific instruction we had been given.

It was freezing. The wind blowing off the ocean had an icy chill to it, while it constantly sent sand blasting over our bare arms, and in Insoo's case, bare torso. It seemed like a couple of hours had passed before we were allowed to sit up and move around. An assistant dashed over carrying a thick duffle coat each for us to wrap up in.

"I thought it would be more glamorous than this," Wonseok muttered, his teeth chattering.

"Just be thankful they're not expecting us to play in the ocean," Insoo told him, his teeth chattering. The four of us looked out to sea, shivered, and huddled closer.

It got a little warmer and the afternoon was spent taking video after video of us dancing. So many angles, so many group shots and solo shots.

By the time they called it a wrap on the first day of shooting, I was exhausted. We were finally taken to the hotel and a small villa. I was actually expecting Wonseok to be with his family at the ... wherever they lived. Instead, he was sharing a room with me.

"I don't want special treatment," he said when he caught me looking. "Also, my dad will just mother me. He's worse than my mom—and she's bad!"

"You know you're not going to get that many opportunities to see them, right?"

"I know," he nodded. He jumped onto the bed and stretched out with a groan. "But I want to sleep. We don't get many opportunities to do that, either. And we have an even earlier morning call tomorrow." He yawned, emphasizing his point.

I was ready to crawl into the bed with him, but I shook my head at him. "You need to take your makeup off."

"I'm not worried about the sheets."

"Worry about your face," I chided him. I walked to the bathroom door. "I'm showering."

The shower also warmed me up. When I was getting out, Wonseok walked in. I gave him a smug smile, then returned to the bedroom. As soon as the shower was running and I could hear him singing in it, I pulled out my secret phone and turned it on. There was a text message waiting for me.

02-3431-5102: **I hope your video shoot went well. Xxx**

02-3431-5110: **It was cold but amazing. I miss you. How did your evaluation go? Xxx**

02-3431-5102: **What were you doing for it to be cold?? Xxx**

02-3431-5110: **Sunbathing. Xxx**

02-3431-5102: **It's January … Even in Jeju it has got to be ten degrees?? Maybe you shouldn't have given me your hoodies. Xxx**

02-3431-5110: **I only gave you one of them …! But yes, it was eight degrees today. They haven't told us anything about the video other than we had to act warm. I'm assuming there's some kind of fire theme. How did your evaluation go?? Xxx**

02-3431-5102: **I have to go. Make sure you keep wrapped up between takes! Xxx**

I stared at the brief conversation with a frown; why wasn't she answering? Did she have her evaluation? Did it go badly?

This was why long-distance relationships were hard. I knew there was something wrong with Yerin, but there was nothing I could do about it.

I rolled over, turning the phone off and sliding it back into the depths of my bag. I rolled back onto my back and turned my head to find Wonseok watching me. "What?" I asked, suspiciously.

He gave me a smile and shook his head.

I turned onto my side, away from him, and stretched out. Something told me I could trust Wonseok. That it would be good to have someone know what was happening to help me cover it up.

But tonight, was not the time for that conversation.

제22 장

Yerin

Dasom had a problem with me and I had no idea what it was. At first it had upset me a little. Then it had annoyed me. Now? Now I was ignoring her as much as I could. I had no idea who she thought she was, but I was not going to let her rule me.

Right now, I was on side of the room, stretching and warming up, and she was on the other, doing the same, chatting with Sojung.

I didn't have a problem with the maknae ... if she was ever left alone for long enough for us to have a conversation. I swear Dasom refused to leave us together; was she scared I was going to steal her best friend from her?

"OK, ladies," Holly called, clapping her hands. "Let's see what you've got."

We'd spent the previous weeks practicing almost sixteen hours a day. Next week was our turn to film our first ever music video and I was beyond excited about that. I just had to get past this evaluation. It was like a final check that we were ready to debut.

Dasom, Sojung, Miyeon and I took our positions. I had practiced so hard I had blisters on my blisters. I knew this routine forwards and backwards. I had this.

The music started and the four of us performed for Holly, Ro Chanheon and two other executives from Atlantis.

I thought it went well. I had no time for Dasom and she clearly didn't like me, but when we were performing, at least, we were able to put it aside for the sake of the routine.

We finished, the four of us breathing heavily, but instead of an applause, the four adults were sharing looks with each other. Something in my stomach twisted.

Holly let out a long, disappointed sigh. "I'm going to push the debut back. You're not ready."

"What?" I demanded.

"You can't do that!" Dasom exclaimed, angrily.

"Actually, I can," Holly corrected her, simply.

Ro Chanheon pointed at me and Dasom. "This song is about getting a boy to fall in love with you. You two look like you would murder one if they stepped within three feet of you. The dancing is supposed to be strong, not hostile. You're all over the place. You're not in sync. Frankly, you look like a cover group who has had no formal training at all."

"Is there something going on that we should know about?" Holly asked.

I shook my head, as did the others.

Holly raised a hand in a half shrug. "Then I'm going to push your debut back. I can't let you go out like you are."

"Please don't push it back!" Sojung cried, looking

like she was going to burst into tears.

"Atlantis can't let you debut as you are," Ro Chanheon said, firmly. "Watching you perform is uncomfortable and it shouldn't be. I don't quite know what is wrong with your group dynamic, but you need to work on it."

"He's right," Holly agreed, although she sounded a little more sympathetic. "Whatever is going on with you guys, you need to work it out, otherwise, I'm going to have to make some decisions I really don't want to have to. Your dancing, singing, and rapping is good. Great, even. But as a group, you're not ready."

She and the other adults left, leaving the four of us alone in the studio. I sank to the floor, devastated. It had never occurred to me that we wouldn't debut. Until that moment, I hadn't realized just how much I wanted this, either. A door slammed, and I looked up to find there was only Miyeon left in the room. She was staring at me with a surprisingly blank expression. "What?" I asked, miserably.

"You look upset," she said, slowly.

"Strangely, that's because I am," I snarked back at her. "Did you think I'd be sat here grinning?"

"No," she said, tilting her head. "But I didn't think you'd be all that bothered."

"What?" I asked, sharply, this time.

"Don't look at me like that, Yerin. I'm not the only one who didn't think you were committed to this."

My mouth fell open, then, I tore my boots and socks of my feet and pointed at the weeping band aids. "Do you think these are here because I'm not committed?" I demanded.

Miyeon looked at my feet, pulled a face, and then

walked out of the room.

Alone …

Once more, I was alone.

But then again, I had felt just as alone when I had been at SLA.

Right then, my mind went to one person: Seungjin. All I wanted to do was tell him how badly the day had gone and let him wrap his arms around me and tell me it would be alright. He was the only one who had ever done that. Unfortunately, my phone was back at the dorm (I didn't want to risk anyone finding it), and besides, Seungjin was busy.

I got to my feet, instantly regretting taking my boots off. As uncomfortable as they were on, my feet had molded to the boot, and walking and dancing was manageable. Now I was barefoot, the pain of the burst blisters was much worse.

I hobbled over to where I had discarded my things.

I might not have a Seungjin to wrap his arms around me, but I did have Seungjin's hoodie to provide me with the next best thing to his embrace. As I slipped it over my head, the door opened and Miyeon walked back in carrying something. A bowl. "Are you going to throw that at me?" I asked her, warily.

Miyeon stopped and snorted. "If that's where your mind goes to when someone approaches you with a bowl of water, I don't want to know how many people you've thrown water over, otherwise I'm going to change my mind about being nice."

"It was only people who deserved it," I shrugged. "And it's only water."

"OK, I'm going to stop you right there. I am

trying to be nice to you, because I'm sure somewhere in there is a nice person, but you really make that difficult when you're constantly being a bitch."

"I am not a bitch!"

"Well you're certainly not a nice person."

I rolled my eyes as I crossed my arms across my chest. "If you don't like me, go."

"Don't tempt me," she said, through gritted teeth. Instead of leaving, she walked over to me and set the bowl of cloudy water on the floor in front of me. While I stared at it, she grabbed a chair and set it beside it. "Sit down and stick your feet in there."

"Why? What is it?"

"Just sit down," she snapped. Without waiting for me to do so, she was already walking out of the room.

I watched the door close behind her, and then I sat down on the chair, peering suspiciously at the contents of the bowl. Steam was rising up from the liquid. After shooting another suspicious glare towards the door, as though Miyeon could see it through the wood. I decided to ignore the water: Miyeon didn't like me. How did I know she hadn't put something in there?

Instead, I turned to the side so I could ease my feet back into my shoes. I wanted nothing more than to slip my shoes into some comfortable running shoes, but these pumps were Gucci.

I gritted my teeth and walked back to the dorm.

No one else was there when I got back. I took advantage of the quiet and took a long, hot shower—sitting—and then, once my band aids were changed, I put on my pajamas and curled up on my bed.

Now Dasom was trying to ruin my life. It was all her fault.

No, it's not.

I frowned at the little voice in my head, arguing with me.

OK, maybe she had a point. Part of this was my fault too. It wasn't just rapping and dancing I needed to work on, but my acting skills too. What was the advice Seungjin had once given me?

Fake it until you make it.

There were plenty of rumors of other idol groups where their members didn't get on until later in their careers. The same could happen now. Or it could never happen. All I really had to do was convince the public— and Atlantis—that everything was fine.

I had been doing that for the rest of my life recently anyway. Why not just add one more thing to that list?

Thinking of Seungjin, I got off my bed and pulled my suitcase out from under the bed to find the phone he had given me. While I had the room to myself, I quickly sent him a message, telling him I hoped his video shoot went well.

When I didn't get a response, not that I was expecting one just yet, I sat back on the bed, opening a new message window. **Hello, father. It's Yerin. I have a new phone number.**

I stared at the words and deleted them.

I hadn't spoken to my father since the message on Christmas Eve. Even though we'd all had our phones taken off us when we'd moved into the dorms, we were allowed access to them once a week to call our parents—under supervision of our manager.

After the first couple of weeks where I'd had no missed messages from either, nor had my mother or father answered the call, I'd stopped collecting it. Even Kareun hadn't tried to get in touch. It was less painful not to go.

I stared at my reflection in the blackened screen and sighed.

The sound of someone at the door had me scrambling to stuff the phone into my pocket as Dasom walked in, followed by Sojung and Miyeon. As soon as she saw me, Dasom's face contorted in rage.

"I should have known you'd be here!"

"It's my dorm too!" I snapped back at her.

"Considering this is all your fault, I'd expect you to be in the studio practicing."

I got off the bed and stood. She was still taller than me, but at least she wasn't towering over me as much. "Do you have a hearing problem?" I asked her, looking at her in disbelief. "They said *we* weren't ready."

"It's only been a few weeks," Miyeon interjected, trying to be diplomatic.

"A couple of years isn't going to help her talentless ass," Dasom snarled at her.

I puffed up my chest. "I got into the same entertainment company as you," I pointed out. "They had plans to debut me in this group. And I'm not the one who should have debuted a few years ago but didn't," I finished.

Dasom snapped, shoving me backwards. My head smacked against the side of the bed before I fell onto my mattress. "No, but you come from a family who has a history of destroying other people!"

"Dasom! Stop it!" Sojung yelled. She looked like she was going to cry.

She wasn't the only one, but I sure as hell wasn't

going to do it in front of anyone else. I leaped off the bed, pushing Dasom away from me, and then Miyeon was in between the two of us. "Fighting is the surefire way of making sure we don't debut at all!" she informed us.

"Maybe I don't want to debut!" I lied, before storming out of the room.

I stormed outside, ploughing past a few faces I recognized from school, but not realizing it was Sungil, Jaehoon and King until I was so far from the dorms I had no idea where I was. I paused, looking in a shop window to check my reflection.

I was wearing clothes I was going to sleep in— yoga pants, one of Seungjin's oversized hoodies, and my slippers. My hair was still damp from my shower, and I had no makeup on.

Wonderful.

On top of that, a gust of wind decided to remind me it was late January and the temperatures were barely above freezing.

The problem was that I didn't want to go back to the dorm.

I didn't want to go to SLA, but it was close. I was willing to bet my mother would still be there and I could go back home with her. Home was a better option to the dorms.

I stuck my hands into my pockets, bowed my head against the wind, and walked the remaining distance to the academy. I paused at the gates, looking up at the familiar buildings. When I had signed with Atlantis, they had said I was supposed to continue attending SLA and make sure I graduated, but we had been so busy preparing for our debut, I hadn't stepped foot on the grounds since I'd left it.

I didn't miss it.

It was a strange feeling: emptiness. I had ruled this school when I had been here, but all of the good memories I had, and I had a lot—I hadn't been a person who hated school—had been tarnished in the last few months.

I closed my eyes, trying to find the good memories from that time ... most of them involved Seungjin. They brought some warmth to me and a smile to my face.

The smile evaporated as I remembered why I was here.

Just like I hadn't been here for weeks, I also hadn't spoken to my mother for that length of time. We'd never had the relationship where we'd go shopping together, or get our nails done together, but things had never been this bad between us.

Right now, all I wanted was a hug from my mother and for her to tell me it was going to be OK, even if there was nothing that she could do about it.

I walked through the grounds to the main school building. Although it was late, it was still open. I waved at the security guard and walked inside. Just like the outside, nothing on the inside seemed to have changed either.

The light in my mother's office was on. I gently knocked on the door and entered. My mother was sitting behind her desk, reading through a handful of papers, but she looked up when the door opened. Instead of a welcoming smile, I got a scowl. "Yerin? What are you doing here?"

"I wanted to come home," I told her.

"You can't."

I stared at her, not sure I was understanding her. "I can't?" I repeated.

"You committed to Atlantis. You need to stay there and debut."

"Mother, I just need a night away, at home. I … I can't go back there … not tonight." I told her, trying to stop my voice from breaking.

My mother stood, walking around the desk to me, and for a moment, happiness surged through me as I thought she was going to give me the hug I desperately needed from her right then.

"Yerin, you agreed to be an idol, and you agreed to everything that goes with it—including the knowledge that you wouldn't be able to return home."

My lips slowly parted as my mouth fell open. That wasn't how being an idol worked. You didn't just stop talking to your family. Yes, seeing them and talking to them wasn't going to be easy or regular, but it didn't mean you had to cut them out of your life. And if it did? Surely a mother would jump at the opportunity of having their only child stay with them?

More importantly … "You're the one who told me to be an idol," I whispered. "You said to be an idol and help you and the school out."

Mother folded her arms, looking at me with disapproval, like being upset was inappropriate and an insult to her. "You didn't enter into this thinking you would be afforded luxuries like this. Stop acting weak. Stop … And for goodness sake, stop crying, Yerin.

Visiting my mother was a … luxury?

"I'm here now," I told her. "I will go back tomorrow morning. I just had an argument with one of the girls—"

"Ugh!" she exclaimed. "This is just like you. You are just like your father: running away from your problems. Blaming them on other people. When will you grow up and act like a responsible adult?"

"I'm not running away!" The words came out more like a shriek, but I couldn't stop them. "And Father didn't run away—you banished him. You drove him away instead of standing by him!"

"Your father drove himself away!" Mother yelled at me. "Your father not being here is better for him and us anyway. I do not need a scandal—not when I'm trying to save my reputation and manage this school. Your father made a choice, and now he is sticking my it."

"What about you when you made the choice to marry him?!"

The answer to my question was a slap; sharp and stinging on my cheek. "Our marriage wasn't a choice: it was a necessity. Just like you being an idol. Some things are more important, Yerin. When you grow up, one day you will understand that. Now, get out of my office and back to Atlantis Entertainment. I do not want to see you again unless it's approved by your manager. Do *not* do anything to ruin this, Yerin. I will not have another embarrassing failure in this family."

Despite the biting pain on the side of my face, I straightened my back. "Don't worry, mother. I will not be back."

Feeling colder than I had outside, I left the room. In the back of my mind, I was wondering if this was going to be the last time that I ever saw my mother again.

제23 장

Yerin

I looked around, trying to work out where I was. I'd left the school, walking almost blindly, not paying any attention to where I was going. For the first time in my life, I had no idea what to do. I didn't know where I was supposed to go. I still couldn't go back to the dorms, SLA and home were out of the question too.

I almost snorted at that: *home.* I didn't feel like I had a home anymore, either.

I paused, looking around. I was just by Roosters—a fried chicken shop not too far from SLA. The only thing I had on me was the phone Seungjin had given me. I hadn't set up any accounts with it, which meant I had no money.

However, the clock told me it was past curfew for SLA, which at least meant the people in Roosters wouldn't be anyone who would recognize me. It also looked busy enough that I might be able to stay in there a while without being asked to leave for not buying anything.

At least it would give me somewhere warm to sit

while I tried to work out what to do next.

I waited for a group of people to enter, not too much older than me, and followed them in, taking a table next to them. The owner was busy behind the counter and didn't pay us much attention.

Just what did Dasom mean, my family destroyed others? She hadn't been a student at SLA, and frankly, if a student was dumb enough to be failing, that was their own fault, not my mother's.

Mother ...

I put my elbows on the table and sank my head into them.

I was surrounded by people but I had never felt more alone.

I stared out of the window, vaguely aware of the conversations around me, but not really paying attention, lost in my own thoughts.

It was a vibration in my pocket which brought me back to Roosters. I pulled out the phone, my heart soaring when I saw the response from Seungjin.

02-3431-5110: **It was cold but amazing. I miss you. How did your evaluation go? Xxx**

I couldn't help but smile, imagining Seungjin having fun filming: I was genuinely happy for him. This was exactly what he deserved.

Then what did that mean for me? Was this what I deserved? The smile fell from my face. I desperately want to tell him everything, but I didn't want to do anything to spoil his good mood. The fact he was texting and not calling told me he was probably not in a position to be able to do that, and I also didn't want to do anything that would risk him doing something stupid—like calling me.

I ignored the question. **What were you doing for it to be cold?? Xxx**

02-3431-5110: **Sunbathing. Xxx**

I stared at the phone, arching an eyebrow. Even though Jeju was further south, it couldn't have been that much warmer than Seoul. **It's January … Even in Jeju it has got to be ten degrees?? Maybe you shouldn't have given me your hoodies. Xxx**

I didn't want to give him any of his hoodies back, but I also didn't want him to catch a cold.

His response came back quickly: **I only gave you two of them …! But yes, it was eight degrees today. They haven't told us anything about the video other than we had to act warm. I'm assuming there's some kind of fire theme. How did your evaluation go?? Xxx**

There it was again. I started tapping out my reply… and then I deleted it. Seungjin was happy. This could wait until he was back in Seoul. If nothing else, it would be easier to explain in person rather than over a phone. **I have to go. Make sure you keep wrapped up between takes! Xxx**

I turned the phone off and slipped it back into my pocket before I changed my mind. When I looked up, a paper tray of honey and sesame chicken wings were being pushed in front of me. "I didn't order these."

"I know," the owner agreed. "You haven't ordered anything in the couple of hours you've been in here."

"I … I'll go," I told him, getting to me feet.

He held a hand up. "Stay and eat. Your friends have already left anyway," he nodded his head towards the now empty table.

"Oh … thank you." I slipped back into the chair and looked longingly at the chicken. It had been breakfast when I had last eaten and now delicious looking food was in front of me, I found I was hungry. "Thank you, ahjussi."

"Yoo Chaewon."

"Huh?"

"My name. In case you need me." I stared blankly at him. I didn't know him at all. "I like to think of my customers as friends and family. Ahjussi seems a little too …" he shook his head. "Chaewon."

I nodded my head, once, and he smiled, leaving me alone with the chicken.

The chicken tasted as good as it smelled. I'd walked past Roosters quite a lot while at SLA and yet I had never been in. Those had been wasted opportunities.

I was about halfway through the basket when Miyeon settled into the chair opposite me. "What are we going to do with you?"

"Excuse me?"

"I can't work you out," she continued, reaching over and helping herself to my chicken.

"What on earth does that mean?"

"It means that somewhere, deep, deep, *deep* down underneath that bitchy exterior there has to be a nice person trapped in there, dying to come out."

"*Excuse* me?" I asked again, staring at her disbelief. "Do you know who you are talking to?"

Miyeon let out a long sigh. "OK," she set the half-eaten chicken wing down. "First of all, that's got to stop. Yes, I do know who you are: you are one quarter of a girl group. The same girl group I am in. You are no better or no worse than anyone else in this group. Plus, saying nonsense like that is going to going to act like a repellent to potential fans."

My mouth fell open. "Dasom——"

Miyeon held a hand up. "Dasom is treating you the same way you have been treating everyone else. The same way you still treat everyone else. All the two of you are doing is repelling everyone away from you. The only difference is Dasom has Sojung." She lowered her hand. "And if you two keep it up, you're going to repel Atlantis too."

"I am not——"

The hand shot back up. "No, Yerin, it's time to listen and be quiet, because if you want to debut, which strangely, I think you do, you really need to hear what I am telling you."

She dropped her hand and waited. More out of shock than anything, I gestured for her to continue.

"I don't know what's going on between the two of you, and if it wasn't for the fact it was stopping everyone, *myself included*, from debuting, I would say it wasn't my business, but you made it my business. So, what's going on?"

"I don't know."

"You're not helping things, Yerin!"

"I really don't know!" I yelled back, slamming my hands on the table. "I'd never met Hoo Dasom before I joined Atlantis and from the moment she met *me*, she decided she didn't like me—not the other way around."

Miyeon sat back, staring at me. With a small sigh, she placed both her hands on the table, palms down. "Then why did she say your family destroys people?"

"I wish I knew!"

"I can't help unless you tell me what's going on," she pressed.

I gritted my teeth together and glowered at her. "For the love of—I don't know!"

Miyeon stood, reaching for my hand. "Come on." Tugging me to my feet, she led me to the back of the restaurant, past the few tables to the counter. "Chaewon, we're borrowing the back room."

Chaewon waved us into the back without question. Half-dazed, I followed Miyeon into a storeroom where she promptly sat me down on a bag of rice. Once she had returned from closing the door, she stood in front of me. "I have a boyfriend. His name is Ryu Gunpyo and he's the leader of my former busking crew. Or at least, I think he's still my boyfriend."

"I am not the person to ask for relationship advice," I told her, dryly.

She rolled her eyes. "I'm not asking for relationship advice. I'm telling you a secret. I am *trusting* you."

"Why?"

"Because if we're going to debut together, we need to trust each other."

I stared at her. There was no way on earth I was confessing to dating Lee Seungjin. I was not going to do anything that put his position at Atlantis in jeopardy. Again.

"Ryu Gunpyo is the reason I knew you were here. He saw you sitting by yourself and sent me a Kakao message asking if you were one of the girls in my group and if you were OK. Which is my second secret: I have a secret phone too."

"What has this got to do with me?"

Miyeon crouched down in front of me. "I'd really like it if you told me what you just saw on your phone which made you look like you had just discovered the world was about to implode. I'd really like it if you'd let me be your friend."

I sighed, looking at the screen. What did I have to lose? I didn't seem to have any friends anymore. My parents didn't want me. My group didn't like me. And when what my father had done finally came to light, Atlantis wouldn't keep me anyway.

So, I told her. Everything—except for the parts with Seungjin.

When I had finished, Miyeon pursed her lips, and then she sat down beside me, pulling me into a hug. "You're not alone, Yerin. I know I can't do anything about your parents, but that's your parent's business."

"It is my business when they seem to be the reason Dasom doesn't like me. And when it makes Atlantis change their minds about me," I said, miserably.

"We don't know for certain if it is the reason Dasom doesn't like you," Miyeon said, firmly. "We need to confirm that. And as for Atlantis, it's not what is stopping us debuting: you are. And we can work on that."

"I'm not some project you can fix up, you know."

Miyeon rolled her eyes. "Shut up, Yerin."

She stood and held her hand out to me. I eyed it suspiciously. "What?"

She let out an exasperated sigh. "Do you know how infuriating you are? We can't stay in Chaewon's store all night. It's time to go home."

"I'm not going to the dorm!" I protested, shaking my head. There was no way on earth I was staying in the same room as Dasom. Not tonight.

"It's a good job we're not going back to the dorms then, isn't it?" She was still offering her hand. I got up without her assistance, but I did follow her back into the restaurant. "Thank you, Chaewon!" she called as she led me outside. She glanced at her watch and smiled. "The buses are still running."

I shot her a look of disgust. "Bus?"

"Too good for a bus?"

I rolled my eyes. "I take the bus from the dorm to the practice studio all the time, dumbass." I pointed down at myself. "I'm in my nightclothes."

"You look like you're in a boyfriend's stolen hoodie," Miyeon corrected me as we walked to the bus stop we needed. "And you've been walking around in them for hours now."

I was, and I wasn't going to tell her that. It was also all that I was wearing—without my coat, and with slippers on, I was freezing. Thankfully, we didn't have to wait long for the bus. Miyeon paid my fare and we took a seat at the back of the empty vehicle.

"Where are we going?" I asked as the bus eventually crossed the river to the north side of the city.

"Home," she shrugged.

Home, I finally discovered, was Miyeon's parents' house in Itaewon. I stared up at the block of flat. Although there were still a lot of lights on, it was late. "Aren't your parents going to be upset about you coming in so late?"

"Not as upset as Atlantis will be if they discover we're not there." We stepped into the elevator and

Miyeon hit the button for the eighth floor.

I shot her a sideways glance. "You could have gone back to the dorms, you know?"

"I know," she nodded. "But you couldn't."

"Why are you being nice to me? You don't like me."

Miyeon turned her head and gave me an unimpressed look. "Do you ever listen when people speak to you? I told you: I'm sure there's a nice person somewhere deep, deep down inside of you. I'm determined to find her." The elevator pinged open. "Now hush, or you'll wake everyone up."

We followed the path along to her door and she quietly opened it. After discarding my slippers, I followed Miyeon to her bedroom. It wasn't big. It had a single bed, a rail with a few items of clothing on it, and a desk. But with all the photographs of her and her family and friends over the walls, it seemed a lot cozier than mine.

Miyeon pulled some bedding out from under her bed and laid it out next to it. "You can take my bed," she offered.

I considered it, and then slowly shook my head. "It's your bed."

"Suit yourself," Miyeon shrugged.

I sank onto the makeshift bed and yawned. It was past midnight and I ached. I was ready to lie down and let sleep win, when Miyeon let out a gasp, jumping off the bed and crouching down beside me. "Yerin!"

"What?" She grabbed my foot, tugging it towards her. "You're bleeding!"

"I burst a blister," I said, wincing as she prodded it. "Miyeon, that's kinda gross!"

"No, letting your feet get in this state is gross!" Miyeon got up and disappeared out of the room. While she was gone, I peeled off my socks. The band aids were still there, but a different blister had burst. At some point, it seemed I'd stopped being able to differentiate between each area of pain on my feet.

Miyeon reappeared in my room with a bowl of liquid and set it down just off the bedding. "Scoot down here and put your feet in there. I can't believe you didn't do this earlier."

I moved down and poked a toe in the liquid. It was warm, only steaming because the room was cool. It also didn't burn my foot off, so it wasn't acid either. The action had Miyeon rolling her eyes at me. "It's not poison."

The moan that started to escape me turned into a hiss as the water hit the blisters. But after a while, it eased off. "What is this?"

"Saltwater," Miyeon replied. "When you're spending as much time dancing as we are, you've really got to look after your feet. You must be in so much pain!"

Not at the moment. This was bliss.

"Stay there." Without a word, Miyeon left the room once more. When she finally returned, she was carrying a handful of items. When she got close, I discovered that amongst them was a towel and more first aid items.

She sat down in front of the bowl and peered at my feet. "You should have taken those band aids off," she told me, pulling a face. "Let the saltwater get to the blisters properly."

Reluctantly, I plucked a foot out of the bowl,

pulled a band aid off, then switched feet to repeat. I was surprised to find my feet were already feeling better. "Is it really just saltwater?"

"Epsom salt," Miyeon nodded, as though that would mean something to me. "You really need to start looking after your feet better. They're important when you need them to do your job." She rubbed at the back of her neck, staring thoughtfully at my shoes. "Don't you own any dancing shoes?"

"They're Gucci," I pointed out.

Miyeon snorted. "The last I checked, Gucci didn't do a line of shoes for dancers."

"The last I checked, idol groups were all dancing in designer labels."

Miyeon closed her eyes briefly. "Yerin, stop going on the defensive."

"I'm not!" I objected.

"Then take this as advice from a dancer and not an attack on you: you need to look after your feet. You need to wear your sneakers a lot more."

"Ro Chanheon said we had to dance in heels."

Miyeon reached into the bowl and took a foot out, drying it off with gentle dabs. She peered at the sole. "That looks better already." It felt it too. She grabbed a fresh band aid and applied it.

"Thank you," I muttered.

Miyeon looked at me with her eyes wide. "As if you know that word!"

I shot her a withering glare.

"Seriously, Yerin, look after your feet. Chanheon wants us in heels, yes, but only for his practices. Have you not noticed that none of the rest of us wear heels when we're practicing without him?" I shook my head.

"I'm sorry; I should have noticed sooner. You must have been in so much pain."

"Something like that," I muttered. "Are you done?"

Miyeon nodded. "Go to sleep. I'll clean this up. I'll set an alarm so we can get back to the dorms in time for our run." She picked the bowl and trash up shaking her head. "And you go running on those feet ..."

I was asleep before she came back in the room.

Z

I was awoken by an unfamiliar alarm in an unfamiliar room. It took a few moments of staring at a stuffed Mon.G, the mascot for Monsta X, to remember I had gone to sleep in Miyeon's apartment. I sat up, sleepily, and rubbed at my eyes as I waited for Miyeon to turn the alarm off. When she didn't, I threw Mon.G at her head.

"I'd rather you threw Hyungwon at me," she grumbled, finally cancelling the alarm.

"I thought you had a boyfriend?"

"Hyungwon," she shrugged with a yawn, as though that was a reasonable answer.

At four in the morning, I didn't care.

I rolled the bedding away and then Miyeon and I walked out into the living area. I was surprised to find her parents awake, eating breakfast. They seemed just as surprised to see us. "Miyeon?"

"Hi mom," she greeted her mom cheerfully, wrapping her arms around the smaller woman. I wasn't sure how old she was, but she looked worn. There were a lot of wrinkles around her eyes, but they had a friendly glint to them.

Her dad looked at me with a surprised expression. "And here was me worrying about the day you would bring Gunpyo home."

"Yerin is a trainee with me," Miyeon explained with a roll of her eyes. "We needed a break, so we hid here last night."

"Is everything OK?" her mother asked in alarm. "You can both stay here as long as you need to. I don't care about those contracts."

A lump made a sudden appearance in my throat. That was what I had wanted my mother to say to me last night, even though I'd had every intention of returning to Atlantis.

"We're going back, mom!" Miyeon exclaimed. "That's why we're up early."

"What about breakfast?"

"We don't have time. We need to be back at the dorms by 5."

Miyeon's dad looked to the clock with a frown. "Have something to eat. Your mother made too much breakfast as usual. I'll drop you off on the way into work."

The next thing I knew, I was sitting at the table, eating breakfast with Miyeon's family. Although there were a lot of question about how Miyeon was doing at Atlantis, they kept including me in the conversation.

Strange.

I looked around the apartment, trying to work out what they did for a living. It wasn't a particularly modern apartment, but it was homey. A newer model television, but a mismatching sofa suite that had seen better days.

It wasn't until Miyeon's dad put on a jacket that I worked out what he did, at least; he was a bus driver.

A bus driver?

Miyeon's father was a bus driver?

And yet, for the first time, I didn't care.

제24 장

Yerin

February

The decision to push back our debut was final.
However, we were promised that if we were
ready by the end of March, we could debut in
April.

"CHA YERIN, WERE YOU BORN WITH
TWO LEFT FEET?!" Ro Chanheon bellowed across
the room. I winced, but made myself continue dancing,
silently cursing Gucci for his uncomfortable shoes.

I had no idea how idols made dancing in high
heels look so effortless because it wasn't. I always wore
heels, and yet this was pain. My feet had gotten to the
point where they were burning before I started dancing.
Knowing I would get no sympathy from Ro Chanheon,
I'd bound them up and gritted my teeth.

"No, that's it," Chanheon snapped. "I am done
for the day. You lot can practice more." He turned and
glowered at me. "Especially you."

Dasom waited until Chanheon was out of the

room before she stormed up to me. She looked as exhausted as I felt. We were all in workout clothes, aside from our heels, and our clothes were soaked. But she wasn't here to give me any sympathy. "We have an evaluation at the end of this week. You had better get your act together before then."

"Get out of my face!" I snapped at her.

"I don't have time for this."

She started marching to the door. "It's not just me," I yelled after her. "Our problem is we're always out of sync."

Dasom turned on her heel and stormed back to me, shoving a finger at my collar bone. "No, the problem is you. You and your stupid, lying, family."

Sojung, darted between the two of us, her eyes wide, round and alarmed, like a tarsier. "Dasom, stop it, please."

"What is your problem!" I cried. Once upon a time, I would have hit her. Instead, I yelled a few curse words at her, then realizing it was a waste of air, threw my hands in the air. "In fact, I don't even care anymore," I declared. "If you want to practice; stay. If you don't; leave."

"You have as much respect for people as your father does!" Dasom lunged at me, shoving Sojung out of the way. As Sojung went flying, Dasom's fist hit my nose with a sickening crunch. I dropped to the floor tentatively trying to touch my nose as I felt blood pour out from it.

Before I could say anything, which would have been hard because all I could focus on was the pain and the blood, my attention was dragged to Miyeon who was screaming Sojung's name. I looked over, seeing

Sojung on the floor, not moving. "What the hell did you do?" I asked, staring in horror at Dasom.

Dasom had gone an unnatural shade of grey and was just standing there, unmoving.

"Get some help!" Miyeon was yelling.

I scrambled upright, ignoring the blood, ignoring the pain in my head and my feet as my blisters protested at me moving on them, and stumbled to the door. I burst out into the corridor, breathing though my mouth, trying not to inhale the blood. "Help!" I shouted.

I rounded a corner, almost falling, but I was caught—by Seungjin. I had no idea why he was here, and I didn't care. "Yerin?"

"Help!" I gasped at him.

Seungjin stepped back so that he could look at me, but it was someone else who spoke. "What happened to you?"

I glanced over at the younger boy who looked like he was going to pass out. Clearly, he didn't handle blood well. "Not me. Sojung. In our practice studio."

Seungjin, refusing to let go of me, turned to the other boy. "Wonseok, go get help. I'll look after Yerin."

Wonseok took off at a run. I tried to lead Seungjin back to the studio, but he held me firmly. "Yerin, what the hell happened to you?"

"Sojung!" I said, my words turning into a sob. "I think she's dead!" I could feel my body as it started to shake. My face and feet weren't hurting anymore, but I was sure I was about to throw up. "We need to get to Sojung!"

Seungjin looked conflicted, but he allowed me to lead him back to the studio. I pushed open the door, unsure as to what I was going to find. Relief flooded me when I found Miyeon holding Sojung. Sojung's eyes were closed, but she was moaning. I almost collapsed into Seungjin's arms in relief.

Moments later, the door flew open as our manager, Yan Kiae burst in accompanied by an Atlantis medic and Wonseok. With Sojung on the floor, their focus was on her until two paramedics came in.

There was a blur of noise and movement and Sojung was wheeled out on a stretcher, accompanied by Kiae. It was only because Seungjin waved the Atlantis medic over that anyone finally realized that I had been injured. Seeing as it wasn't hurting anymore, I was sure it was just going to need a clean, but the medic shook his head. "That's broken," she informed me, turning to Seungjin. "She needs to go to the hospital too. Will you help me take her down to my car and I will take her myself."

Without giving me the opportunity to say I could walk down by myself, Seungjin scooped me up in his arms. "I'm coming too," he declared.

The medic didn't object. Instead, she led us both down to the underground parking lot. Seungjin gently put me in the backseat before running to the other side of the car to get I beside me. He slid over to the middle seat and gently pulled me to him, taking care to not touch my face.

It was when we were halfway there that things seemed to move at a normal speed. I hadn't realized until then, but from the moment I had left the studio to find help, it had been like everything had slowed down and had been moving in slow motion.

With the speed came the pain. Slowly at first, building like air filling a balloon, until the pain in my nose was strong enough to have tears in my eyes.

If the tears weren't already there to start with.

"I thought she was dead," I muttered again, and again into Seungjin's chest. He just held me, his hand gripping my shoulder firmly.

2

Not only did I have a broken nose, I needed an operation to fix it. Without ever wanting one, I'd been given a nose job. I'd spent a week in a hospital room by myself with no one to keep me company for most of the day. Even Vice Chairwoman Holly hadn't been to visit me. She had been in New York when everything had happened: we weren't the only group causing her problems.

Miyeon had been to visit me as much as visiting hours had permitted. Word had, of course, gotten out at Atlantis, but had somehow escaped the press. For now, our group was ...

Who knew?

The best Miyeon had managed to get out of everyone was that we were waiting for Holly to get back to Seoul.

Sojung had been in the same hospital but in a different room. It had again been Miyeon who had informed me that Sojung had hit her head as she'd fallen and knocked herself out. After forty-eight hours supervision for concussion, she had been discharged. She had been to see me, burst into tears and apologized profusely.

Dasom, on the other hand, had not been to visit me. Not that I expected her to.

"She's gone," Miyeon said, suddenly.

She had arrived a while ago with a laptop loaded to stream the day's episode of M Countdown, sat down on the chair beside the bed with her feet up on my bed, and we'd watched it together.

Seeing as Monsta X's comeback stage was about to start, I leaned forward and hit pause before I missed anything and turned to Miyeon. "Who?"

"Dasom," she replied. "The Vice Chairwoman is supposed to arrive back tomorrow morning and I think she quit before she was thrown out."

"Good," I grunted. "I hope I never see her again. She made my life miserable." Miyeon arched an eyebrow at me. "What is that look for?"

"I was just going to let this slide, but considering I have no idea what our future now holds, and I hope that it will make you a better person, I'm just going to say it: your actions at SLA weren't much better than Dasom's, Yerin."

"Excuse me?" I stared at her in disbelief. "I never nearly killed anyone."

Miyeon removed her feet from my bed and stood. Her posture wasn't threatening, but it was firm—her back straight and her hands on her hips. "Until we signed with Atlantis, you spent the entire time we were at SLA ignoring me because I was a scholarship kid. My mom is a postal worker, and my dad is a bus driver. They both work full time, and they both work hard. I'm not ashamed of that and I never have been. Yet you, who had never met them, was."

"I liked your parents!"

"Would you have liked them if I'd have told you what they did before you met them, back when we were at SLA?"

I thought about it and slowly shook my head. "Probably not."

"Exactly. You judged people based on their parents, which is exactly what Dasom did with you. And I know you refuse to talk to Lucinda until she tells you what her parents do."

"Only because I don't get why it's such a secret!" I objected. But she was right.

"And then there was that unbelievably mean thing you did to TK, which not only would have affected him, but his dad too."

"I did that for—" I stopped myself at the last minute. "His brother was the reason Bright Boys disbanded."

"Right or wrong, Hyunseo is the reason it got disbanded. He may have had his reasons, but he still hit someone. Either way, that was between Hyunseo and TK's brother—neither of which are TK, nor TK's dad."

I glowered at her. "Did you come here to make me feel better or worse?"

Miyeon looked surprised, and then pleased. "I didn't want to make you feel bad, but the fact you do makes me feel better. It means I was right and there *is* a decent person in there." She lowered her arms and shrugged. "She's just hidden behind a spoiled princess."

"I thought you were my friend?" I asked. Was I really a spoiled princess? How could I be? I shared a room with three other girls, my Gucci pumps were now last season and thanks to all the dancing, in desperate need of re-heeling, and my nose job was the result of a fight not out of choice; I'd actually liked my nose.

"I am," she said, firmly.

I blinked. I hadn't really thought she felt that way. "You are?"

"Do you really think I'd come hang out with you if I wasn't? In fact," she leaned over and started playing with the laptop, "To show you how much of a friend I am, I'm going to skip Monsta X's comeback stage for you."

My mouth fell open. "Excuse me?"

"Shut up and watch." She hit play and sat back.

The next thing I knew, I was watching as special pre-debut stage for 1SO: Fire. I watched, mesmerized. Because I'd been taken to the hospital with no pre-planning (obviously), I hadn't brought my phone with me. Aside from Seungjin accompanying me when I had been admitted, I hadn't seen him since. "How?"

"I know, right? I've heard Atlantis are one hundred percent invested in this next boy group. The word is getting out. They've even got a special show outside of Atlantis tomorrow. And this is just the first unit." Miyeon turned to me, her eyes glinting in excitement. They don't even have a complete lineup and I can tell they're going to be big. Can you imagine what it will be like for us?"

No. I couldn't.

My face was a mess. The doctor had told me that I wouldn't be ready for heavy exercise, aka dancing, for at least another six weeks. That put us back *again* with a debut date. Then there was the fact we were down a member. Would they be adding a new person? Would they be ready to debut?

And then there was the other glaringly obvious thing …

"I've been here a week. Outside of you and

Sojung, the only person who has been to see me is Kiae. Atlantis won't debut me. It's my fault …" I trailed off as Miyeon got up and started looking through all the drawers beside her. "What are you doing?"

"Looking for the crazy pills they've prescribed you."

"Miyeon!"

"No, I'm serious," she said sitting back down. "You're talking crazy. I've told you that the Vice Chairwoman is going to handle this, and she's on her way back from handling a problem in America. Did you know one of Onyx's members was attacked and is in a hospital in Toronto?"

"No!" I stared at her, wrinkling up my nose in disbelief, then wincing at the pain. My nose was still too tender for extreme facial reactions. "What?"

"The point is, she's not forgotten about you, she just had to deal with other crazies on the other side of the world first. And as for this being your fault, even if there is some history between her parents and yours, the fact is Dasom chose to hit you. There are plenty of groups with members that don't get on—we can't all be best friends with everyone—but they don't show it. You and Dasom could have gone years not getting along but being able to work with each other. She messed that up; not you."

"I could have tried harder," I muttered.

"Yes," Miyeon agreed. "You could have. But you haven't exactly had anyone tell you when you're being a jerk until now."

"And that's where you come in?"

"Yep; because that's what friends are for. They tell you when you're being a jerk. They don't encourage that behavior."

"You're my friend?" I repeated my earlier question, still shocked at that.

Ignoring my surprise, she pushed herself onto the bed beside me and hugged me. "The way I see it is we're going to debut together, probably spend the next five years, at least, sharing a room, and be in the same group for several decades to come," she explained. "You can either ignore that and we work together, or you can accept the fact that we're friends, but I'm a better example than Geom Kareun. Who I've not seen since we signed with Atlantis."

"I don't think that sounds too bad," I mumbled.

"Which part?"

"Any of it."

제25 장

Seungjin

Performing on M Countdown had been a dream come true. Even when we'd debuted with Bright Boys, we'd never made it onto M Countdown. To make it even better, we even had a small group of fans—despite the fact we didn't have an official fandom name—doing fan chants with the song.

For the first time since Bright Boys had disbanded, I felt hopeful. I'd had a feeling of dread that I'd been unable to shake, that no matter how much work we put into this, and no matter how many ideas Holly had, fans wouldn't be able to forgive Hyunseo, and ultimately me.

Maybe it was because I was the only original Bright Boys member in this unit, or maybe they really had forgiven us since Hyunseo had been cleared, but all the feedback was positive.

While I'd forgotten how tiring filming a music show was, I was grateful. A four-minute performance took most of the day. We had to arrive, change, get our makeup done … then there was the first run-through for us, and a second for the camera crew. Then we had to wait for our turn to perform.

When it was all over, reality hit.

"Hyung," Wonseok hissed at me. "That's Itzy!"

I looked up as a five-piece girl group walked past us. Insoo, Kota, Wonseok and myself all stopped and politely bowed as they walked past.

"Yuna is even more beautiful in person," Wonseok sighed.

I hadn't noticed. It wasn't that she wasn't pretty, because she was ... she just didn't compare to Yerin. No one did.

Something churned uncomfortably inside of me, despite the post-show high. We continued along the corridor, following Oh Seokbeom back to the shared dressing room so we could gather our things.

Although I didn't say it, I was desperate to leave.

We had a performance the following day, which meant tonight was ours. And I had one place I wanted to spend it: the hospital.

Yerin was still there and I hadn't been able to see her since her manager had taken me back to the dorms almost a week ago. It was killing me.

If things went well tomorrow, today was likely my last chance to be able to sneak into the hospital without anyone knowing who I was.

Only, things weren't that simple. I had to wait an hour before we could leave the television studio. Then, Ok Seokbeom announced he had to collect something from Seo district of Incheon. We drove away from the dorms to collect ... it was a small shoebox sized crate and apparently a prop to be used for one of the other units.

Unfortunately, on the way back to the dorm, we then got stuck in traffic jams that stretched for miles after a major wreck on the highway. I stared out of the window, morosely, watching the late afternoon slip away from me.

"Are you OK, hyung?" Wonseok asked, leaning over to rest his head on my shoulder.

I nodded, even though I wasn't. It was one thing to have no free time because of the job, but this was supposed to be our free time. Rare like unicorns … and I couldn't tell anyone why I was irritated.

It was almost two hours before the traffic started to clear. By that point, there wasn't even any trace of a wreck to glower at as we passed.

Just when I thought my secret plans couldn't be derailed any further, Seokbeom announced he was taking us for barbeque to celebrate our first pre-debut stage. Much as I loved meat and it was a rare treat as a trainee, it also meant at least another two or three hours before I could get to the hospital.

"My father is expecting me tonight," I lied, apologetically. I spent all day, every day with these guys.

"Do you need taking to your house?" Oh Seokbeom asked, suspiciously. "You never mentioned anything earlier."

"I was caught up in the show," I told him. "And no, thank you, hyungnim. I said I would meet him at Atlantis when we were finished."

Thankfully, my father was the one person Oh Seokbeom would never question: a rare advantage to being the son of the Chairman.

I could see the doubt lingering in Seokbeom's eyes. Even Wonseok was watching me suspiciously.

"Enjoy your meal," I added.

"We will drop you off at Atlantis," Seokbeom finally agreed, giving the instruction to our driver.

"What gives, hyung?" Wonseok hissed at me.

"There's something I have to do," I admitted.

Thankfully, he didn't press.

A short time later, I was walking into Atlantis. I moved out of the line of sight of the doors, waiting for the minibus to drive off, and then I pulled my hood up and mask on and made my way for the rear exit where I promptly flagged down a taxi.

Hours later than I planned, I was walking into the hospital, keeping my head down as I navigated to the private ward that I knew Yerin was in. Unfortunately, because it was long after visiting hours, I couldn't ask which room she was in. Instead, I was wandering the corridor, checking each room plate, trying to look as inconspicuous as possible with the large bag I was carrying.

When I found the door, I glanced up and down the deserted hallway, just in case, and then gently knocked on the door. "Hello?" Yerin called from inside.

I pushed open the door and carefully closed it behind me. "Hi Yerin," I greeted her.

Her response was let out an ear-splitting shriek and hide behind her pillow.

"It's just me!" I hissed at her, pulling my mask off. "Lee Seungjin!"

"I know! That's the problem! What are you doing here?" she asked, still hiding behind the pillow.

"I came to see my girlfriend," I told her. I moved over to the side of the bed and grabbed the corner of the pillow, trying to tug it out of the way. "What are you doing?"

"My face is all swollen and bruised. You can't see me like this!"

"I know." I sat down on a chair by her bed, setting the bag down beside me. "I was here when you were admitted. Whatever it's like now, it's going to be miles better than what it was."

"I look a mess."

"You look beautiful. You always do."

"Seungjin," she wailed. "I look like I was in a fight. I had rhinoplasty and the swelling hasn't gone down yet."

"I don't care if you had surgery to remove your nose, you'd still be beautiful to me."

Her eyes peeked over the top of the pillow to stare at me, full of disbelief. "Are you telling me I'd be attractive if I looked like Voldemort?"

"Maybe don't shave your head *and* lose your nose," I offered. The pillow dropped another millimeter. "Yerin, you're beautiful. A bit of bruising and swelling won't stop that. You're Cha Yerin."

The pillow was finally lowered to her lap and Yerin met my gaze. Although the swelling wasn't as bad as it had been when she had been admitted, her face, particularly under her eyes, was still puffy. It was also red and bruised like faded anger.

I'd never wanted to hit a girl before, but if Dasom had walked into the room, at that moment, I would have done. "I'm sorry."

"What for?"

"I should have said something about Dasom: warned you."

Yerin titled her head as she frowned. "You

did…"

Had I?

If I had, I should have said something to someone else. I knew that Dasom had a history, and more importantly, I knew Yerin was struggling with her. Then again, how could I have said something? Yerin was pre-debut. If I had said something, it might have resulted in her being taken out of the group.

"I'm sorry," I said again.

Yerin looked away, glumly. "I'm the one who should be apologizing."

I gaped at her. "For what?" I demanded.

"You had your debut pre-debut stage and I wasn't there to see it."

I left the bag beside the chair and stood, moving closer. "I didn't find out until yesterday, so I'm not sure what you could have done. If you weren't in the hospital, weren't you supposed to be filming your own music video anyway?"

Yerin nodded, although she still looked glum. "I know, I just wanted to be there for it."

"When do you get out of the hospital?" I asked her, thoughtfully. "We have our first official stage tomorrow outside of Atlantis?"

"I don't think I will be out of here tomorrow," she pouted. "The doctors don't like to give me much information."

Impulsively, I leaned over and kissed her pouty lips—gently, just in case I hurt her healing face.

"What was that for?"

I shrugged. "I can't help but want to kiss my girlfriend."

"I'm hideous," she said, flatly.

"You're beautiful," I corrected her. "A little bit of bruising doesn't change the fact that you're Cha Yerin."

She stared at me, eyes blinking slowly, and then she straightened her back and sat up. "Yes, I am." Her hands reached out, grabbing my sweater and twisting the fabric in her grip as she tugged me close to her. "I am," she whispered as she kissed me.

If there was any pain in her face, it didn't stop her moving her lips against mine, teasing gently at them. If she wasn't in pain, I was certainly happy to kiss her properly. I deepened the kiss, moving onto the bed beside her to get a better angle.

Cha Yerin was the kind of girl I wanted to kiss all day.

Being with her was both comforting and reassuring, and yet it had my heart racing. I finally pulled away, a small smile on my face. "I have a present for you."

Yerin's eyes lit up. "What?"

I leaned down, gathering the bag off the floor and handing it over. With eyes lit up like a Christmas tree, Yerin took it off me and peered in. She let out a squeal of delight as she pulled out the Queen Margaret Gucci bag. There was another excited squeal as she realized there was a shoebox in there too and pulled it out. While the Gucci top handle bag was placed on her sheets with the care the paper bag was tossed to the side.

She pulled the lid off and lifted one out. "They're the latest," she said in a breathless whisper. "They match the bag." Her eyes drifted to mine, tearing up. "Thank you, Seungjin."

"Your last pair looked a little worn," I told her.

She nodded, guiltily. "Miyeon said I shouldn't be

using my Gucci pumps to dance in, but I definitely won't use these."

I gaped at her. "You ... you were dancing in your... in *practice*?"

Yerin nodded. "Mr Gucci would be turning in his grave, I know."

"That's not ..." I shook my head, still amazed. "Yerin, you're spending most of your day as trainee practicing. You should be wearing comfortable shoes."

"Miyeon has already provided the lecture for me," she grumbled. Then, she picked the second shoe up and hugged the pair. I arched an eyebrow. "These will be treasured."

"These will be the first pair in your new collection. You will soon be able to buy your own again."

The smile slipped form Yerin's face. "I don't know what will happen. No one from Atlantis has been able to tell me what's going to happen next."

"You are talented and amazing," I assured her. "They'd be stupid to not debut you."

"I hope you're right," she admitted, fixing her gaze on me, looking suddenly embarrassed. "I really want it, Seungjin."

I took the shoes out of her hand, slipping them back into the box, and then I set them gently on the chair beside the bed. After depositing the small handbag on top, I shuffled so that I was sitting beside Yerin and wrapped my arm around her shoulder. She leaned into me, resting the side of her head against my chest. "Don't give up yet. I can't believe I'm saying this, but give Holly a chance."

She glanced up at me and arched an eyebrow.

"How are things with your sister?"

"Not much has changed," I told her. "I mean, yes, she has done what she has said she will so far, but as far as me and her go ...?" I shrugged.

"She's not spoken to you?"

"She said she would wait for me to go to her. I just don't know if I want to." I puffed up my cheeks and blew out a breath. Since being back at Atlantis, life had gone from zero to a hundred in a space of a couple of months. I hadn't really had much time alone with my thoughts, and when I had, they'd mainly been consumed with Yerin. There had been a handful of occasions where I had considered calling her, but I didn't know what to talk about.

"I understand that."

"Have you spoken to your father?"

Against my chest, Yerin's head moved. "He changed his number," she mumbled.

Mentally, I kicked myself. Then I imagined kicking her father.

"Seungjin, I know it's not my place, but ... maybe consider trying to talk to your sister. If she's letting you set the speed, I think she really wants to get to know you."

I stared at the wall opposite the bed. I just couldn't work out what I wanted to do. The fact she was here wasn't her fault. Dad had brought her back. But no sooner had she appeared, it seemed, my brother had been banished to China. Sejin wasn't taking my calls either. That might not have been Holly's fault, but I couldn't shake the feeling him being in China had something to do with her.

Then again, I knew Sejin. He could have brought

it on himself.

If I chose not to speak to her, things would carry on exactly as they were. That wasn't a bad thing. If I did choose to speak to her, things would carry on exactly as they were. But I would also have a sister to talk to.

"I don't know what to do," I admitted.

There was no response.

I glanced down, craning my neck to look at her face; Yerin was asleep. It was late, and she was still in a hospital. I started to extract myself from her, trying not to wake her, but an arm shot up, grabbing my sweater. "Stay," she mumbled, sleepily.

It *was* late …

Making sure I stayed on top of the covers, I slid down so that we were both lying. Half asleep, Yerin moved against me, curling up into my side before finally succumbing to sleep.

My hands traced patterns on her arm, watching her. She really was beautiful.

Z

"What the—?"

I jerked upright at the screech, the sudden light making my eyes water, my heart pounding. Before I could register that Cho Miyeon was stood in the entrance to the room, staring at us like we'd been caught doing more than just sleeping, Yerin had shoved me off her. I went flying onto the floor on the far side of the bed, only just avoiding smacking my head on the chest of drawers.

There was a bustle of sound and then I could hear Miyeon in the hallway. "Kiae-unnie, Yerin is still sleeping. Let's get a breakfast smoothie for her."

"Miyeon!"

"Shhhh! You'll wake her!" The door shut and I could hear the conversation moving away from the door.

I waited until I couldn't hear them before popping my head up. My heart was still racing. "What was that?"

"I think that was my friend covering for us." Yerin looked as confused as I did.

However, now was not the time to worry about it. Miyeon had given me an opportunity to escape and I was going to do it before we got caught. "I should go."

"I love you."

The two of us froze.

"I ... uh ... go!" Yerin instructed me.

"Yerin."

"Now!"

I was torn between wanting to stay and tell her it was OK; that I loved her too ... but I didn't want her to think I was saying it because she said it.

... I loved her too ...

Oh.

I gave her an awkward smile and all but ran from the room.

When had that happened?

제26 장

Yerin

The car ride back to the dorms was the most uncomfortable ride I'd ever had. My heart was beating a rhythm against my rib cage so quickly that it could have been the bass line for a drum and bass song.

Why had I done that?

Why had I said that to Seungjin?

Yes, it was true, but these were words that made boys run away.

Especially those about to become world-famous idols.

I was insane.

I was in love.

Is that what they meant when they said love makes you do crazy things?

It wasn't a new feeling. It had been growing for months. But his words last night—and the fact he had stayed with me—it had just …

My heart had been swelling, like it was going to explode.

All I wanted to do was crawl into my bed and pull the covers over my head. Not that hiding under my covers would hide me from my feelings. Nor would they hide me from Miyeon.

Miyeon, was sat next to me and hadn't stopped staring at me.

She managed to wait until we were in our room and had made sure that Sojung wasn't in the bathroom, before rounding on me. "Lee Seungjin?"

"Seungjin's—"

"Don't even try to convince me he's just a friend, because friends do not buy million won shoes for friends. They also don't stay the night. In the same bed. In the hospital."

I fixed her an impatient look as I folded my arms across my chest. "Seungjin's my *boyfriend*," I told her. "And he slept on top of the covers."

Miyeon's mouth was already hanging open at the admission of my lack of single status.

"Lee Seungjin?"

"What's wrong with Seungjin?" I demanded, defensively. If she said a bad word against him, I was going to use one of those new Gucci pumps to kick her butt.

Miyeon sat down and continued to stare at me in confusion. "He always seems so ... rigid. By the book... you know? Someone who wouldn't break the rules by dating." She scratched at the back of her head. "But in terms of him dating you? I can definitely see that."

"Good. Considering we are."

"How long?" she asked, still amazed.

"Not long," I admitted, sitting down beside her. "You can't tell anyone."

"You're talking to the girl who also has a boyfriend," she pointed out. She shook her head before grinning and holding a hand up. "Damn, Yerin. Lee Seungjin?" When I just stared at her, she reached over, lifted my hand and hit against hers. "Don't leave a girl hanging."

"It's not like that."

"Like what?" she asked. "You're not madly in love with him?"

"Yes, but—"

"Then that's all I need to know." She flopped backwards, giggling. "Yerin and Seungjin lying in a hospital bed," she sang.

"Songwriting might not be the future career for you."

"Oh!" she exclaimed, sitting bolt upright. "The future! I was supposed to tell you! Holly wants to see us after lunch. Go get a shower."

I swiped at her. "You could have led with that!"

"I could have, but you led with Seungjin and you dating, so ... no. Now go shower! You smell of hospital."

I sniffed at my clothes as I ducked into the small bathroom. Taking care not to let the water spray on my face, I had my first shower in a week. It was bliss.

It was also hard work. The doctor had spent twenty minutes telling me and my manager what I could and couldn't do for the next few weeks. Not only was physical exercise off the table for another month, there would be no singing (or rapping) as the vibrations could cause me pain and discomfort—who knew? He also warned me that I was likely to find my energy levels had dipped considerably.

As I'd spent a week in a bed with minimal exercise, I had thought he had been exaggerating at this. Only, a fifteen-minute shower had exhausted me. Although I managed to dress myself, I had to let Miyeon dry my hair for me.

I put a light layer of makeup on, even though that had been a recommendation *not* to, but I wanted to look and feel human again. Plus, the bruising was ugly. It didn't matter that I had every intention of hiding it all underneath a mask. I just needed to feel like me if I was going to find out what was happening.

With strict instructions to look after me, Manager Kiae returned to take us to Atlantis in the car rather than letting us get the bus. The next thing I knew, we were driving around the building to get to the parking lot entrance. "What's that?" I asked as we drove past a stage. It had been set up outside of the main entrance and already had attracted a crowd.

"I definitely told you this yesterday: it's the stage for 1SO: Fire's official stage." She frowned. "The last I heard, they were definitely a pre-debut unit, so can you call it a debut stage for a pre-debut group?" She shrugged and then grinned. "Either way, it's for that." She leaned over. "Do you want to watch it with me after the meeting?"

"Do you think we'll be able to?"

Miyeon nodded, firmly. "It's later this afternoon. The Vice Chairwoman will want to watch it, so our meeting will be done, and we will be watching and supporting our sunbaes. I heard Minhyuk from H3RO will be there too!"

My excitement for the show evaporated as we walked into Holly's office. Sojung was already there, sitting on one of the couches. I looked over at her, trying to gauge her mood. She didn't seem upset. She didn't seem ridiculously happy either. I had no idea what that meant.

"Cha Yerin, how are you feeling?" Holly asked, hurrying over as soon as she saw me. "I'm sorry, I didn't get back into Seoul until just as you were being discharged."

"I'm OK," I shrugged. My nose was still tender, and I was terrified of sneezing, but it *was* OK.

She led us over to the couch. Miyeon sat down beside Sojung and I sat on the other side of Miyeon. "First things first. Hoo Dasom has been let go from Atlantis. I'm sorry if she was your friend, but that behavior is completely unacceptable. It does mean that this will affect your debut. Assuming you all still want to debut with Atlantis."

"I do," Sojung said, quietly. "But Dasom is still my friend."

"From the company standpoint, Dasom is not allowed on Atlantis property. She's currently at the dorm with another manager collecting her things. I cannot dictate who your friends are, but she is not allowed anywhere near Atlantis or Yerin, which means she shouldn't turn up at locations or even the same coffee shop. I don't want to have to go down the legal route and get a restraining order, but I will," Holly told her, firmly. "The rest is up to you girls."

"Dasom is from Pohang," Sojung said. "She said she was going back home. She won't be here." She looked over at me. "I spent years training with her. She always had my back—she was always there for me. She shouldn't have hit you, but I can't just turn my back on her."

I dropped my gaze to my lap, toying with a stray thread on my skirt. I didn't like Dasom. I never had. I never would. But Dasom wasn't the issue: Sojung was. It wasn't that I didn't like her. I'd never had the chance to get to know her. I just wasn't sure how she felt about me being the cause of her best friend being kicked out of Atlantis.

"I don't have a problem with Sojung," Miyeon announced with a shrug.

I pursed my lips. This was the girl I was going to spend the next seven years of my life with. I glanced over at the maknae asking myself one question: was this going to be a problem?

For me, no.

I straightened my back and flipped my hair over my shoulder. "If Sojung is happy to stay in the same group, so am I," I responded, looking back to Holly. "But I don't want to run into Dasom again."

"Hoo Dasom was informed she wasn't to return to any Atlantis property," Holly repeated. "She was also told not to come near you, or she would face legal action. I will see to it that your instruction is upheld if required." She got to her feet. "I have new paperwork for you."

She walked out of the room, leaving the three of us sitting awkwardly on the couch.

"I'm sorry," Sojung said, quietly.

I looked over at her with a questioning look. "Is that directed at me?"

Sojung nodded her head, her bob brushing against her chest, her head was hung so low. "I knew Dasom didn't like you but didn't say anything."

"I don't get why," I muttered, bitterly. "She was angry at my parents and I get that, but why me? I didn't cause my parents to fire hers."

"Really?" Miyeon arched an eyebrow as she turned in her seat to look at me. "You're going to say that with a straight face?"

"What does that mean?" I demanded.

"You still don't see it, do you?" she groaned. With an exasperated sigh, she reached over and patted my knee. "Don't worry: we'll work on that."

I gave her a pained smile, before looking back to Sojung. "Does that mean you don't think I'm the reason Dasom's not here?"

Sojung's eyes widened like saucers and she shook her head. "I love Dasom. She was there for me when we weren't selected to debut with Cupcake, and she's helped me a lot while we've been trainees, but she's the one who hit you. She promised me she wouldn't let us *not* debut, and I really wanted to believe it. You can't be friends with everyone, but I thought she'd be OK with you." She bowed her head again. "I want to debut more than anything, but I don't want to do it with a group I wouldn't be happy with. I still want to debut with you two."

"Let's just start again," I started, just as the door was opened. Holly walked in with two girls. Sojung, Miyeon, and I stared at them in confusion.

"I'm not sure if you've all met before," Holly said. "I think some of you will know Jeon Mintae as she has been a trainee here for a few years."

Jeon Mintae looked the same age as Dasom. She was about the same height with a beautiful heart-shaped face. Her black hair had been pulled back in a low ponytail. She was wearing a leather jacket that was three sizes too big for her, with denim hot pants, fishnet stockings and some hightops. She looked like she had already debuted.

Only, I was aware that she was still a trainee. I had seen her face on the Atlantis trainee roster, but it had said she was focusing on acting.

"Minty," Mintae said.

"I don't have any," Sojung said, automatically.

"My name," Minty clarified.

"Minty will be joining you as another rapper," Holly told us. She turned to the other girl. Her eyes were a little rounder, and her skin had a darker tone to it. I knew before she spoke she wasn't Korean. "This is Adele Tham. She auditioned with our global auditions in Thailand."

"I am from Singapore," Adele said, a slight accent to her words. "My Korean is not good, but I am learning. Please have patience with me."

Aside from the accent, you couldn't tell.

"OK, girls, I'm going to let you get to know each other better, but first, I want you to look at the new paperwork." Holly waited for Minty and Adele to sit down on the second couch before holding up a single sheet of paper. She turned it over.

GROUP NAME: Glitter
FANDOM NAME: Glamour
COLOR: #f04bc1 (Pink sherbet)
DEBUT DATE: September 22nd*
LEADER: Minty

***Depending on abilities and group cohesion.**

The five of us read it, but it was Miyeon who reacted the most vocally. Miyeon squealed and wrapped her arms around me. For once, I didn't mind. I was just as excited.

Holly grinned, lowering the paper. "We have a plan and we have a new song. You girls have four months to learn this. If you can come together and work as a group, we will get you in the studio and record that album. I just wanted you to know that there really is a plan to debut you all."

"We won't let you down," Minty promised.

"Why don't you girls head out for some ice cream? There's a new ice cream parlor a few blocks away which has amazing milkshakes." She handed Minty some money and then ushered us out. I hovered in the doorway, and it took the Vice Chairwoman a moment to realize I was still in the room. "Is everything OK, Yerin?"

I closed the door behind me and walked over to her desk. "The doctor said I wouldn't be able to sing or dance for a few more weeks," I admitted.

"I know, and it's fine," Holly assured me. "You should know by now that being an idol isn't just about being able to sing and dance ... or rap, in your case. You can still learn the lyrics to your song, and you can still sit in on the dance classes. Physically, you can take it easy for however long the doctor tells us. This is why we've pushed your debut day out. I still expect you all to graduate high school, and I will be getting language tutors in so you can all pick another language to learn. Don't worry, Yerin, there's still plenty to do."

"You're really OK with this?"

"I'm not OK with the situation that caused this," Holly said, shaking her head. "But your health is important. Take as long as you need to heal. This is why I wanted you to have this information." She looked at the piece of paper she had held up to us with a thoughtful expression. Then, she pushed it towards me. "You can pin this up in your dorm room."

I had barely picked the sheet of paper off the desk when the door to the office suddenly burst open and one of the members of H3RO, Dante, strode in. He stopped the moment he saw me, looking briefly guilty.

"This is why we knock," Holly sighed in exasperation.

"This is why we use locks," Dante countered. "Which is what I will be using ..." he glanced at me. "For our conversation."

Holly's head fell into her hands.

I took the hint and walked out, making sure to give both Holly and my sunbae a respectful bow as I passed them. I didn't envy the job of the Vice Chairwoman. There were just too many idols to keep happy.

The rest of Glitter were waiting for me outside of Holly's office.

Glitter.

That put a huge grin on my face.

"Is everything OK?" Miyeon asked. I wasn't sure if was because I looked slightly insane, or because I had spoken to Holly.

I held up the sheet of paper. "Something to hang in our dorm."

제27 장

Yerin

The excitement wore off as we walked down the street to the ice cream parlor that "I guess we should make the most of this," Minty sighed. We had ordered a Berry-Praline ice cream cake to share between the five of us. The description said it served four. The thing in front of us looked like it would feed eight.

Nobody moved. Custom dictated the youngest would serve, and although I was sure Minty was older than me, I wasn't sure where Adele fell.

"I'll serve," Adele said, brightly, picking up a knife.

"I suppose we should introduce ourselves?" Miyeon suggested as Adele started slicing up the cake. "I'm Cho Miyeon, and I'm eighteen."

Minty was the eldest. She was twenty and had been convinced by her manager, and then by Atlantis, to join us as our other rapper. Sojung remained the maknae, but with only a couple of weeks between her and Adele's birthday, there wasn't much in it.

I was convinced Adele was a genius. She spoke four languages, although she was adamant that she wasn't good enough at Korean to say she was fluent … while saying so in perfect Korean.

I knew within minutes that Minty was the perfect person to be our leader. She was calm and softly spoken, but she was able to keep us in check.

Something just clicked with us. We devoured the first slice of ice cream cake, but then we were so busy talking—and laughing—that we lost track of time.

We were in our own little world, oblivious to our surroundings. Including who else was in the ice cream parlor.

"These things can only be found on the island I'm from, Pulau Ubin, and normally, they don't come in the houses, but my nenek left a window open and it flew in one night. They're massive!"

"What's a nenek?" Sojung asked.

Adele screwed up her nose, trying to find the translation, but failing. "My mom's mom?"

"Grandmother," Minty supplied.

"Yes, grandmother," Adele nodded. "It was almost as big as my nenek, my grandmother," she continued.

"Bats aren't that big," Miyeon disagreed, pulling a face.

"We call them flying foxes and they have a wingspan over a meter long!"

"I would have run out of there screaming," Sojung said, her eyes wide with horror. "I don't like bats. I really don't like monster bats!"

"Oh, look what we have here."

The table went silent as we all turned and found

Dasom staring down at us, her arms folded and a scowl on her face.

"Hello, I'm Adele," Adele said, not picking up on the awkwardness and apprehension radiating from three of us at the table.

"You were told not to come near us," Miyeon said, calmly. "I think it would be for the best if you left."

"I think you should shut up," Dasom growled back at her. She had the air of a cobra about her, like she was about to strike at any moment.

I watched her with a wary eye. The swelling in my nose was just about gone and I didn't want another rhinoplasty operation, but I was not going to start a new life scared of the old one.

"Dasom-unnie, I think you should leave," Sojung told her, apologetically. "I don't want you to get into trouble."

Dasom's lip turned up in a sneer. "I see you've had no trouble forgetting where your loyalties lie. Do the last four years mean nothing to you?"

"Everything," Sojung told her. "They mean everything."

"Then what are you still doing here? Come with me? We can join a new agency together: one that doesn't let trash in with it," she added the last bit with a pointed look at me.

I was about to stand up and say something, but under the table, Miyeon's hand settled on my thigh. She gave me the gentlest shake of her head, and I stopped myself. Whether it was her intention or not, this was a good way to see just where Sojung's loyalties lay.

Sojung, who's eyes had been fixed on Dasom until that point, dropped her gaze. "I'm sorry, unnie, but

I'm staying here."

"Pil Sojung!" Dasom cried. When Sojung refused to move, the surprise was replaced with narrowed eyes and an ice-cold glare. "Fine. If you're choosing the trash, you might as well look like them."

Before any of us could stop her, Dasom had snatched up the plate of melting ice cream cake gloop and poured it over Sojung's head to the sound of her shrieks.

The only time I experienced time freezing was when I was kissing Seungjin. Lost in his arms with his lips on mine, I would lose all concept of time. Occasions like that were few and far between with our schedules, and the feeling was welcome.

As I watched the ice cream fall on Sojung's head, time seemed to freeze for me. No, it slowed. It was like I was watching a movie in slow motion. Only, the movie was horror.

And it was me with the leading role, not Sojung.

Déjà vu hit me, like a cannonball, hitting the bottom of my stomach with as much force.

I'd done this.

I'd done this and *more*.

I'd done this and *worse*.

I was taken out of that ice cream parlor and taken back to SLA and the day I had ordered everyone to dump their food on the floor. In my head, the floor was replaced with images of TK, TK's father, Lucinda, and all the cafeteria staff.

Dasom was a bully, and I could see myself in her.

"No!" I yelled, snapping myself out of my daymare. Before I could move, Minty, who had been sat opposite Sojung, was on her feet. While Dasom was busy pouring the sloppy, sticky mess over Sojung, Minty reached out, grabbed Dasom's hand and twisted it behind her back before pushing her face down onto the table, and the convenient mess Dasom had created.

Dasom let out an unintelligible screech, struggling against Minty's grip. While Miyeon and Adele rushed over to help Sojung, I moved around to Minty. "Let her go."

"Yerin, she—"

"She has an issue with me, not Sojung," I said, calmly. "Let her go."

"Yerin—"

"Please, Minty. This is between us."

She shot me a dubious look, but Minty let go and stepped back, putting herself between Dasom and Sojung. I was thankful for that.

"You ruined my life," Dasom spat at me.

I slowly shook my head. "No, you ruined your own life."

"You have no idea what I've been through—"

"No," I agreed, cutting her off. "I don't have a clue what you've been through. Just like you don't know what I've been through. You're not the only one hurting because of my parents. And honestly, I don't blame you for hurting me." We looked nothing alike, but somehow, I felt like I was talking to myself as well as— or maybe instead of—Dasom. "Hurting someone else makes you feel like you've got some control over your life. Hurting someone else makes you feel better when someone else is hurting too. But you're only hurting yourself."

"Oh, shut up!" Dasom let out a war cry of a scream and lunged at me.

With lightning fast reflexes, Minty's hand shot out, wrapped around Dasom's ponytail, bringing her to an abrupt halt. As her foot slipped on some of the ice cream she'd slipped, Dasom's legs went out from under her and she fell backwards to the ground with a heavy thud.

Minty crouched down over her. "I don't know the details of why you're not in this group anymore; not yet at least. But it has only taken five minutes for me to know that I don't like you and that you're toxic. This is my group now. I will be informing Atlantis of your actions today, but, so help me, if you come near any of my members again, I will make you regret it."

Minty stood up and looked at us.

"I think I love you," Miyeon muttered, in awe.

Even I was staring at our new leader with a combination of admiration and a smidgen of fear.

As if she sensed it, Minty softened her expression. "You may not be blood, but you guys are my family now, and I'm going to do my best as Glitter's leader to protect you and do the right thing."

I wasn't sure what to make of that. You couldn't just pick your family.

But I sure was glad to have someone else on my side.

We went back to the dorms to help Sojung clean up. Miyeon helped her shower seeing as Sojung was crying too much to do anything. When she emerged, although with red and puffy eyes, she had finally stopped crying.

Minty and Adele had been given the bedroom next to ours—it was barely big enough for the bunkbeds—and were busy unpacking.

I'd spent the time pacing back and forth, trying to work out what to say. Even when I'd turned my attention to changing my clothes for 1SO: Fire's show, I was still playing conversations over and over in my head; trying to work out the best way to word how I was feeling.

I wasn't sure what I was feeling.

Or maybe I was … I just had no experience in telling people these kinds of things.

In the end, it was Seungjin who helped.

Not directly. He didn't appear in my room like a knight in shining armor to fight my battles.

Not that this was a battle.

But he wasn't here to tell them what I was thinking, because only I could do that.

Instead, I put on the Gucci pumps he had bought me and imagined they were full of power like the ones Dorothy had, filled with the same power to take me to my family.

Or, at least, the family Minty had spoken about.

"I don't think I should be in this group," I announced.

Our bedroom was full. Minty and Adele had come into our room, also in fresh clothes, so we could all head back to Atlantis.

"What logic brought you to that conclusion?" Miyeon asked me. She folded her arms and leaned back against the door she was standing in front of, as though to physically stop me from running away.

I wasn't going to run away.

I was going to tell the truth and then bow out gracefully.

I sucked in a deep breath.

"The reason Dasom doesn't like me is because one or both of her parents used to work for my father. The company was going out of business because my father was embezzling from it. They lost their jobs."

"Then that is between your father and her parents," Miyeon shrugged.

I turned to look at her and frowned. "You keep saying that, but it's not. My father did something that affected her family. It sounds like what he did hurt a lot of families. There are consequences to those actions."

"I get why she'd be mad at your father, but I still think it's unreasonable and irrational for her to vent that at you," Miyeon disagreed.

"Irrational, maybe, but if someone hurts your family, you're going to want to hurt them back, even if that means hurting their family. At the very least, you're going to hate that person and their family."

"But Dasom isn't part of Glitter," Sojung pointed out. She gave me a small smile. "It's just us, and I don't blame you."

"Me neither," Minty agreed, while Adele nodded her agreement and Miyeon gave me a pointed look.

"But there are a lot of people in this city who will. It won't take much for them to find out who I am. Then Glitter's reputation is damaged before we even debut."

"I haven't seen or heard anything about anyone embezzling in the news."

I looked at our leader and raised a shoulder. "My father resigned from the company and fled to the US. I'm not entirely sure his company found out, and if they did, they probably don't want to risk their shareholders considering there would probably be a huge lawsuit and some hefty payouts."

"Then, if they're not going to say anything, how will the public know?"

"My parents got divorced," I added. "My mother told my father not to come back, and my father …" a huge lump had formed in the back of my throat, forcing the rest of my sentence out in a whisper. "He told me not to try and see him, and then he changed his number." I had no way of getting in touch with him at all anymore.

Miyeon walked over to me, took my hands in hers, and led me over to my bunk to sit us down. "Look, I get you're worried about your reputation, but divorce isn't as taboo as it was even ten years ago. You come from money, and yes, that's a whole lot of archaic traditions, but the rest of us? We don't care. Divorce happens."

"My parents are divorced," Minty told us, suddenly. "I was brought up by my aunt. So, if they hate you for that, they're going to hate me more."

"See, we're good!" Miyeon said, enthusiastically.

We weren't good. "I'm not much different from Dasom."

All four sets of eyes were on me.

"What makes you say that?" Miyeon asked.

"What she did to Sojung? I did that to TK—and my motives weren't any purer than hers."

"Finally," Miyeon sighed, leaning over and hugging me.

I wriggled away from her and frowned. "What does that mean?"

"That means there is some good in you," she declared. "You are redeemable."

"What does *that* mean?" I repeated, still not

understanding Miyeon's code.

"What has happened, has happened. I don't condone it, but you can't change it. What you can change is yourself, and how you react to people and situations going forward. You can do it. You can be a better person."

"You make it sound easy," I grumbled.

Miyeon let out a snort. Or maybe it was a bray. "Easy? You're a spoilt princess brat. It's not going to be easy at all. Luckily for you, you have me around to keep you on the right path," she draped an arm around my shoulder. "And if you don't stay on it, I'll dump kimchi on *your* head."

"I have no idea what's going on here," Minty interrupted us. "But whatever you're doing, can you do it without wasting anymore food? We already lost a perfectly divine ice cream cake today."

"Deal," I laughed.

"Um, I don't know what you're talking about either," Sojung added. "But I don't think you're like Dasom. And like Minty said earlier: we might not be a family by blood, but we're still family. We might not know each other yet, but we will. And we'll have your back."

I still didn't understand what Minty had meant by that, but given the looks the others were giving me, they did.

Maybe I would too, one day.

제28 장

Seungjin

"We have a crowd," Wonseok said, hopping from side to side with a nervous energy which was starting to rub off on me. We were in the Atlantis building, sheltered from view by mirrored glass windows, watching the crowd that had been gathering all afternoon.

The rain had held off, but it was still cold out. Despite this, there had to be three hundred people out there. A large portion of them were carrying homemade 1SO: Fire fan signs. Another portion had bought some of the official merchandise, despite its limited selection.

It was an amazing feeling.

It was an intimidating feeling.

I was doing well to keep as calm as I was, because the number of butterflies inside of me were multiplying. The other three hadn't debuted before. They didn't have to be perfect like I did. There were still posts on the internet, talking about the Bright Boys scandal; one of the members (me) was confirmed to be working up to debuting again, and the unconfirmed rumors, with the public at least, were other former Bright Boys members were also hoping to do the same.

"It's not like we haven't performed in front of a crowd before. We were on M Countdown, remember?" Insoo said to Wonseok.

Insoo was one of the calmest people I knew. The only person who was calmer was Kota and he was currently sitting with his legs crossed, meditating at the side of the room. As our unit leader, I had faith in him. He reminded me of Hyunseo a little, but he would react to situations a little less passionately, rarely raising his voice.

Then again, Hyunseo had been like that too, before …

"Remember?" Wonseok asked, chuckling. "How could I ever forget that?"

"Exactly," Insoo agreed, before turning to our Japanese member. "Kota?" Insoo called, gently.

Kota poked an eye open, before both blue eyes were staring at his leader. He'd been given contacts for this and they were striking. Eerie, but striking. "Yes?"

"It's time."

Before Kota could get up and join us, Oh Seokbeom had walked into the room. "It's time to go down."

How did Insoo do that?

We followed our manager down to the backstage area. While H3RO's Minhyuk was onstage talking to our crowd (and there were definitely some H3RO fans in that crowd), Insoo gathered us round. "This is it, guys: our debut stage. We might not be debuting officially with this unit, but it is our unit's official debut, and that's just as important. Hwaiting!" He stuck his fist out and the rest of us mimicked him. "Hana, dul, set …"

"1SO: Fire!"

We bounded onto the stage and took our positions.

We had three songs: our title song and two additional numbers. We'd spent hours practicing on them, and I knew, when I would watch the video that Oh Seokbeom was recording for us, our performance would be everything that it needed to be. There wasn't a note off key, a lyric forgotten, or a step misplaced. We were on fire.

When we walked off stage, I wanted to do it all over again.

Unlike the M Countdown performance, the audience had been there to see us. They had known about the show, and they had turned up for us.

The applause and the screams were the best kind of drug that a person could become addicted to.

Not only was I addicted, I had no intention of quitting.

We were taken back into the Atlantis building where we were ushered into one of the dance studios to be rewarded with cake and soju. Or, at least Kota and Insoo were. Wonseok and I were stuck with non-alcoholic drinks.

I didn't mind. I was still buzzing from the performance. Even the hairs on the back of my neck were still standing on end.

"You guys were amazing!" Jun exclaimed, bounding over. "This place needed some good vibes and this was it."

I knew he meant well, but that put a slight

dampener on things: Onyx had returned home, only for half of the members to be in an accident. Hence why the only member present was CX.

I listened to Jun as he excitedly gave me a detailed account of the show—from the wings where he had been watching us and the audience. Apparently, there had been a lot more signs with my name than I had originally realized: the bright lights on the stage made it hard to see too far back. I'd seen a few, but they had been evenly split between us all. "They made up fan chants, Seungjin. It was amazing. You were amazing. You're going to do well when you really debut."

When Minhyuk pulled him away, I walked over to Yongsik—no, CX—and hugged my former group mate. "Calling you CX feels weird, hyung," I told him.

He looked surprised, as though he had forgotten his own name. "I guess I'm used to it now."

"How was the world tour? Aside from the end?" I asked, tagging the end part on awkwardly.

"Hot," CX responded. "Passionate. And more than I expected."

I stared at him, pulling a face. "That is the most random collection of words to describe a world tour, hyung. Hot? Was there no air conditioning? It's February—just how hot was Europe?"

"London was hot," CX said, vaguely.

"London? As in the UK? In February?"

CX looked at me like I was mad. "The UK was cold. But inside the apartment was hot. Surprisingly hot. I could do that again …"

I stared at him in confusion. "Are you OK, hyung?"

As if he was finally realizing I was there and a part

of his exceptionally weird conversation, he shook his head. "Sorry, Seungjin. Let's just say that I'm happy."

"I'm glad," I told him truthfully. We had all been devastated after Bright Boys had disbanded, but Yongsik—CX—had been the only one who hadn't been given a clear plan. It had worked out well for him. "I'm sorry the rest of your tour got postponed."

"Don't worry: we'll be back out to finish it off, soon." He clapped me on the back and gave me a huge grin. "You're going on a world tour too. That performance? If this is what a unit can produce, I can't wait to see the rest of the group. And neither will the rest of the world."

Much as I was willing to ask him for more details about his tour, I had spotted someone lingering at the edge of the room: Yerin. The room was full of management and other idols of varying popularity. Even if she was still a trainee, she had every right to be in there, just like me.

I hurried over to her, picking up a bottle of banana milk along the way (whoever had included those in the drinks selection deserved a pay rise). "Hello, beautiful." I offered the drink to her, refraining from wrapping my arms around her. There were far too many people around to be thinking things like that.

"They put you in the right unit because you guys were on fire," she told me, looking at me with a look which was smoldering. Who was the one on fire?

"You really can't look at me like that," I chided her.

Yerin stabbed the foil lid with the straw and looked up at me while she sipped her drink, blinking at me with a faux innocence? "You mean, like I think you are the best looking, most talented person in this room, and I want my own personal show of your body rolls? That was supposed to be a PG-13 performance, not something X-rated."

I barely gave it a second thought as I leaned over, close to her ear. "Meet me in the conference room in five minutes," I murmured. The hell with it. I was making out with my girlfriend tonight.

Yerin's eyes fell on something across the room, and she shifted uncomfortably. "Can we make it ten minutes?"

"Sure?"

Distracted, she stepped past me. Curiosity won out and I followed her through the crowds to the far side of the room, surprised when she came to a stop in front of King, Lucinda, (what was she doing here?), TK and Miyeon. At first, I thought she had gone to speak to her groupmate, but her attention was on TK.

"TK, do you have a moment?"

"Not alone with you," Lucinda retorted, answering for TK.

Yerin nodded. "That's fair." She glanced over her shoulder, surprise lining her face when she saw me behind her, but carried on scanning the crowd around us, before looking back to TK. "I am sorry," she said. While she shifted uncomfortably, her words were strong. "I had a … an eye-opening experience recently, and I realized just how horrible I was back at school."

Lucinda snorted. "Near death experience? Or are you afraid your nasty behavior is going to stop you debuting?"

Miyeon kicked her shin. "Hear her out!" she hissed, ignoring Lucinda's yelp of objection.

"It's OK," Yerin told Miyeon. "I mean, she is partly right: I am worried about how my past behavior will affect my debut. I was horrible. Not my parents, but me."

"What have your parents got to do with this?" Lucinda asked, rolling her eyes. "Don't tell me; you're rich enough to have help and they're evil to them to because they're the help?"

"Almost correct," Yerin agreed. "We *were* rich enough to have help, and my parents were awful to them. But something happened with Hoo Dasom and she's no longer at Atlantis."

TK's gaze flicked to me, then to Yerin. This wasn't a surprise to anyone but Lucinda. It's hardly a secret when someone leaves the company. Even the rumors which had been flying around, internally of course, had been fairly accurate.

"The point is, I'm taking responsibility for my own actions. And that's starting by apologizing to you," Yerin turned to Lucinda. "And to you too."

Lucinda's mouth actually fell open as she gaped at Yerin.

"I'm not going to say it's OK, because it's not. However, I accept your apology," TK told her.

If it wasn't for the context, watching the American would have been amusing, seeing as now her eyes were almost bulging out of her head. "Just like that?" she spluttered, turning to TK. "You're accepting her apology after everything she did? Next you'll be telling me you're best friends with Seungjin."

TK shrugged.

"Are you serious?"

"I spoke to Seungjin weeks ago," TK explained.

"I said the same thing to him as I did to Yerin. It's not OK, but I accept the apology. I understand why they did what they did. I'm not going to be best friends with Seungjin, but we are likely to debut in the same group. We can be professional and civil towards each other."

It was true. We had had a conversation a while back, and we weren't going to be best friends. I wasn't even sure we could call it friendship at all. I did know I was going to try to make it up to him. Somehow …

Lucinda looked between the group of us, shaking her head. "What I went through is nothing compared to TK and there's no way I'm just going to let it go like that."

"I understand," Yerin said. "I'm not sure I could either. It doesn't change my apology though. I am sorry for how I treated you. I'm going to work hard on not being that person anymore."

"I guess I'll believe it when I see it," Lucinda muttered. She glanced at Miyeon. "You're going to stay my friend, and I love you, but I don't want her around me."

"It's OK, I'm going," Yerin said. She gave Miyeon a smile. "I'll see you later."

She said goodbye and walked away. I arched an eyebrow as I caught King briefly rest a hand on the small of Lucinda's back, then hurried after my girlfriend.

I was just about to join her at the door when sense snapped into me and I realized leaving the party together wasn't a smart move. Instead, I hung back, only to be joined by my dad.

"You did well today," he told me.

He'd never told me that when I was in Bright Boys. Not once. It was why I had always been convinced he'd never wanted me to be an idol and had only signed me because I was his son and he didn't want to look bad when I went to another entertainment company. "Thank you," I said, suspiciously.

"I mean it, Seungjin. You did well today. You looked like a real idol."

I suppose I should have taken that as confirmation that I had been right, but I didn't. Honestly, I was thrilled he felt that way now. "Thank you," I repeated, more confidently this time.

"Have you spoken to your sister yet?"

I clenched my teeth together before I blurted something out. He wasn't talking about today. "We both have conflicting schedules," I finally managed a diplomatic answer. "When is Sejin coming home?"

Dad looked away, shaking his head. "It will be some time before Sejin returns to Seoul, son. Shanghai will keep him busy for some time." He turned back to me, ruffling my hair like I was six years old again. "You focus on music for now … and maybe consider talking to your sister."

I gave him a non-committal shrug, before bowing my head and leaving him to talk to another company member.

I'd left Yerin waiting long enough and did my best to leave the room as discreetly as possible. Thankfully, she was still waiting for me when I entered the conference room.

Yerin was beautiful.

Standing at the window, staring out at Seoul's nighttime skyline, I could see her profile. Her nose had changed slightly. Only a fraction of an angle at the tip. Otherwise, she was the exact same Yerin I had fallen for. I walked over to her, wrapping my arms around her as my chest pressed up against her back. "I don't think I've told you how beautiful you look today."

"You don't need to," she muttered, leaning back against me.

I nuzzled up against her neck, inhaling her scent—strawberries, and something which was distinctly Yerin, but I had no idea what it was. "Don't tell me," I said, stepping back so I could turn her around. I flipped my head, pretending I had long hair. "You're Cha Yerin and you know you're beautiful."

Yerin swiped at my arm. "Is that supposed to be an impression of me?"

I grinned.

Yerin rocked her head as she put a hand on her hips. "That was an appalling impression of me. You really need to put more effort in that hair flip. Like this." She whipped her hair over her shoulder with more dramatic flair than she usually did.

And it was sexy as hell.

I pushed her up against the glass as she wrapped her arms around my neck. "You didn't need to tell me because I can see it in how you look at me," she told me, her eyes shining. "Nobody looks at me the way you do."

"Good," I growled, gruffly. "But that also means they're idiots. Give it time, and I'll be beating your fans away."

"September."

"You have a debut date?"

She bobbed her head as she shrugged. "It's not confirmed, but it's what we're working towards. We're … Glitter." She gave me the biggest smile, her eyes once again lighting up. "Our group is going to be called Glitter."

"I like it."

"And we have two new group members. Minty and Adele." The grin slipped a fraction. "I'm sorry, this is your day."

"I want to hear," I assured her. "I think this is the happiest I've seen you."

"I am happy," she agreed. With a long sigh, she turned her head to rest her cheek against my chest. "Thank you."

"Why are you thanking me?"

"Because if it wasn't for you, I wouldn't have signed with Atlantis. I think I would have gotten on that plane and tried to find my father and missed this opportunity. It has been nothing like I thought it would be, but singing soothes my soul. I feel peace." She looked up at me. "I guess that sounds strange, but even when my legs ached, or Dasom was getting me down, or when I think about how my father ran away without a goodbye … when I was singing, I felt at peace. I still do."

I did know. I knew exactly what she was talking about. It was the reason I had tried so hard to debut. Music was powerful. It didn't need lyrics, and it didn't need words that you could understand, but it had the power to change someone's life—if only for three and a half minutes.

But, I was beginning to realize why so many songs were love songs.

If a song could change your life for a few minutes, a person could change your life for an eternity.

Yerin changed my life.

She made my world.

"I love you," I told her.

Her eyes were shining again. "I love you too."

I leaned down to capture her lips with mine. Lips that had the power to change the world.

Like the lack of space between us was still too great, I wrapped my arms around her tighter, pulling her soft curves against me so she moaned into me. I deepened the kiss, my hands sliding along the bottom of her shirt, seeking out the warm, soft skin beneath it.

My hand slid upwards, over her ribcage towards—

"Lee Seungjin? Are you freaking kidding me?"

제29 장

Seungjin

I spun around, hiding Yerin behind me, finding not only Holly standing in front of me, but Insoo, Kota and Wonseok. While my sister looked like she was going to have an aneurism, the others looked like they had just witnessed the end of the world.

Just like that, I felt all hope escape me. My future as an idol was over.

Holly rubbed at her temples. "Who is that behind you?"

I shook my head. My future was over, but Yerin still had a chance.

"Cha Yerin."

My head whipped around as Yerin stepped out from behind me. "It's my fault, not Yerin's."

"Don't make it sound like I'm doing something against my will," she scolded me.

Holly held a hand up. "Is this a one-time thing, or something more?"

Neither of us said anything.

"OK then …" Holly looked at us wearily. "Yerin,

go back to the party. I'll speak to you later."

"It's not Yerin's fault!" I objected. "She shouldn't get into any trouble."

"Yerin, go back to the party," Holly repeated, ignoring me. "I will get someone to bring you to speak to me later."

"Yes," Yerin said, bowing her head at the Vice Chairwoman before hurrying out of the room.

Holly moved over to the conference table and slid into one of the chairs. "What are you doing here?" I demanded.

"If you bothered to check your phone, you would know that I wanted to discuss the next steps for 1SO: Fire. But I suppose we'd all best have another discussion first. Sit down." She watched as we all moved over towards the table, before sighing. "If you could do it without looking like I'm going to push you out of a window or something, that would be great."

I don't think any of our expressions changed.

"I'm going to ask you all a question, and I want you to answer honestly. Who here, besides Seungjin, is in a relationship?"

"I'm not in a relationship," I lied.

Holly rolled her eyes, but ignored me. "Is this the truth, or are you all too scared to answer me?" She shook her head. "I am happy to announce that you are the first four members of Zodiac. There will be three more units having a moment to shine and introduce themselves to the world, but I will announce the members after their pre-debut debut stage," Holly frowned. "I have got to come up with a better way of describing that," she muttered to herself. "As such, you are not allowed to discuss this with the other trainees.

You will find out who the other members of Zodiac are when they do. Hopefully, it will include all unit members, but we will also be taking their wishes into consideration."

"Wait, we made it? *I* made it?" I asked, eyes wide. "Seriously?"

Holly looked amused. "Why? Did you think your girlfriend would stop that from happening?"

Actually, yes.

"You still have a month of promotions to complete. We need to keep the hype up and the public interested, but what I saw today has convinced me the four of you are what I want in Zodiac."

"Is that why we are the element of fire?" Insoo asked, like a lightbulb had switched on.

"It is indeed," Holly said, proudly. "Each of the star signs have an element to them. Now, this is something I want the public to guess as we go, to try to draw up a bit of mystery about the group, so no spoilers, please. We will continue to have the one 1SO social media account and we will convert that to Zodiac when we announce the full group. It also means we will be taking charge of all social media posts. You will be able to post and take over, but only under supervision. For the next month, you are 1SO: Fire."

"You're really debuting us?" I asked again, still struggling to believe it. "All of us?"

Holly leaned forward, clasping her hands together as she rested them on the table. "This industry demands celibacy."

I cringed. We'd gone from relationships to sex and that was not a conversation I wanted to have with my sister—regardless of the fact she was my half-sister and I barely spoke to her.

"Idols are not allowed to date and you're to remain single to fans, so they can dream that they have a chance with you. I both agree with it, because every girl and boy has that fantasy, but at the same time, I think it's unhealthy for you guys, and I think it can get unhealthy with fans too."

"You don't mind us having a girlfriend?" Kota asked.

"I don't, but the industry does."

"That doesn't answer the question," I told her.

Holly shot me a look. "It does." She let out a long sigh. "I've spent a long time talking this over with the Chairman and the legal team and this is the best deal I have negotiated. For the seven years you are signed with Atlantis, you will not be allowed to date publicly. I'm not stupid. You've got hormones and urges."

I swear I nearly dry heaved at hearing her say that.

"What we require is that you inform the company and you keep it private so that the public does not find out. If they do find out and you have told us your relationship status, we will tell the public that although you are advised not to date, you are not breaking your contracts or any rules imposed by Atlantis Entertainment, and we will support you."

"Are you serious?" In the history of Atlantis, this had never been a thing. I knew of two idols who had been in relationships over the years and they had been asked to leave by my brother.

"Yes. Anyone want to change their answer to my question about dating?"

I raised my hand.

"I thought you might," she nodded. "Look, I

mean it when I say I both agree and disagree with it. You guys have these jobs and I don't think the public truly understand how stressful and intense they can be. Yes, you have each other, and we at Atlantis will do all we can to help when you're feeling stressed, but there's something about having a girlfriend—or boyfriends—that," she tapped at her heart. "They help keep you sane and grounded in a different way than your friends and family. I'm not going to stop that. *But ...*" She sighed, raking her hand through her hair. "I've seen how quickly the public can turn. Just look at what happened with Pentagon."

Pentagon was group who had debuted a few years ago. Two years after that, the press had discovered that one of their members, E'dawn, had been dating his label-mate, sunbae and special unit co-member, HyunA. In the end, the pair had been forced out of their company.

"Your fans might be different, and they might not," Holly continued. "I don't want us to lie to them. I don't want you to lie to us. There was a lot more going on there than them just dating, and I don't want us, Atlantis, to be in the position to have to react the same way. We'll stand by you, provided you trust us. We don't care what kind of relationship you have. We don't care if you date guys or girls. We just need to know."

"Not that we're not grateful," Insoo said, his nose wrinkling slightly as he considered his words. "But what happens when Atlantis is affected? Will you still stand by us when stocks plummet?"

"I will," Holly said, firmly. "We will. The reason why Lee Woojin set up this company was because his friends were idols. There is a picture of them hanging on his office wall. Their company failed them, and he created Atlantis in their honor. We're not going to fail you." She sank back into her seat with a sigh. "But, we are a company, and if we can avoid dating scandals, it would be helpful."

"What about Onyx?" Insoo asked.

I looked at him with an arched eyebrow. Had I missed something?

"That is being discussed with Onyx," Holly responded, vaguely. "And things relating to Zodiac will stay with Zodiac until a decision has been made too."

CX hadn't mentioned anything … was one of them dating? I really needed to check the news sites when I left here …

"The Zodiac contracts will include dating clauses, in which you will agree to inform us of your relationship status." Holly stood. "I have kept you from your congratulatory party for long enough. Go enjoy the rest of your evening." She paused and looked at Insoo. "Insoo, would you come with me to my office? There's something we need to discuss."

Although he looked confused, Insoo nodded, following Holly out of the room. I watched her walk away, confused. Sejin had told me not to trust her; that she would try to take everything away from us … but… despite everything, I was still here. If anything, she seemed like she was on my side, giving me opportunities.

The only thing she seemed to have taken away from me was my brother.

The moment the door closed, Wonseok turned and looked at me, giving me an accusatory glower. "You have a girlfriend and you didn't tell me?"

I shrugged. "I didn't know that would happen."

"Ugh! I should have known when you went running to her rescue!"

"Do neither of you really have girlfriends?" I asked, curious. In all honesty, I didn't think they did ... King, on the other hand ...

Sure enough, both Kota and Wonseok shook their heads. "But there is someone I like," Kota said. When both Wonseok and I looked at him, he actually blushed. "My tutor. Maybe I'll ask her out?"

"Do it!" Wonseok exclaimed. He started laughing and then stopped, turning to me. "Why are you not telling your girlfriend that you can date without having to worry about Atlantis?"

That was a very good point.

To the soundtrack of Wonseok's laughter, I ran out of the room.

And almost collided with Yerin. "What happened?" she demanded, anxiously. "Did she kick you out? She can't do that! She's your sister. And we didn't admit to anything!"

I swooped in, wrapped my arms around her and kissed her.

Yerin pushed me away, eyes darting around in a panic as she checked if someone was watching. "You can't—"

"They don't care." I cut her off. "Atlantis don't care if we date, so long as we tell them, and we hide it from the public."

"What?"

"They know and they're all right with it."

Yerin stared at me. I could almost see her processing the words. Then it set in and she launched herself at me, kissing me like she thought she would never have been able to do it again.

I didn't care, kissing her back just as desperately.

I couldn't get enough of this girl.

And now I had no limit on her.

Somehow, things had fallen into place.

And Cha Yerin had fallen into place beside me.

The End

The story of ~~Bright Boys~~ Zodiac will continue in 'The Leader Who Fell From The Sky.'

Keep up to date with all of the gossip from Atlantis Entertainment:

Sign up to Ji Soo's Newsletter

In the meantime, if you enjoyed this story, please consider leaving a review. Those few minutes will really help an author out!

The End

SONGS MENTIONED

1) Wanna One – IPU (I Promise U)
2) 4-Minute – Crazy
3) Pentagon – Runaway
4) EXO – Ko Ko Bop
5) EXID – DDD
6) BTS – Fake Love
7) Tablo ft Taeyang – Tomorrow
8) Jessi – Gucci
9) Monsta X – Alligator

CHARACTER BIOGRAPHIES

Two new groups are coming from Atlantis
Entertainment ...

Name: Zodiac (조디악)
Fandom: TBC
Colors: TBC
Debut: Soon?

Stage Name: Insoo (인수)
Birth Name: Chang Insoo (창인수)
Position: Vocals, rapper
Birthday: December 3
Age: 21
Zodiac sign: Sagittarius
Height: 175 cm

Weight: 57 Kg
Blood Type: A

Insoo facts:
Born: Incheon, South Korea
Family: father, mother, older sister

Stage Name: Kota (코타)
Birth Name: Yokota Heiji (横田平治 / (헤이지 요코타)
Position: Dancer, vocals
Birthday: December 24th
Age: 22
Zodiac sign: Sagittarius
Height: 182 cm
Weight: 62 Kg
Blood Type: O

Kota facts:
Born: Tokyo, Japan
Family: father, mother

Stage Name: Seungjin (승진)

Birth Name: Lee Seungjin (이승진)
Position: Dancer, Visual, Vocals
Birthday: April 20th
Age: 18
Zodiac sign: Aries
Height: 180 cm
Weight: 69 kg
Blood Type: B

Seungjin facts:
Born: Seoul, South Korea
Family: father (Chairman of Atlantis), mother, older brother (Vice Chairman of Atlantis), older sister (Vice Chairwoman of Atlantis)

Stage Name: Wonseok (원석)
Birth Name: Hong Wonseok (홍원석)
Position: Vocals, maknae
Birthday: September 16th
Age: 17
Zodiac sign: Virgo
Height: 176 cm
Weight: 65 Kg
Blood Type: AB

Wonseok facts:
Born: Jeju, South Korea
Family: father, twin brother (Hong Wooseok)

Name: Glitter (광휘)
Fandom: Glamor
Colors: #f04bc1 (Pink sherbet)
Debut: September 22

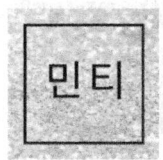

Stage Name: Minty (민티)
Birth Name: Jeon Mintae (전민태)
Position: Leader, Rapper
Birthday: January 31
Age: 20
Zodiac sign: Aquarius
Height: 168 cm
Weight: 52 kg
Blood Type: A

Minty facts:
Born: Sinan, South Korea
Family: Brought up by her Aunt

Stage Name: Yerin (예린)
Birth Name: Cha Yerin (차예린)
Position: Rapper
Birthday: July 18
Age: 18
Zodiac sign: Cancer
Height: 162 cm
Weight: 52 kg
Blood Type: A

Yerin facts:
Born: Seoul, South Korea
Family: Father, Mother (Principal of the Seoul Leadership Academy)

Stage Name: Miyeon (미연)
Birth Name: Cho Miyeon (조미연)
Position: Main dancer, vocals
Birthday: April 7
Age: 18
Zodiac sign: Aries

Height: 165 cm
Weight: 48 kg
Blood Type: AB

Miyeon facts:
Born: Seoul, South Korea
Family: Father, Mother, younger sister

Stage Name: Adele (아델)
Birth Name: Adele Tham (아델 탐)
Position: Vocalist, dancer
Birthday: February 23
Age: 17
Zodiac sign: Pisces
Height: 157 cm
Weight: 46 kg
Blood Type: AB

Adele facts:
Born: Singapore, Singapore
Family: Father, Mother, two older brothers
Speaks English, Malay, Chinese, and Korean

Stage Name: Sojung (소정)
Birth Name: Pil Sojung (필소정)
Position: Main vocalist, dancer
Birthday: September 6
Age: 17
Zodiac sign: Virgo
Height: 157 cm
Weight: 46 kg
Blood Type: B

Sojung facts:
Born: Jindo, South Korea
Family: Father, Mother, older sister

ACKNOWLEDGEMENTS

The Zodiac series is my pet project. I love this series. It's not my most popular one, and I'm not sure it ever will be. I think most authors would abandon a series as unpopular as this one, but I can't do that. Each of the characters and members of Zodiac have a story to share, and I can't wait for you to read them.

Which means I start the acknowledgements by acknowledging and thanking you! You're reading this. It makes me so happy! (Seriously!!) I hope you'll stay with me as I share the stories of the rest of the members of Zodiac. Hyunseo is up next—you will find out what really happened that night he punched TK's brother. You might also find out who was with Baekhee in the library …! But I digress, because I was saying thank you. Thank you for reading, and I really hope you enjoyed reading it as much as I enjoyed writing it. I did worry a little with Yerin; she's not an easy character.

While I had a lot of fun with the two best people in my life, Cheryl and Sarah, plotting this book out, this story took a sharp turn somewhere up a mountain and never quite made it back to the original outline. Thank you both, for spending so much time with me trying to get a handle on where this was going (especially in relation to the rest of the books). For the rest of you, you might be beginning to see just how interwoven the books are. It took a lot of time to get this right!

Something I'm questioning the more books I write is, 'who am I?'. I realize this sounds strange, but I was born and raised in Texas, and I have spent my entire education in a Texas school. You'd think I'd be American, right? If you could see how much British words, phrases and grammar has seeped into this book (prior to the version you're reading now), I'd bet you'd question it to. I've worked in hotel with British and Australian colleagues, and I accept I've picked a lot up from them, but some of the things highlighted—I've been using them for as long as I can remember! So, no, I don't know who I am anymore. With that in mind, I need to thank Adena for sending me such long lists highlighting them. Seriously, girl—thank you from the bottom of my heart!

My beta team is amazing. Courtney, the speed at which you read these astounds me, and I thank you for your feedback—your comments make me go back and tweak or add chunks (you made this book even longer—this one is on you!!) to make the story better. Or at least, I hope it made it better! Claire, you were right and I changed it, and hopefully no one else will ever notice! Thank you!!

My ARC team are equally as amazing. I write this knowing that so many of you will read this before the book actually publishes. I know some of you will read this in a day. I just don't know *how* you manage it! Thank you for giving up your time—you guys kick ass!

Of course, I can't go anywhere without drawing your attention to the beautiful cover from Natasha. I cannot wait to see the completed series (although I'm going to have to as this will take me several years to complete!). I love getting an email from you, knowing the mockup and then the final image is attached. There's always a squeal of delight and then a rush to something with a bigger screen than my phone to stare at the pretty. Thank you for creating such beautiful covers!

For this book, several thanks must go out to those who

helped inspire the characters (visually): Kai from EXO and Rosé from BLACKPINK for Seungjin and Yerin. You'll never read these books and you'll never know this, but your faces are the faces I see when I write these characters.

Actually, for those curious, I finally created Pinterest boards to catalogue all the visual inspirations for my books—feel free to have a look:

https://www.pinterest.com/jisooleeauthor/

ATLANTIS ENTERTAINMENT NEWSLETTER

Would you like to be kept up to date on the antics of the idols and artists at Atlantis Entertainment? Sign up to the Atlantis Entertainment Newsletter, managed by the silent Chairwoman of Atlantis Entertainment, Ji Soo.

Ji Soo will keep you updated on the Atlantis Roster, as well as providing you with a healthy dose of K-pop, some Korean culture, and if she can persuade her 할머니 (that's Korean for 'grandmother', pronounced halmeoni) to part with some cherished recipes, some of those, along with some reading recommendations. There may even be a few insights into her crazy life. But probably not, because her life is very boring …

Find out more at:

www.JiSooLeeAuthor.com/newsletter

ABOUT THE AUTHOR

International Bestselling author Ji Soo Lee spends most of her days lost in a K-Pop haze, which inspired her to start writing stories about her idols at Atlantis Entertainment.

Under the name Ji Soo Lee, you will find YA contemporary romances, with romance levels like a K-Drama.

Under J. S. Lee, Ji Soo writes steamier stories, mainly of Reverse Harems.

WAYS TO CONNECT

Facebook
Author Page:
https://www.facebook.com/OfficialJiSooLee
Atlantis Fan Group:
https://www.facebook.com/groups/AtlantisEnts/

Bookbub:
https://www.bookbub.com/authors/j-s-lee

Amazon:
https://www.amazon.com/J.-S.-Lee/e/B07H353S3L

Instagram:
https://www.instagram.com/ji_soo_lee_author/

Website:
www.jisooleeauthor.com